RISKY
BUSINESS

Upside Books examines events in business and management through the lens of technology. *Upside Magazine* is the preeminent magazine for executives and managers eager to understand the business of high-tech.

Published

High Tech, High Hope: Turning Your Vision of Technology into Business Success, Paul Franson

Risky Business: Protect Your Business from Being Stalked, Conned, or Blackmailed on the Web, Daniel S. Janal

Forthcoming

Silicon Gold Rush: The Next Generation of High-Tech Stars Rewrite the Rules of Business, Karen Southwick

PEOPLE · TECHNOLOGY · CAPITAL

RISKY BUSINESS

*PROTECT YOUR BUSINESS FROM BEING
STALKED, CONNED, OR
BLACKMAILED ON THE WEB*

DANIEL S. JANAL

John Wiley & Sons, Inc.

New York • Chichester • Weinheim • Brisbane • Singapore • Toronto

Published by John Wiley & Sons, Inc.

Published simultaneously in Canada.

This publication is designed to provide accurate and authoritative information in regard to the subject matter covered. It is sold with the understanding that the publisher is not engaged in rendering professional services. If professional advice or other expert assistance is required, the services of a competent professional person should be sought.

Library of Congress Cataloging-in-Publication Data:

Janal, Daniel S.
   Risky business : protect your business from being
stalked, conned, or blackmailed on the Web / Daniel S. Janal.
      p.   cm.
   Includes index.
   ISBN 0-471-19706-8 (cloth : alk. paper)
   1. Computer crimes. 2. Internet (Computer network)—Security
measures. 3. Computer security. 4. Fraud. 5. Extortion.
  I. Title.
HV6773.J35   1998
364.16′8—dc21   97–44832

Contents

Foreword

Like most innovations that threaten to change the status quo, the emergence of the Internet has polarized society. Baby boomers remember when television was described as a pernicious influence that would introduce children to immorality and vice, shorten our attention spans, divert us from reading and other necessary skills, undermine our allegiance to authority; in short, ruin our entire generation. The new medium was described as a "vast wasteland" that would turn our brains to mush as we sat glued to the "boob tube." By benefit of hindsight, we can now say that most of these dire predictions did not come to pass, though there is undoubtedly some truth to many of them. Television, showing us images like grown men setting police dogs loose on frightened children who happened to be of a different color, did undermine our allegiance to authority. It introduced us to immorality with indelible images of Joseph McCarthy berating witnesses whose "crime" was association with people of whom the senator did not approve.

Now the Internet promises to allow a new generation of children even more freedom to think for themselves. And to shake up complacent adults whose opinions were formed in the television era. By enabling instantaneous communication with virtually all corners of the world, the Internet should help us trample stereotypes and judge an individual by his or her thoughts—not race, gender, or religion. Access to a wide range of information, from airline schedules to the magnitude of the latest California earthquake, means all of us can make up our own minds without depending on politicians or parents to interpret for us. So the Internet is avidly embraced by techno-Edenists who see it as the highway to a better world yet hated and feared by others who see it as a magnifier of all the evils of humanity.

Into this debate steps *Risky Business,* a clear-headed, cogent analysis of what the real dangers of cyberspace are and how businesses and individuals can effectively protect themselves. Author Daniel S. Janal is a professional speaker and Internet marketing consultant and teaches at the University of California at Berkeley Extension. As he says, "This book is not designed to scare the hell out of you nor to convince you not to enjoy the benefits of the Internet." Rather, its intention is to provide some guidance so that yo can take advantage of the Internet without unreasonable fear or panic.

In 14 highly readable chapters that avoid techno-speak, Janal addresses such issues as cyberstalking, online fraud, competitive spying, security violations, Internet access and employee e-mail policies, copyright questions, domain names, and crisis management. *Risky Business* is a wide-ranging prescription for dealing with the risks of cyberspace that can, and should, be read by consumers, businesspeople, parents, children, managers, and employees. The author covers technical and legal subjects in understandable, down-to-earth fashion, but even experts in the field will find value in this book's exceptional grasp of its subject and pragmatic advice.

There's no doubt the Internet does present criminals, hucksters, hackers, pornographers, vandals, and other mischief-makers with a whole new field in which to prey upon their victims. Like self-defense classes, what *Risky Business* does is give potential victims a way to fight back. It suggests preventive measures that can be taken to ward off trouble and legitimate responses when problems occur. Janal not only gives a list of practical tips with every chapter, he also provides contact information such as phone numbers, e-mail addresses, and websites for lawyers, law enforcement officials, and government agencies. For anyone who's online or even contemplating being online, *Risky Business* is a must-read. Of the plethora of Internet-related books being published, it is one of the few that will retain its usefulness and become a foundation of the essential Internet reading list.

Risky Business is the second offering in the Upside series of business technology books jointly produced by Upside Media, Inc. and John Wiley & Sons, Inc. Upside Media is the parent of *Upside* magazine, which has been providing "authoritative, insightful, provocative and opinionated analysis of the business of technology" since its founding in 1989. "Through its magazine, website, books and events, *Upside* is the essential resource for technology executives, entrepreneurs, investors and savvy observers who want to cut through the hype and focus a critical eye on the most important business driving the world's economy." We're proud to present this book as a valuable addition to our mission to cover technology intelligibly and truthfully.

DAVID BUNNELL
Publisher and CEO, Upside Media, Inc.

KAREN SOUTHWICK
Editor, Upside Books

Preface

While the Internet offers a cornucopia of wonderful, positive ways to change the world for the better, it is not without its perils. The villains of the real world manipulate the new tools of the Internet to wreak havoc by stalking people for sexual or monetary advantage and by vengefully attacking organizations and destroying their good names. One purpose of this book is to demonstrate that all these frauds, con games, libels, extortions, character assassinations, and other dangers exist. However, this book is not intended merely to scare the hell out of you nor is it designed to convince you to forgo the benefits of the Internet. Instead, its primary purpose is to identify the problems and propose workable solutions that you can use to protect yourself, your family, and your organization from the dregs of society who have technologized their warped view of reality and now ply their trade on the Internet.

This book is designed to help:

> ➤ Senior management at corporations, nonprofit agencies, associations, trade groups, small businesses, and educational institutions who need to create policies for the fair treatment of employees and to build

defenses that protect their organizations from lawsuits, fraud, and attacks from cyberscammers.

➤ Middle management who need to set standards for employee use of the Internet in a fair and consistent manner.

➤ Public relations, advertising, and marketing executives who must control their organizations' images in the media and protect their good names.

➤ Employees on the front lines who deal with irritated customers seeking revenge against the company or its employees.

➤ People who create their own websites and wonder about the legalities of copyright, plagiarism, libel, and other legal concerns.

➤ Parents and children who are concerned about protecting their privacy and safety from thieves, sexual predators, and fanatics.

This book is divided into four parts for easy reading and convenient reference. The writing style of each chapter is friendly, informal, and supportive. Throughout, masculine and feminine pronouns (he or him, she or her) are used interchangeably. Unless stated otherwise, however, all the information provided herein is equally applicable to both men or women. Interviews with experts provide succinct analysis and advice in a conversational style that is easy to understand. Although there's a lot of solid legal information and advice, there's no legal jargon here. Even the technical information is written for everyday consumers and business managers, not computer jockeys.

Part One is the Introduction. Each chapter serves a specific purpose:

➤ Chapter 1 suggests the scope of problems you might face in cyberspace during your business day—and gives you assurances that you will be able to outsmart criminals.

Because many businesses require their managers and workforce to operate online, the next three chapters deal with threats to your personal safety:

➤ Chapter 2 explains online stalking.

➤ Chapter 3 explores identity theft.

➤ Chapter 4 deals with impersonation.

Each of these chapters describes the problem and how it can hurt you, and proposes ways to protect your privacy and fight these attackers.

Part Two contains two chapters that explore threats to your financial well-being:

➤ Chapter 5 shows examples of online fraud and how consumers and businesses are being ripped off—and what you can do about it.

➤ Chapter 6 explains security violations and technical abuses that can affect individuals and organizations. This chapter is an introduction to a vast body of knowledge that can only be appropriately examined in depth in technical tomes.

Part Three deals with security. The next five chapters delve into internal threats to your organization's security:

➤ Chapter 7 presents employee Internet access policies that could save your company time and money, and provide protection from legal hassles. Sample policies and procedures are included for your review.

➤ Chapter 8 shows how to use e-mail effectively in building customer relations and marketing—two troublesome areas for many companies.

➤ Chapter 9 thoroughly covers questions about copyrights online—what you can copy and what you need permission to use.

➤ Chapter 10 addresses competitive spying and trade secrets.

➤ Chapter 11 describes the entire process of applying for domain names and protecting your right to use them.

Part Four, the final three chapters, detail the external threats to your organization's reputation and are a helpful addition to the corporate communicator and public relations official's bookshelves:

➤ Chapter 12 introduces you to attack websites, rumor mills, and other communication perils on the Internet and in newsgroups.

➤ Chapter 13 presents information and advice on how to combat online investors who try to manipulate your company's stock price.

➤ Chapter 14 offers a model plan for public relations crisis communications to protect your organization from attack websites, stock manipulators, and threats to your reputation or products.

DANIEL S. JANAL

Author Biography

Daniel Janal is a speaker, author, and marketing consultant specializing in Internet marketing. The *L.A. Times* called Mr. Janal "an online marketing expert." He can be reached at dan@janal.com, www.janal.com, or 510-648-1961 during normal business hours in California. Mr. Janal is the author of two best-selling Internet marketing books: *Online Marketing Handbook,* and *101 Businesses You Can Start on the Internet.* He also has written *How to Publicize High Tech Products and Services* (10K Press/Janal Communications, 1991), considered the definitive training manual for public relations novices. He is the co-developer of Publicity Builder software (JIAN, 1993).

He has provided online marketing consulting services for The Reader's Digest, Panasonic, and Biltmore Estates. He was on the publicity team that launched America Online. He has delivered online marketing training seminars to the publicity staffs of American Express/IDS, U.S. Postal Service, and IBM. His public seminar clients include AT&T, Pacific Bell, DCI Expos, and Ragan Communications. He has addressed trade groups and associations including Public Relations Society of America, Credit Union Executives Society, and National Ski Areas Association. He lectures at the University of

California at Berkeley. He has addressed audiences in Mexico, Canada, and Brazil.

Mr. Janal has provided public relations consulting services for more than 100 software publishers, hardware manufacturers, and publishing companies over the past 13 years, including launching Grolier's Multimedia Encyclopedia, the first piece of consumer software available on CD-ROM. Other clients include AT&T Multimedia Software Solutions, Bell Atlantic Creative Services, Prentice-Hall Home Software, and The Learning Company.

He has contributed articles to trade magazines, including *PC Laptop Computing, InfoWorld, Accounting Technology, PR Tactics, Ski Area Management,* and *Credit Union Executives Society.*

Before starting a career in public relations and marketing, Mr. Janal was an award-winning newspaper reporter for the *Today* newspaper in Cocoa, FL, news editor of the *Port Chester (NY) Daily Item* and business news editor for the *Rockland County (NY) Journal-News.* He has won writing awards from the National Education Association and the Hearst Foundation. He holds a bachelor's and a master's degree in journalism from Northwestern University's Medill School of Journalism.

Part One
Introduction

Chapter 1

Cyberspace Is a
Scary Place

Cyberspace can be a scary place:

➤ Cyberstalkers can find your home phone number and address, and print a street map to your house.

➤ Child molesters invade chat rooms, searching for naive children and luring them to real-world meetings.

➤ Crooks can open shop on the Internet—and never send the products you ordered and paid for.

What a growing number of people realize is that cyberspace can be dangerous for businesses, organizations, nonprofit groups, educational institutions, and associations:

➤ Upset employees can rake your name through the mud, telling a trumped-up story to thousands of your hard-won, loyal customers.

➤ Rumors spread like wildfire as employee scuttlebutt spreads through your company e-mail system—and then leaps outside the company to a newspaper reporter's e-mail box with the simple stroke of the "forward" button.

➤ Seemingly harmless questions posted on a newsgroup bulletin board can lead your competitors to deduce information about your new product line and other trade secrets.

➤ Thoughtful employees, who want to get the job done, copy software illegally—and put your company at tremendous financial risk of copyright violations.

➤ A careless remark sent via e-mail becomes a major piece of evidence in a lawsuit involving your organization. Attempts to erase it, and the computer logs, can land the company in even hotter water.

➤ In a matter of minutes, an online calamity can destroy years of hard work.

➤ Scam artists in the real world steal credit cards and buy products from online merchants, defrauding honest, hard-working people of their livelihoods.

The potential for fraud, extortion, and personal attacks exists everywhere in the real world. These threats carry over to the Internet as well. Some con games are age-old: The only thing new is that they are online instead of on the phone or in the shopping mall. Other scams are new and stretch the envelope of the Internet's technology as well as our current laws and regulations.

■ THE COST OF INTERNET CRIME

Exact figures on the cost of Internet-related crimes are hard to come by. No one has conducted surveys of the costs of crime in cyberspace. In fact, some security experts who consult with financial institutions say their clients would rather eat their losses than have the world find out that their systems are less than 100 percent secure. So we may never know how many bad credit cards are passed online or how much money has been withdrawn from online banks fraudulently.

In February 1997, the Federal Trade Commission reported that in nearly 100 federal district court cases brought by the agency between October 1995 and December 1996, fraudulent sales in these actions cost consumers more than $250 million a year and more than $700 million over the life of the schemes.

A survey by the Computer Security Institute, a San Francisco association of information security professionals, reported in March 1997 that computer crime reached $100 million in 1996. A total of 563 major U.S. corporations, government agencies, financial institutions, and universities responded to the survey. While the study was not limited to the Internet, it offers interesting statistics that show how organizations are being attacked, from inside and outside, through computer security systems or through negligence and misuse of company resources.

Some 75 percent of respondents reported losses due to security breaches ranging from financial fraud, theft of proprietary information and sabotage, to computer viruses and laptop theft. Those reporting financial losses cited the following causes:

➤ Unauthorized access by insiders—16 percent.

➤ Theft of proprietary information—14 percent.

➤ Financial fraud—12 percent.

➤ Sabotage of data or networks—11 percent.

➤ System penetration from outside—8 percent.

Concerning losses directly related to the Internet, the study found 31 percent of the companies found employee abuse of Internet privileges (e.g., downloading pornography or inappropriately using electronic mail) cost companies about $1 million.

There are no nationwide statistics on how many children have been lured into dangerous liaisons with molesters. But you can hardly pick up a newspaper without reading about some child's terrifying experience, or about a clever police sting operation that nabs a deviate before he can do more damage.

All of this damning evidence can lead you to believe that cyberspace is as scary a place as the real world. But the Internet allows thieves to commit crimes faster and more efficiently than in the real world. Because of the increased pace of communication, the ease of distributing information vast distances, the effortlessness of sending thousands of pieces of e-mail, the appeal of starting a conversation with a stranger in a chat room, and the anonymity of all transactions, the Internet attracts some unsavory users.

■ PROTECTING YOUR BUSINESS

Organizations and individuals need to be aware of a whole new Pandora's box of issues ranging from legal to moral on the Internet. Even swindlers are inventing new ways to take advantage of honest, hard-working people.

Fortunately, for every scam, there is an antidote. For every criminal, there is the stronger (and smarter) arm of the law. In this book, you will learn about the many potential threats to people and organizations through exposure on the Internet. Then you will find out how to protect yourself by drawing on the advice of lawyers, law enforcement officials, government agencies, nonprofit groups, and public relations and investor relations professionals.

This book is meant to scare you—but in a positive way. I hope to motivate, or alarm, you to take action to protect yourself and your organization. Although the threats are real, there are ways to reduce your chances of being targeted by fraud as well as ways to protect yourself if someone makes the attempt.

When you have finished reading this book, you'll be aware of the problems that exist on the Internet and know how to defend yourself and your company against such attacks. But don't stop there. Family members, to protect themselves, should read this book as well. Organizations also should make this book required reading for employees to prevent silly mistakes that could harm an employee and the company, or expose the company to lawsuits.

■ THE SMALL PRINT

Every situation is different. Your individual situation may require a precise answer that cannot be provided in a generic book. You might need to talk to a lawyer or police officer to find the solution that best deals with your circumstances. All information in this book is offered at face value and as a generic approach for many situations. For that reason, contact information (phone number, e-mail address, and Web addresses) for lawyers, law enforcement officials, and government agencies are listed wherever possible and practical.

■ THE NEXT STEP

Your journey to self-empowerment on the Internet begins now. As you read the situations and advice in the book, think about how these examples fit you or your organization. Make notes on the points you need to address with your family, management committee, information services department, lawyer, or communications staff to provide the level of security—and peace of mind—you need to use the Internet to your full advantage.

Chapter 2

Cyberstalking

Reaching out and touching someone can lead to nasty situations on the Internet. Online perverts can stalk you, your spouse, or your children. These unscrupulous individuals can find out where you live and print a map showing the exact location of your house. Even worse, you might be giving out precious personal information about your family and clues about your personality without even realizing it.

This chapter considers the frightening subject of cyberstalking:

➤ How to define cyberstalking.

➤ Real-life horror stories.

➤ Advice on how to protect yourself by stalking yourself.

➤ Tips for protecting yourself.

➤ What to do if you want to meet your cyberpals in real life.

➤ What to do if you are being stalked.

➤ A listing of online resources.

■ WHAT IS CYBERSTALKING?

"Cyberstalking is a new, high-tech version of an old terror, 'stalking.' It can take many forms including threatening, obscene or hateful e-mail, spreading vicious rumors about you online, and electronic sabotage like e-mail bombs (overwhelming your system with possibly thousands of e-mails)," says Mark Grossman, who leads the Computer and Internet Law Department of Becker & Poliakoff, P.A. He is also the Computer and Internet Law columnist for the South Florida *Daily Business Reviews* and a regular contributor to the *Legal Times, San Francisco Recorder, PC World Magazine, PC World Online,* and other publications.

Imagine waking up one morning, retrieving your e-mail and reading a threatening and anonymous letter. "You're a slut and I hate you." Or maybe it's "I love you and if I can't have you, then nobody should." Then, later that day, a friend calls to tell you that she found a newsgroup posting that includes your name, birthday and Social Security number. (An Internet newsgroup is like an electronic bulletin board where potentially millions of people can read a posted message.) Finally, just in case you still had an appetite, you find out that someone is impersonating you in e-mail and sending your customers messages that include child pornography. These are examples of what's meant by cyberstalking. The fact that all of this took place in cyberspace makes it no less terrifying if you're the victim. Cyberstalking is a crime that's about a frightful invasion into your personal space and a feeling that somebody is watching and hovering over you. If the things that I just described happened to you, I guarantee that you would feel terrified and helpless.*

---

* Mark Grossman, "Cyberstalking: The Newest Form of Terror," published on his website, May 9, 1997. He can be reached at CLTW@MGrossmanLaw.Com. His home pages are http://www.becker-poliakoff.com and http://www.mgrossmanlaw.com.

In 1991, California became the first state to pass an anti-stalking statute. Since then, every state has passed similar statutes. In Dallas, a state district judge granted a temporary restraining order against a cyberstalker who was found to have caused emotional distress or threatening bodily harm. Since officials didn't know where the person lived, they posted the restraining order online (*Dallas Morning News,* October 15, 1996).

"The rub here is insensitivity and a lack of understanding by the authorities," Grossman says. "Stalking is generally a hard-to-prove crime. It often lacks physical evidence and is a crime only because of the 'emotional distress' of the victim."

According to Grossman, the simple and sad fact is that cyberstalking often escalates to what some authorities call "in real life" stalking. Renee Goodale, president of Survivors of Stalking (http://www.soshelp.org/), an antistalking resource center, goes so far as to say that virtually every case of cyberstalking escalates beyond just cyberstalking.

■ REAL-LIFE HORROR STORIES

While lawyer Grossman paints an alarming view of life in cyberspace, he is not exaggerating. The front pages of newspapers carry reports of online malefactors who molest naive children or try to extort the richest man in America. Here are some recent cases of stalking and attacks online. Fortunately, many of these cases were solved and the perpetrators caught:

➤ A Massachusetts teenager in 1996 was charged with a hate crime after allegedly sending anti-Semitic death threats to a former teacher via e-mail.

➤ A college student in Michigan was charged with interstate transmission of a threat in 1996 when he wrote to an acquaintance about raping, torturing, and murdering a classmate.

➤ A New Jersey woman was the victim of a cyberstalker who harassed her online and then stole $2,500 from her checking account. He also called her on the phone, recited her Social Security number, knew the names of her family members, and described her neighborhood.

➤ Even Bill Gates, the richest person in America, was the target of a stalker. FBI agents arrested an Illinois man at his parents' house and charged him with extortion. The man had threatened to kill Gates and his wife if the executive did not meet the stalker's demands for money.

➤ A Washington state woman used a chat room to trap a man who had molested her 12-year-old son. She coordinated the effort with the Mercer Island Police. After learning his online nickname, she posed as a teenage gay boy. Police made the bust by sending an undercover officer to pose as the fictitious boy. The man pleaded guilty to second-degree molestation.

Sadly, countless other cases don't end as cleanly. Newspapers regularly report tragic cases of rendezvous between children and adult molesters, rapists, and murderers. While many pen pals pursue healthy, happy relationships online, you should use great caution when talking to people online and agreeing to meet them in person. People are not necessarily who they say they are, and their motives might not be innocent. Be vigilant when you are online and guard your personal data.

■ STALKING YOURSELF FOR PROTECTION

How much information can a stalker find out about you? One way to find out is to use online resources with yourself as the subject. That's right. Stalk yourself. That way, you'll know exactly what the bad guys know.

Use a search engine like Yahoo!, InfoSeek, or Excite to find information about yourself. Type in your name and see what comes up. You might be astounded. If you have a personal website or a family website, it will be recorded automatically on several search engines. Even if you didn't register it yourself, the search engines will register each page anyway.

Now look at the content on each page. Are you giving away personal information such as your name, address, phone number, names of spouses and kids, personal interests, and business information? Do you have pictures of yourself and your family online? Now the stalker knows your children's names and what they look like.

Imagine this scenario at a nearby playground: "Hi Johnny, I'm your father's friend from work at The Whozit Company. That's where he works, isn't it? Fred asked me to pick you up and take you rollerblading today. That's your favorite sport, isn't it? That's all right, Mrs. Neighbor, I know the Whatzit family. I house sat for them last winter when they skied at Steamboat Springs. I even fed their Burmese cats, Dolley and Llama."

Have you posted messages to newsgroups? They are all recorded online. All of them. Forever. And ever. Want to see? Use Deja News, www.dejanews.com, and search for your name. You'll find every message that contains your name. Next, search on your e-mail address. You'll find every message you ever posted. Now strangers can read every message you ever posted online including your political views, medical history, and personal interests if you mentioned them in a discussion. Do you really want the world to know that you posted a message in the HIV-positive newsgroup, the abortion rights newsgroup, or the gun control newsgroup? Anyone can develop a profile of your life.

Now go to a white pages service, like 411, www.four11.com, or Bigfoot, www.bigfoot.com, to see if your phone number and address are available online. These services get their information from the local phone companies. If your number is unlisted in the real world, it will be unlisted online as well. These services also list your e-mail address, so if someone wanted to stalk you, but didn't know your e-mail address, the person could use this service to find out.

Anyone who knows your address can print a map of your home or office with a service like Mapquest, www.mapquest .com. This product is usually pretty cool and a great service to people who need reliable travel directions fast. Unfortunately, bad guys can use it, too. Ask yourself these questions:

➤ Do you have a signature file (also called an online business card in Netscape Communicator 4.0)? A signature file usually contains your name, contact information, and perhaps your favorite quote. This signature is automatically attached to every piece of e-mail and every newsgroup message you write. When you post messages on newsgroups or mailing lists or send e-mail, that signature file can tell the world all about you. What information is listed? Is it too revealing? Maybe you shouldn't include your home phone number or address.

➤ Are you a public figure, or famous in your industry? Have you spoken at a conference? If so, the conference might have a web page where it has posted your contact information and picture.

➤ Have you written an article for a trade publication? If that magazine is online, the editor might have reprinted the article online.

➤ Are you a college student or teacher? Your contact information, age, and major might be listed in an online college directory. Some schools even print photos along with mini bios. Can you have your information removed?

➤ Have you filled out a personal profile on America Online? Now 10 million people can read about you. Have you registered with Firefly, www.firefly.com, a service that tries to match people with similar interests? You told the truth in your profile; did your new "buddy?"

➤ Has your company printed a personnel directory on its website? You could be listed and found with a search engine inquiry.

So far you've spent zero dollars. You can find your own credit file from TRW or a similar company for less than $100. A stalker who is a particularly good liar might be able to get it as well ("Hello, I'm calling from Arlington Apartments. We're doing a credit check on Jane Jones. Here's the information you need . . .").

■ TIPS FOR PROTECTING YOURSELF FROM STALKERS

If you participated in the preceding drill, you may be astounded by the amount of information about you online. To prevent stalkers from knowing more about you than you'd like, here are tips for protecting your private life from strangers who see your personal home pages, e-mails, postings on newsgroups, and conversations in chat rooms.

➤ Personal Web Pages

Personal web pages seem to be all the rage these days. National Internet service providers (ISPs) are promoting their services to individuals and families by offering them a personal page to tell the world about themselves. America Online, CompuServe, and Prodigy all offer personal home pages for their members (those pages can be viewed by anyone via their Internet browser). The Pollyanna-like ads proclaim that you can use your personal web pages to find new friends, keep in touch with family members and old friends, and maybe even find a new job.

How smart is this? Not very.

You could have every cadger in the world trying to contact you online or in e-mail to sell you something or tip you off to a stock or just plain harass you, because that's what some misfits like to do.

If you'd like to have a personal page for all the positive reasons, go right ahead. But play your cards close to your vest. Don't list your home phone number; use your office number. Don't print your home address; use a post office box number. Don't print pictures of your kids or their ages because deviates will find this information. They can print out maps that show where you live and use the information on the page to build rapport with your kids—and trap them. Tell your friends about your great vacation when you see them or talk to them on the phone. Don't print it on your web page.

➤ Signature Files

Signature files are great ways to tell the world about you. But don't tell them more than you want them to know. Don't list your home phone number. Feel free to use your e-mail address as the preferred way to be contacted. If you'd like to take the relationship further, then you can supply a phone number and send it by a private e-mail instead of posting it on a public bulletin board.

➤ Newsgroups

One of the biggest mistakes people make about posting messages on newsgroups is that they think they are engaging in a one-to-one conversation with a friend or colleague. In reality, their messages are being read by thousands of people. A stalker could easily find out about you and how to contact you if you reveal too much information in your message, or in your signature file.

➤ Chat Rooms

While the previous headings could be fodder for stalkers who are willing to work hard to find victims, chat rooms are easy feeding grounds. They are the singles bars of the online world. Almost by nature, chat rooms tend to gravitate toward talk about sex. Many chat rooms on America Online or the Internet are really social groups for people who want to meet new people. The chat rooms have names that appeal to different groups, such as teens, single parents, people in their 30s or 40s, or followers of different religions.

Although many chat rooms are for professionals discussing arcane material, stalkers scour those areas as well. In fact, I was once a guest in a chat room for a professional magazine on CompuServe. In the middle of the interview, I received a private message from someone with a woman's name who asked if I wanted to go into a private area and talk dirty. After a brief pause to collect myself, I said, "No," but as this story indicates, the stalkers have no shame and will go to any lengths to find someone who will cooperate with them.

Here are several ways to defend against online stalkers:

➤ Women should be especially wary of online chats. A chat room labeled for women only might attract men masquerading as women. To find out if you are talking to a woman, ask gender-specific questions that only a woman would be likely to answer correctly (e.g., makeup procedures or fashion trivia).

➤ Women should be careful about using feminine names to identify themselves. If a woman goes to a chat room, she will probably get asked if she wants to "talk dirty." Some women use men's names or neutral words to avoid this problem.

➤ Men are not immune from stalkers. Deviants can attack men online as readily as women.

➤ Don't select provocative names.

➤ Don't enter sex chat rooms if you don't want to talk about sex.

➤ Don't believe anything you read in a personal profile. People lie.

➤ Don't believe anything anyone writes in a chat room. People lie about their age, sex, and interests.

➤ Filter what you read with common sense. People generally write in a way that suggests their age or experience. Do they say they are kids, but sound like adults? Do they say they are adults, but write like teens?

➤ Never give out personal information when meeting people for the first time in chat rooms.

It is true that many people have met the loves of their lives in a chat room or on online forums. If you follow these tips, you'll have a better chance of separating the slime from the sublime.

➤ Online Phone Directories

Online phone directories get their information from your phone company. They don't create or research the information themselves:

➤ Ask your phone company to not print your address or full name in the phone book. For example, ask to be listed as "J Smith, NO ADDRESS" instead of "Janet Smith, 123 Main Street, My Town, USA."

➤ Get an unlisted phone number. This option costs a few dollars a month.

➤ Ask the online phone directory to remove your listing entirely. Some will do this, some won't.

■ WHAT TO DO IF YOU WANT TO MEET YOUR CYBERPALS IN REAL LIFE

So you've found a person you want to get to know better. That's great. But realize that no matter how much the person has told you online, you really don't know a whole lot, and you don't know whether it is the truth. You also don't know whether the person is an accomplished con artist.

RISKY BUSINESS' SEVEN TIPS FOR MEETING YOUR CYBERPALS SAFELY IN THE REAL WORLD

If you want to meet someone, follow these steps to protect yourself:

1. Call on a phone to verify information, age, and sex.

2. Consider calling from a pay phone, so your phone number can't be traced.

3. If you call from home, use caller ID blocking.

4. Don't ever give out your phone number. Ask for the other person's number. That way the person won't be able to call or abuse you by phone.

5. Trust your instincts. If you feel this person is bad news, hang up.

6. If the person passes your tests, and you want to meet face to face, select a public place such as a restaurant or shopping mall. Don't meet at your house or office. Don't get into a car with the person.

7. Don't reveal your last name.

If you follow these steps, you will have continued to protect yourself because the stalker won't know your phone number or where you live.

■ CHILDREN AND STALKERS

Because of the extreme potentials for danger, parents should warn their children about the dangers of cyberspace. There have been cases of children being given free airline tickets to meet their new online pals—never to be seen again.

Children can reveal personal information in the most innocent ways. During a business meal, a friend told me that

RISKY BUSINESS' EIGHT TIPS FOR PROTECTING YOURSELF IF YOU ARE BEING STALKED

If you are being stalked in a newsgroup or online chat, here are activities you can perform to protect yourself:

1. Tell the person to stop. This might not work, since some stalkers like a response, any response.

2. Ignore him.

3. Set up a blocker, an online tool used by many chat programs to block a person from sending you a message.

4. Set up a filter on your e-mail program to delete any messages from the stalker, or messages that contain offensive words in the subject line.

5. Just say goodbye. Leave the chat and go to another room, or return to that chat with a different name.

6. Tell forum administrators on CompuServe or America Online. They have the power to turn off the stalker's service.

7. Keep track of the chats, copies of e-mail, and other evidence that you can present to the police or the ISP. Show how the harassment affects your life and show the steps you are taking to stop it.

8. Call the police. Several states have antistalking laws that include cyberstalking.

These tactics might stop a stalker from harassing you. Trust your instincts when you meet people online—and don't be afraid to ask for help from online monitors and hosts, or from real-world police.

his 10-year-old daughter told him that if Johnny called, it was for her. He asked her who Johnny was and where she met him. She said she met him online in a chat room. Sure enough, a few minutes later, the phone rang and Dad answered the phone. It was Johnny and he sounded about his daughter's age. He asked Johnny to put his father on the line. He then told Johnny's father what had happened—and the dangers that Johnny had put his daughter in by asking her what school she went to and other personal information. The other father said he would talk to his son about it. What his daughter didn't realize is that while she was talking to Johnny about what all kids talk about, hundreds of adults and other kids were listening in. Maybe one of them was taking notes.

This story illustrates an important fact. Children need to be aware of the dangers of going online. They must understand that:

➤ Not everyone online is their friend.

➤ People aren't always who they claim to be.

➤ They should never try to meet these people alone—no matter how enticing their offer.

➤ Never give out information about where they live or other personal data, including their family password or codes.

Children need to realize that whenever they talk to someone in a chat room, hundreds of other people are listening. That means that while they are talking with someone who is nice and friendly and isn't a stalker, a stalker could be reading the messages and taking notes on where they live, what school they go to, and what time their mother picks them up.

Another concern is that marketers try to use children to obtain information about family incomes and preferences. They do this by asking children to enter contests on websites that ask for family data. Simply by asking for an address, a marketer can find out a great deal about the family's income. While this doesn't qualify as stalking, it merits notice as invasion of privacy, especially since small children don't understand the consequences of marketers on Madison Avenue. By filling out these forms, your family may be exposed to telemarketing pitches during dinnertime or have your private life enjoined in a computer database forever. Children should fully understand whether they may enter contests, fill out forms, or reveal certain types of information.

■ SUMMARY

Cyberstalking seems to be growing along with the Internet. The Internet is not a model community. Instead, it mirrors the real world. Miscreants can ply their trade online with ease since they can hide their identities and spread their maliciousness with little fear of being caught. However, you can take steps to protect yourself—and if you live in a community with enlightened police—actually help to bring down these offenders.

ONLINE RESOURCES

Cyberangels, www.cyberangels.org, provides tips to protect yourself from online harassment.

National Victim Center, www.nvc.org/ddir/info43.htm, describes stalking, stalkers, and what to do about them.

Barton's Den of Iniquity, www.io.com/~barton/harass5.html, despite the weird name, contains good tips on protecting yourself against stalkers.

Survivors of Stalking, www.soshelp.org, an antistalking resource center.

The Stalker's Home Page, www.glr.com/stalk, has links to antistalking sites and resources.

Chapter

3

Identity Theft

Your phone rings. It's a collector from a credit agency. She's wondering why you haven't paid your bill from a major department store. You tell her you don't know what she's talking about. You don't have a credit card for that store and you don't even shop there. She informs you that an account had been opened in your name, using your Social Security number and other personal information that was found to be true after being checked with a credit reporting agency. You're a victim of identity theft.

This chapter:

➤ Defines identity theft and outlines how it can hurt you.

➤ Explains how crooks can find out about you.

➤ Suggests what you can do to protect yourself.

➤ Looks at legal protections and proposed laws.

➤ Provides a listing of online resources.

■ WHAT IS IDENTITY THEFT AND HOW CAN IT HURT YOU?

Identity theft is a crime in which a crook steals your personal data and makes purchases in your name. He might have applied for and received credit cards in your name, or impersonated you in such a way as to convince merchants to sell him products and charge your account.

This act can hurt you by destroying your good name, your sound credit history and could leave you liable for the financial destruction left in the crook's path.

"Theft of identity fraud is on the rise," according to PIRG, a consumer advocacy group. "Most TOI victims never learn how the identity thieves accessed their personal identifying information. Indeed, it may be impossible for a consumer to prevent access to all his or her personal information which is so readily available to thieves (and to junk marketers) from a variety of sources."*

A company called Background Investigations Division, in Chico, California, claims it can use online sources to find service records of the Army, Navy, Air Force, or Marine Corps; trial transcripts and court orders; and credit, driving, or criminal records; and can verify income or educational accomplishments.

Your financial liability for stolen credit cards is limited to $50. However, there are no limits on debit cards. Nor can you ever be compensated for the lost time and aggravation you will have endured to set your credit records straight.

While crooks can find information about you on the Internet, this crime is not limited to cyberspace. It can happen in real life as well. A section later in this chapter explains how to thwart thieves on cyberspace and in the real world.

---

* PIRG website.

RISKY BUSINESS IN THE NEWS

Kurt Vonnegut's Identity Is Stolen

In his magnificent short story, "Who Am I This Time," author Kurt Vonnegut tells the story of two star-crossed lovers who meet at a local community theater when they try out for parts in the play. Ironically, they connect in their roles, but not in their real lives because they have no personalities. They decide to adopt the identities of Romeo and Juliet and fall in love.

Ironically, Vonnegut was the victim in an identity theft hoax that made the front pages of many newspapers in the United States in August 1997 and was the subject of an ABC News *Nightline* show. It seems that a prankster sent an e-mail to his friends that contained what was reputed to be Kurt Vonnegut's commencement address to the students of the Massachusetts Institute of Technology (MIT). People liked the witty article so much, they forwarded it to friends around the country and eventually, around the world. The message sounded so much like Kurt Vonnegut that when his wife received it from a friend, she thought he had written it and had wondered why he hadn't told her. He told her that he didn't write the piece nor had he spoken at MIT.

The article had been written by Mary Schmich, a columnist for the *Chicago Tribune* several weeks earlier. She had no idea the article had been sent to millions of people by e-mail or that people thought that Vonnegut had written the article.

While this hoax was harmless (if you discount copyright violations), it shows that people will believe what they read online—even if it isn't true! What would have happened to Vonnegut's reputation if someone sent a nasty message and attributed it to him? As you can see, identity theft can have a dangerous side as well.

■ HOW CAN CROOKS FIND OUT ABOUT YOU?

If you didn't already do so, carry out the activities suggested in the section "Stalking Yourself for Protection," in Chapter 2, to find out whether you are giving crooks easy access to the most private financial aspects of your life. With this information, crooks can easily impersonate you and trade on your identity.

➤ Online Purchases

If a waiter in a restaurant can steal your credit card number while ringing up your order, then online crackers can steal your credit card from unsecured websites with sniffer programs. Guard yourself by purchasing only from companies that use the latest standards in security. If you are typing in your password or credit card number in a public space or office environment, be on guard for "shoulder surfers" who look for your number. If your card is stolen online or in the real world, your losses are limited to $50.

➤ Registration Forms

Crooks can also find out about you by setting up phony websites that ask you to enter a contest, get a free sample, or register to be on a mailing list. You fill out your personal data and now they have a file on you. It is not surprising that many people don't fill out these forms or fill them out with phony data. Many legitimate companies ask you to fill out forms as well, so don't look at all registrations as possible con games. Simply use common sense in deciding whether you really want that company to know about you.

➤ Cookies

"Cookies" are tools that websites use to track your online movement on their websites. By recording what information you choose to read or buy, merchants can begin to learn about you, your preferences, and your buying patterns. This is both a good thing and a bad thing. On the one hand, merchants will know which ads to display and which product selection to offer you. If you read articles about gardening and home repair, the site will display banner ads from merchants hoping to reach that audience. They won't waste your time with banner ads from windsurfing manufacturers. The benefit is that you find information that interests you quickly. On the other hand, your privacy has been invaded. Someone knows something about you—and perhaps you don't want them knowing about that. For example, you read an article about HIV testing. That merchant sells your name to a life insurance company. You apply for life insurance and are denied by the insurance company.

There are no laws against cookies, or collecting personal information. You can set your browser to warn you if you enter a site that tries to collect personal information. You can also delete the file that stores cookie information. It is called cookies.txt.

➤ Merchants Who Sell Your Personal Data

Do you reveal personal information to merchants in exchange for free products or software? That's perfectly acceptable if they promise not to resell your information. Before filling out any forms, read the disclaimers to make sure the merchants won't reveal your data. If they don't make this disclosure, then don't fill out the form, no matter how tempting the offer.

The Electronic Privacy Information Center said that only 17 of the Internet's 100 most popular sites have policies to protect users' privacy.

A Boston Consulting Group survey in June 1997 showed 41 percent of Internet users abandoned websites that asked for

RISKY BUSINESS' FIVE WAYS TO PROTECT YOURSELF FROM IDENTITY THEFT

Are you revealing too much information? Can perfect strangers learn more about you than you care to have them know? Here are tips for protecting yourself in cyberspace:

1. Don't ever give out information that can be used to apply for credit, such as your Social Security number or your mother's maiden name. (One legitimate company, a magazine publisher, asked me for my mother's maiden name to apply for a free copy of their publication. Why on earth would they need that piece of information?)

2. Warn children against giving out confidential information. Many websites targeted at children ask them to fill out contest forms to win prizes—an irresistible option for kids. The sites then have marketing and demographic information about your family that they can use or sell. If your family has a secret password, be sure the child knows not to give it out to strangers. Young children know they should not do this, but studies have shown they will do it anyway if asked by an adult.

3. Use passwords that are hard to guess. Don't use simple words, like "secret," "password," or "test." Change the default setting of passwords. Change your password every few months. Use a combination of letters and numbers, which are harder to guess. Don't write your password on a piece of paper on your desk or in your wallet; it can be stolen easily. Never give out your password to anyone.

4. If you fill out registration forms on merchants' websites, complete as little of the form as possible. You might find you still can get the benefits of registering even if you don't reveal your e-mail address, home address, or phone

(continued)

IDENTITY THEFT (Continued)

number. Avoid filling out registration forms for companies you've never heard of or feel uneasy about, regardless of the reason. If you have any doubts about the company, investigate its credentials. A company like Kodak or IBM is usually above reproach, whereas a company like Joe's Shady Company, Established Yesterday, might not be.

5. Messages you post in newsgroups could reveal a great deal about you. Remember that thousands of people can read these messages; it takes only one warped person to make your life miserable. Use discretion in posting anything online.

Check your credit report to see if fraudulent accounts have been created in your name. You can do this by contacting:

Experian (formerly TRW): 800-682-7654, Experian Consumer Assistance Center, PO Box 949, Allen, TX 75002–0949.

Equifax: 800-685-1111, PO Box 740241, Atlanta, GA 30374–0241. Trans Union: 800-916-8800, 760 West Sproul Road, PO Box 390, Springfield, IL 19064–0390.

---

personal information. The study claimed that commercial transactions on the Internet could jump by $6 billion over the next three years if merchants can convince consumers their privacy is being protected.

■ PROPOSED LAWS

The U.S. Senate is looking at enacting laws to protect consumers. The Personal Information Privacy Act introduced by

Sen. Dianne Feinstein (D) of California and Sen. Charles Grassley (R) of Iowa would:

➤ Prohibit credit bureaus from buying and selling certain personal information not available in the local phone book, especially the "credit headers" on credit reports, which link the reports to individuals. Credit bureaus routinely sell or rent this information to marketers and mailing-list brokers.

➤ Prohibit buying and selling Social Security numbers without consent of the person involved.

➤ Restrict state motor vehicle departments, which often use Social Security numbers for driver's licenses, from distributing license numbers for surveys or marketing.

Senator Feinstein decided to find out what information was available about her and was startled by what she learned, according to the *Christian Science Monitor,* April 30, 1997.* "My staff was able to retrieve my own Social Security number and other personal information from a commercial database in less than three minutes," she says. That experience, along with complaints from constituents, led her to introduce the bill.

Grassley says it takes "minimal information and a few keystrokes" to retrieve a "lifetime" of credit history and other personal information. "For this reason, it is important that we work to make sure some personal information stays out of the hands of people we have never met, whose intentions we don't know," he says.

---

* *Christian Science Monitor,* April 30, 1997.

■ SUMMARY

Credit thieves have moved from rummaging through garbage cans for old credit card receipts and canceled checks to searching online databases, chat rooms, newsgroups, and personal websites. If you unknowingly give out privileged information, you might find yourself the victim of a theft of identity. However, by taking precautions to guard your privacy, you can thwart these thieves. Nevertheless, it is a good idea to check your credit ratings to make sure that thieves haven't compromised you as there might be online sources you don't know about that are giving away vital information. You must be vigilant in protecting your privacy.

ONLINE RESOURCES

Public Interest Research Group, www.pirg.org, offers information on fighting identity theft and other situations. U.S. PIRG, 218 D St. SE, Washington, DC 20003, 202-546-9707, uspirg@pirg.org. For the identity theft guide, send e-mail to watchdog@pirg.org.

Privacy Rights Clearinghouse, www.privacyrights.org, is an organization dedicated to assisting consumers with a wide range of privacy issues. Their informative fact sheet, "Coping with Identity Theft: What to Do When an Imposter Strikes" can be obtained online or by calling 800-773-7748 or 619-260-4160.

Chapter 4

Impersonation

Bill Clinton sends you an e-mail inviting you to a gala dinner reception at the White House. Can you be sure that it's really from the President? Your biggest client sends you an e-mail ordering you to change the background of the new logo from a bold, majestic royal blue to a green paisley. Can you really be sure the mail came from your client? Your boss sends you an e-mail saying you are the biggest dunderhead he's ever met and if you don't improve, you'll be history. Did the note really come from your boss, or from a jealous coworker?

If you use standard e-mail programs today, you can't be sure who the sender is.

It is easy to fake the identity of another person and send e-mail that misleads you in any number of ways. Even if you ask the sender a set of questions, the answers won't confirm identity beyond a shadow of a doubt. Asking for biographical material, such as where the person went to school or when he got married, won't help because that information is public record—anyone can get access to it. If you ask what his favorite color is, he could name any color and you wouldn't know whether it was right or wrong. So how can you tell if a customer is really ordering a product or canceling a contract?

This chapter focuses on impersonation and how it can hurt you, and then suggests ways to protect yourself and your organization. You'll learn:

➤ What impersonation is.

➤ Defenses against impersonators including:

Logical means.

Digital IDs.

Electronic verification.

■ WHAT IS IMPERSONATION?

As the initial examples in this chapter illustrate, any person online can claim to be any other real person or an imaginary person. After all, you can't see him, hear him, or even ask to see a driver's license, as a store clerk would do to verify identification. An organization online can only take the claimant's word that he is the person he claims to be.

This can have dangerous consequences:

➤ A scam artist orders products in the names of people who don't exist. You are left holding a worthless invoice.

➤ An unscrupulous vendor sends himself an e-mail forged with your identification authorizing the final approval of an advertisement or printed brochure. You get the finished product, but without the changes you sought—and he produces the forged e-mail.

➤ A person impersonates a trusted source, such as a newsletter or market analyst, and sends you interesting information about your competitors or market trends. You believe the information is reliable. You act on that information. Because you've made business decisions based on incorrect data sent by an imposter, you may lose money from the purchase of a worthless stock, the shifting of materials and resources in your manufacturing process, or a delay in the hiring/firing of employees. All these actions could have tremendous negative consequences for your business.

➤ A competitor impersonates you by forging your e-mail ID and sends notes to your clients saying you want to triple your fees. The client sends you a note saying she can't afford to work with you any longer. You lose a client and can't understand why.

➤ A fanatic who hates you or your organization impersonates you and sends thousands of e-mails containing racist or sexist remarks. Recipients, thinking the notes are from you, believe the content and organize a boycott.

In a recent case, a former Oracle employee was found guilty of forging e-mail (*San Francisco Chronicle,* January 29, 1997, page B1). She had claimed she was fired from her job, as an executive assistant, after she refused to have sex with the company CEO, Lawrence Ellison. An alleged e-mail allegedly sent by the employee's former boss to Ellison stated, "I have terminated [name] per your request." The company claimed this employee used her boss's password and sent the message after breaking into the company's computer system.

Private citizens can have problems with impersonation as well. People may think they are chatting with a person with certain attributes and then find they are talking with a full-fledged liar. Your 15-year-old daughter might have thought the person she met in a chat room is a teenage girl, just like her, only to find the person is a 30-year-old man on the prowl.

These examples should cause you to scrutinize every piece of e-mail you receive that doesn't sound true.

■ DEFENSES

Since it is easy to forge an e-mail address or lie on a registration form, how can organizations deal with this problem?

"Trusted third party authentication is needed. When users go to use a service, they must authenticate themselves to the company. This will assure the client and the server that the other is who they say they are," says Jim Duncan, jim.duncan@psu.edu, 814-863-8310, manager of network and information systems at the applied research laboratory of the Pennsylvania State University.

> According to Jim Duncan: "It is important to understand the difference between authentication and identification. Identification is based on information that can be obtained from many sources, like a Social Security number. It is not reliable. Authentication requires a shared secret involving strong encryption. A password that is encrypted would be an example of an authentication."*

"A new standard security device is being developed called Kerberos, from Project Athena at MIT, is evolving into the heart and sole of the DCE security service. Many large companies, including IBM, are hoping it become the standard. IBM is building this service into its mainframe computers. Not only will it authenticate the user, it will protect the password as well," he says.

How can you protect yourself and your organization against impersonators? There are logical means and technology measures.

---

* Interview, July 28, 1997.

➤ Logical Means of Verifying Identities

Organizations can thwart impersonators with at least three logical measures:

1. Every questionable piece of material should be verified by phone. If you get a mysterious e-mail from a client changing order specifications or canceling a contract, you can easily verify the information with a quick phone call.
2. Information or misinformation sent by impersonators can be detected by calling an independent third-party source, or by checking that source's website for reliable information (or to see whether they've even posted any information on this subject).
3. Read the header information on the e-mail message to see whether it contains clues, such as e-mail addresses or Internet service providers, to the sender's authenticity.

All these strategies can be given greater credibility by creating company policies that require employees to verify information and identities before acting on the orders in those messages. Chapter 7 provides sample language for such policies.

➤ Technological Measures to Verify Identity

To protect individuals and organizations against online impersonators, companies are rushing to develop technological defenses. The following products aim to authenticate the person who sent the message and verify that the materials have not been altered in transit:

➤ Encryption.
➤ Digital signatures.
➤ Fingerprint/eye print.

Encryption, Definitions Please

One of the most popular methods of securing your documents is *encryption.* It involves converting a plain text message into "ciphertext," which looks like gibberish (XFD-JEKFSKSDJFSDKFW4ER88FT9DK49043). The message is sent via e-mail to the recipient who holds a key for decrypting the message so it can be read. If this e-mail is intercepted, no one can read it. Here are some types of encryption:

➤ The "key" is a string of numbers that decodes the message.

➤ A "private key encryption" or "secret key encryption" is a routine based on using a single key to encrypt or decrypt a message. The sender and receiver must share the same key.

➤ "Public key encryption" is a routine based on two keys: one private and one public. The public key is published in a directory. The private key is secret. Anyone can send a confidential message by encrypting it using the receiver's key, but the receiver's private key is the only one that can decrypt the message.

Secure/Multipurpose Internet Mail Extensions (S/MIME) is the industry specification for secure electronic mail. S/MIME allows you to:

➤ Digitally "sign" your e-mail, which, in essence, means that you can electronically "shrink-wrap" your message. This allows the recipient to authenticate that the message is really from you.

➤ Digitally "encrypt," or "scramble," a message to ensure that only the intended party can read it.

Digital Signatures

As businesses begin to embrace the Internet and engage in electronic commerce, they face critical questions involving the source of the communications they are expected to act on, and the integrity of the electronic messages so critical to electronic commerce, according to the American Bar Association (ABA) website. "The key answer to these critical legal and business concerns is the concept of a digital signature . . . The Internet is embracing digital signatures for all forms of electronic commerce, from electronic contracts to electronic credit card payments, digital cash, and electronic checks. Likewise, states are rushing to enact digital signature legislation to provide the necessary legal infrastructure to facilitate secure forms of electronic commerce."

Digital signatures are important because you can prove who sent the message and that the person agreed to its terms.

"These two things are essential elements to a binding contract," says Mark Grossman, (CLTW@MGrossmanLaw .Com; http://www.becker-poliakoff.com; http://www .mgrossmanlaw.com.) who leads the Computer and Internet Law Department of Becker & Poliakoff, P.A. "Remember that many contracts are not enforceable without a signature. In case of a dispute, a court will probably find that a digital signature is as good as a 'real' signature."

Digital IDs can:

- ➤ Authenticate the identities of all participants in electronic commerce and communications.
- ➤ Authorize access to key information sources.
- ➤ Provide legally binding proof, in an increasing number of states, of messages sent over the Internet.
- ➤ Verify the integrity of the exchanged information.
- ➤ Authorize privileges in a given transaction.

Verisign, www.verisign.com, is one of the leaders in online security and identification verification. Their service works with most major e-mail programs, including Netscape Communicator's Messenger e-mail package. With Netscape and Verisign, you will be able to encrypt your e-mail messages to ensure the authenticity of e-mail messages and protect your e-mailing privacy.

To use Verisign, you will need to take these steps:

1. Acquire the latest version of Netscape Communicator 4.0.

2. Get aVeriSign Digital ID, a simple, online process, that takes only a few minutes.

3. Now you can send secure e-mail.

4. You'll need to tell everyone in your e-mail address book—friends, colleagues, and business associates—to get a Digital ID, too. By sending your e-mail circle of family, friends, and business associates a digitally signed message—accompanied by your Digital ID—you will be providing them with your public key, which is necessary for them to encrypt any future messages addressed to you.

U.S. Postal Service Aims to Add Integrity to E-Mail

The U.S. Postal Service plans to bring e-mail up to the same level of acceptance that hardcopy mail currently enjoys. The USPS is collaborating with two high-tech firms to create first-class mail electronic commerce services (ECS).

With this service, consumers will be able to purchase a home or conduct legally binding business negotiations over the Internet without worrying about the sender being an imposter or the messages being read or distorted by hackers.

The USPS is developing a series of services to mirror those of first-class mail. The first in this series calls for a time and date stamp to represent the electronic postmark. Other services will include return receipt, certified, registered, verification of sender and recipient, and archiving.

Robert Reisner, Vice President of Strategic Planning, said in a press release on the USPS Website, "The Postal Service has been valued as a trusted third party for more than two centuries. By enabling companies like Aegis Star and Cylink to create services for postal customers, we can transfer our trust to the electronic medium."

In addition to designing a postmarking system, Cylink Corporation, of Sunnyvale, California, is developing a Certificate Authority for people to use to prove who they are when sending e-mail or other electronic documents through the Internet and other networks.

"Imagine signing a mortgage today electronically," said Reisner, "and then 20 years from now finding that the authenticity of the document was in dispute. If you used Postal ECS, you would know that you were backed by the authority of the United States Postal Service." This is especially useful for commercial transactions over an open network like the Internet. While the electronic postmark validates a document's existence at a specific point in time, it also authenticates that the document has not changed from the time that the USPS touched the document.

Aegis Star Corporation, of Palo Alto, California, with expertise in archiving services, sends the electronically postmarked message to the recipient via a value-added network. When the recipient receives the electronically postmarked message, customers use Postal Service Mail Reader software to read and authenticate the message and electronic postmark. Customers will be able to change their address, register to vote, register their children for school, and obtain other government forms, all in one transaction.

Electronic Fingerprinting

Veridicom, Inc., of Menlo Park, California, www.veridicom .com, provides products that make it safer and easier to prove who you are—and protect yourself from those who may try to impersonate you—in private and commercial transactions. The Veridicom fingerprint sensor can be used as a stand-alone solution or with other security measures, such as public/private keys and digital signatures, to prevent impersonation, protect users' privacy and provide higher levels of information security, according to company literature.

Using Bell Labs' patented fingerprint authentication technology, Veridicom has developed advanced software and hardware components that verify a person's identity when face-to-face recognition is not possible. The company was founded as a partnership between Lucent Technologies and U.S. Venture Partners.

"Fax machines, telephones, and computer networks allow us to conduct transactions but provide no assurance of who is on the other end of the line," said Tom Uhlman, senior vice president of corporate strategy and business development for Lucent Technologies, in a press release on the company website. "With electronic identification based on your fingerprints, Veridicom has the potential to revolutionize the way information is accessed and day-to-day transactions are conducted."

Veridicom's fingerprint sensor is the new company's first commercial offer. The size of a postage stamp, it is designed to be easy to use: One simply places a finger on the sensor to access information, use equipment, initiate a transaction, or enter a restricted area. This small size makes it ideal for laptop computers, cellular phones, point-of-sale terminals, electronic commerce, banking, credit verification, and many products in access control and personal property protection.

The Veridicom fingerprint authentication product has four principal components: the silicon sensor, which measures the ridges and valleys of the finger pressed against the chip; analysis software, which reconstructs the fingerprint in digital form and searches for unique features (minutia) that identify a person; matching software, which uses special algorithms to match the current fingerprint to the enrollment sample given by the user; and data protection software, which protects fingerprints from unauthorized copying or tampering.

■ SUMMARY

Imposters can bilk your organization out of money and cause damage to its reputation. Using a logical and biometrical measures to verify the sender and the information, organizations can protect themselves from unscrupulous attackers.

Part Two
Financial Well-Being

Cyberspace Shell Games: Fighting Fraud Online

Pssst . . . Wanna make money while you sleep? Lose 50 pounds overnight with new miracle formula? Get rich by selling reports?

And someone online is probably still trying to sell the Brooklyn Bridge. Cyberspace is full of con artists trying to exploit other people's innocence and greed.

Con artists have plied their unscrupulous trade for hundreds of years using voice, then mail, then the telephone, and now the Internet. Businesses as well as consumers are being victimized by crooks of every sort who try to steal money online.

Cyberspace opens another area of creativity where scammers can develop new, devious tricks. Online fraud can make victims of consumers, who make purchases in good faith, only to get rooked in return. However, real merchants also are victimized by crooks who try to buy products with stolen credit cards, or other elaborate scams. This chapter includes examples of cons against consumers and businesses and explains how to protect yourself and your organization from scam artists. You will learn:

➤ What fraud is.
➤ Why you should treat fraud seriously.
➤ About scams against consumers and organizations.
➤ How to fight fraud.
➤ How to use verification services.
➤ What the government is doing to crack down on fraud.
➤ About the dangers of software piracy.
➤ Which organizations protect consumers and merchants against scammers.
➤ How to protect yourself and your organization against online fraud.
➤ The online resources available.

■ WHAT IS FRAUD?

The legal definition of *fraud* is "an intentional perversion of truth for the purpose of inducing another in reliance upon it to part with some valuable thing belonging to him or to surrender a legal right. A false representation of as a matter of fact, whether by words or by conduct, by false or misleading allegations, or by concealment of that which should have been disclosed, which deceived and is intended to deceive another so that he shall act upon it to his legal injury. Anything calculated to deceive, whether by a single act or combination, or by suppression of truth, or suggestion of what is false, whether it be by direct falsehood or innuendo, by speech or by silence, word of mouth, or look or gesture" (*Black's Law Dictionary*, by Henry Campbell Black, St. Paul, MN: West Publishing Company, 1991). Fraud also includes statements that contain lies or omit important information.

■ WHY YOU SHOULD TREAT FRAUD SERIOUSLY

Online fraud is a serious concern to law enforcement agencies.

"Fraud promoters have moved from the back alleys of America to its front porch," FTC Chairman Robert Pitofsky said in releasing the Federal Trade Commission's (FTC's) "Fighting Consumer Fraud: The Challenge and the Campaign" report on February 12, 1997, www.ftc.gov. "Like legitimate businesses, modern con artists now use desktop publishing, the Internet, and sophisticated telemarketing to reach millions of consumers with persuasive messages. Once a local threat, the snake oil salesman now can market fraud on a national, even international, scale." This FTC report documents that the consumer fraud industry is "sophisticated, tenacious, and constitutes a significant economic threat to consumers." "The good news for consumers and legitimate industry," Pitofsky said, "is that law enforcement agencies also have changed with the times."

In 1996, the FTC formed alliances with local law enforcement agencies to bring over 200 actions against fraudulent operators.

■ SCAMS AGAINST CONSUMERS AND ORGANIZATIONS

➤ What's Your Password?

One of the oldest con games online is the ruse whereby con artists claim to be representatives of the online service provider and ask to verify the user's password. Once they have that information, they can sign on to the service and run up bills. The latest example came in May 1997 when two

Stockton, California, 15-year-olds were picked up for purchasing $9,000 worth of computer equipment by using credit card numbers obtained fraudulently. They allegedly posed as America Online (AOL) managers in private chat rooms. According to a police spokesperson, three victims gave their names, addresses, and credit card numbers over the Internet (*San Francisco Chronicle,* May 3, 1997).

In a variation on this theme, con artists ask for the user's credit card number to verify their billing information which was destroyed somehow. Once they have the number, the con artists charge up orders online or with catalog companies. In minutes, you can find your credit card tapped out.

Although online service providers warn users periodically about these scams, there are always people who are unaware and succumb to this approach. Companies should make sure that all employees are alert to this possibility and understand that they must not reveal credit card numbers, passwords, or sensitive company information. They should also be instructed in the proper procedure to follow in reporting any such attempt that they might encounter.

➤ Please Pass the Password

Consumers who pay a fee to register to use a site are legal. However, when they give their passwords to their friends, they are ripping off the business. Companies that issue passwords need to create safeguards so their sites aren't overrun by freeloaders (*The Wall Street Journal,* February 21, 1997, p. B1).

Possible solutions include limiting the number of accesses each day. The owner of an adult site noted that if the same password was used dozens of times a day, it was unlikely the same person was using it.

Passing passwords is so widespread on the Internet, there are even newsgroups where crackers trade, barter, or sell passwords. The alt.crack newsgroup contains more than 5,000 messages. Other newsgroups that are used by hackers distributing passwords include alt.2600crackx, alt.cracks, alt.crackers, and alt.supermodels. Businesses can see if their passwords are up for grabs by using DejaNews and searching for the keyword "password."

➤ Password: Nyet!

In an example of an international scam, America Online found so many fraudulent users in Russia who used stolen credit cards and passwords that it finally decided to cut direct access to its service for that country as of December 1996. Local users now must use a Russian Internet service, such as Glanet, Russia Online, or Matrix to access their accounts. This action placed a line of defense for AOL against scam artists.

➤ Dial-a-Scam (Part One)

Another widespread fraud against consumers and businesses occurred when people were sent e-mail and were asked to call a number in the 809 area code with the come-on that they might be the recipients of billions of dollars of unclaimed money. This was a pay-per-call service billed at a high rate to the caller's phone. People were shocked to see large charges for calls. This type of scam was covered widely in the traditional media as well as postings in newsgroups and e-mails on the Internet and commercial online services. This scam has been seen since the 1980s in traditional media and spread to the Internet in 1997, according to the Better Business Bureau, www.bbb.org.

According to the National Fraud Information Center, the best advice is never to return calls to unfamiliar numbers. If it's not clear whether a number is domestic or international, check the map in the front of the phone book that shows the U.S. area codes or call the operator.

➤ Dial-a-Scam (Part Two)

Pornography has been described as a victimless crime. But online surfers might find themselves victimized. A typical scam lures people to porn sites with the offer of free pictures, if you download a file. However, there is no file to download. The site hangs up on your ISP connection, turns off the modem speaker, and redials a long-distance phone number in Moldova, part of the old Soviet Union. Viewers find a huge charge to their phone bills several weeks later. Sometimes, the charges run as high as $30 a minute. The phone companies do not forgive the charges. You can protect yourself and your company by:

- ➤ Using a software program that blocks pornographic sites (see Chapter 7).
- ➤ Being aware of the scam and not falling for this ruse.
- ➤ Having a company policy prohibiting porn site viewing.
- ➤ Challenging questionable phone charges.

➤ A Scam Waiting to Happen: Online Gambling

Here's a scam just waiting to bite people. Gambling sites are springing up all over the Internet and all over the world. You had better believe these sites won't give fair odds. Since these companies are based in foreign countries, including the Cayman Islands, they don't have to honor U.S. laws.

➤ Man Bites Dog: Con Artists Attack Merchants

While many trees have given their lives telling consumers about scams on the Internet, little has been written to defend merchants who find themselves victimized by scam artists.

Scammers defraud online ordering systems using several methods. Here are some of these scams and suggestions for protecting your company from abuse:

➤ *Making purchases with stolen credit card numbers.* Merchants should always check the credit card number for validation and take advantage of the address verification check as well. This service notifies you if a customer's shipping address or phone number differs from that of the caller.

➤ *Denying receipt of the property.* Use a delivery service that requires a signature, such as Federal Express, UPS, or the Express Mail service from the U.S. Postal Service.

Telephone operators working for mail-order companies can detect tell-tale signs of fraudulent orders by listening for tense or strained voices, immature voices, and requests to leave packages on a doorstoop without signatures.

Online merchants can't hear the stress levels in those voices so they are easily victimized. Here's what one company did to reduce its fraud rate to a negligible amount.

■ FIGHTING FRAUD: CYBERSOURCE

From the very start, CyberSource, the parent company for Software.Net believed this new enterprise would be a sure winner on the Internet. The company would sell software from its site and would offer the key selling point of downloading software to provide instant gratification for shoppers.

Ah, but there was the problem. Once a crook has your product, you are out of luck.

Dollars attributed to fraud exceeded the dollars attributed to legitimate sales, according to Bill McKiernan, president of software.net, based in Menlo Park, California, www.software.net.*

---

* Interview, May 1997.

"What we learned the hard way with software.net is that fraud is out of control on the Internet. When you fill products electronically, the fraud rate goes much higher than the rate for mail fraud."

Ironically, many thieves were not trying to get the software for their own use, but to demonstrate that they were smart enough to break the code.

"They tend to be teenage boys," said McKiernan. "What we have found is that they are stealing things not so much to pawn them and get cash, but for sport. It is about who can steal the most software. It is a trophy. They will try to steal a $7,000 network management program from IBM which they will never use, but which has a lot of value to them."*

The problem for software.net is that publishers wanted their share of the sale, even if a stolen credit card was used. The company was on the line for big bucks because they had inadequate methods of checking on credit cards.

"At software.net, we found that fraud was a huge problem. We were doing more fraud than legitimate sales," he said. "We were on the hook for paying the publishers as well. . . . We get an authorization code that says the transaction is okay. Then we find out 45 days later that the cardholder cancelled the card. We get a charge back from the bank," he said. "Merchants don't realize that they are responsible for fraudulent sales. The bank won't reimburse them—even if the bank had approved the sale. Consumers have more protection from credit card issuers; they are liable only for $50, but most banks don't charge that for fear of alienating their customers. . . . When you are dealing in a mail order situation, the bank is not liable, the merchant is liable 100 percent. This is unlike a face to face transaction; the bank is liable.

"They are smart enough to know that if they buy something online and have it delivered to their house, they will get caught. With a digitally delivered product, there is more

---

* Interview, May 1997.

anonymity in that transaction. They will get hold of a valid credit card number. They will go on shopping sprees on the Internet. One of the things we've found is that these guys have a very good communications network. They tell each other the card numbers."

Although software.net sells more than $1.5 million of software a month (as of July 1997), the start-up phase was rocky because of fraud.

"We launched in November 1994. We were in very deep trouble. We looked at a couple of solutions at the time. We thought about cutting off electronic software delivery and only doing physical fulfillment, but that goes against company plan.

"We also thought of creating a membership plan so we could have time to check out their credentials. But that would hurt the customer's desire for instant gratification," explained McKiernan. Software.net instead developed a "fraud screen system," an artificial intelligence system that checks the creditworthiness of each potential customer. The artificial intelligence code ran though hundreds of thousands of transactions in the database and analyzed every transaction. The software found more than 100 variables that could identify thieves.

"Some are obvious, like time of day in the local time zone. If someone is calling at 2 A.M. from Boston, that's not great. We also look at where the user is dialing in from compared to the billing address. If they dial in from Miami, but the billing address is in Seattle, that's unusual. We analyze these characteristics and create a score for each transaction. If the score falls below our criteria, we reject it—politely—but we reject it."

The countries with the highest fraud rates are the former Eastern bloc (including Poland and Romania) as well as pockets in the United States.

"We can watch them come in to the site and see them change identities and credit cards. One guy in Israel has used over 500 names and identities.

"With mail order, the sales representatives are the screening mechanism. If someone says, 'Leave it on the porch, no signature required' or has a harried voice or a child's voice, you know something isn't right. A computer can't do that. That's why we needed the fraud screen."

The fraud screen seems to be working.

"Our fraud rate is now under $1/2$ of 1 percent, so it is very manageable," McKiernan said, and then added "Our *attempted* fraud rate hasn't gone down that much."

Software.net fights fraud through the police and courts as well.

"We are able to track them down," he said. "It takes a lot of time and energy. Sometimes we'll call them up at home and tell them we will tell their mother. Often times, that is enough. But we will use the police."

Sometimes the police cooperate, and sometimes they don't.

According to McKiernan, "In Newark, which has dozens of phony names and cards, the police were not cooperative. In the big cities you rarely get any attention. In Modesto, we got the local police involved. They were very aggressive. They set up a sting and arrested four teenage boys. The event got big media coverage. They were bright kids. They were ordering sporting goods on the Net. They had stolen a few thousand dollars of stuff. It was more than just a prank."

Software.net realized they have created not only an effective tool for their own use, but a powerful tool for other online merchants as well. Its parent company CyberSource provides back office and commerce services for online retailers. If you want to sell things from your site, CyberSource can do export control, fraud verification, and fulfillment, and offer an EDI (Electronic Data Interchange) link to fulfillment house. They have as clients more than 100 companies that like the turnkey service and the protection from fraud. Most of their clients are software publishers and resellers of information.

Fraud will always haunt retailers.

"Fraud will take a new look. Fraud is nothing new. It is probably the third oldest profession," concluded McKiernan. "But our software fraud screen gets smarter every day."

■ VERIFICATION SERVICES

In addition to CyberSource, other companies offer ways to protect merchants from unscrupulous customers. This is an issue that must be addressed.

"You have to think very carefully how you are going to address the fraud issue," advises McKiernan. "Once you ship it, you can't pull the bits back."

➤ Cryptolope

IBM has developed a tool called Cryptolope, www.cryptolope.ibm.com, which is an electronic package that holds an encrypted version of a text document or an electronic commodity, such as music, film, art, software, graphics, or multimedia products. The entire transaction is private and protected.

➤ Trust Marks

TRUSTe has devised "trustmarks" that will inform consumers about what kinds of personal information is being gathered from customers and how that information will be used. The association was created by AT&T, IBM, Oracle, Netscape Communications, Tandem Computers, Lands' End, and the Electronic Frontier Foundation. The accounting firm of Coopers & Lybrand will audit companies to ensure they live up to the standards.

➤ Insurance for Merchants

Insurer USF&G, www.shareholder.com/usfg, provides coverage for merchants who use Verisign's Digital ID. This insurer, with $14.5 billion in assets, will protect merchants by authenticating the IDs. It also protects consumers in case merchants lock out consumers who want to make a transaction, which could affect people placing stock market transactions at stock brokerage sites.

■ GOVERNMENT AND ONLINE SERVICES CRACK DOWN ON FRAUD

Government agencies, local law enforcement officials, and online services are treating online crime as a serious offense. They have cracked down on con artists and have achieved awesome results. Here are overviews of key cases.

➤ America Online Nabs "Happy Hardcore" Hacker

America Online was the victim of Nicholas Ryan, a Yale University student and computer hacker also known as "Happy Hardcore" who illegally accessed AOL allowing hundreds of people to use the service for free. The network quickly upgraded its security measures to prevent AOL4FREE or any similar software from working.

Ryan pleaded guilty in federal district court in Alexandria, Virginia, to a felony offense under the Computer Fraud and Abuse Act in January 1997. After uncovering the illegal activity, America Online had assembled evidence against Ryan and then notified the Secret Service, which also investigated the case. This is the first successful computer fraud prosecution involving an Internet online network.

"We hope this conviction sends a message to our members that AOL is dedicated to stopping hackers and their activities on the service and creating a safe and enjoyable online experience," said Tatiana Gau, vice president for Integrity Assurance at AOL. "It also serves as a warning to any would-be hackers that AOL has zero tolerance for this kind of behavior. We have made a pledge to provide our members with the highest level of security and privacy, and they can be confident that we are doing so."

➤ "Clever" Cracker Caught

Police say almost all crooks are stupid. Consider the case of a San Francisco Bay area man. He allegedly broke into a major Internet provider's computer and collected 100,000 credit card numbers, according to an FBI spokesperson. However, he allegedly tried to sell the credit card information to an undercover agent for $260,000.

Authorities won't say how the thief maneuvered this break-in, but observers speculate it happened in one of two ways:

➤ He intercepted numbers as people placed orders over the Internet. This can be avoided if merchants use Secure Sockets Layer (SSL) or SET, two data encryption codes that are built into the Netscape and Microsoft browsers.

➤ He broke into the computer where the numbers are kept. Merchants or ISPs can prevent this by using firewalls and other security measures to keep prowlers out.

➤ U.S. Post Office Stops Internet-Mail Order Scam

Companies making false claims can find themselves out of business. Advanced Computer Resources was a company advertising on the Internet that consumers could purchase a new Pentium computer for the unheard of price of $295. Since the company asked respondents to reply to a post office box, the incident fell under the U.S. Postal Service mail fraud rules. The company address was a mail drop only, according to the Better Business Bureau. The USPS investigated the case and closed the business down in December 1996.

➤ Federal Trade Commission Takes Action against Credit Repair Agencies

The FTC staff has been cracking down on fraudulent credit repair companies on the Internet. It began searching the Internet for credit repair advertisements, and sent e-mail messages to 47 credit repair companies. The FTC sent those companies information about the federal laws and directed them to its website for additional information. The FTC also has a web page to educate consumers about credit repair, www.ftc.gov.

FTC Takes Action—Again

The Federal Trade Commission, and the North American Securities Administrators Association (NASAA), U.S. Postal Inspection Service, and attorneys general from 24 states have begun cracking down on several websites that made wild earnings claims. In March 1997, the agencies sent 215 notices to website operators warning them that they had better have evidence to back up their earnings claims.

Officials made follow-up inspections in April 1997 and found seven sites had been changed to remove the earnings claims; and another 37 sites had been taken down completely. Twenty-four of the ads had been placed on newsgroups and will disappear automatically. Of the 191 actual websites, 23 percent were changed or taken down. The threat of action apparently was enough to close the sites or have them temper their claims.

The FTC said evidence of false or unsubstantiated earnings claims can land a firm in court for alleged violations of the FTC Act or state statutes against deceptive business practices.

> "The Surf Day (created by the FTC, an online event to bring attention to online fraud) approach to policing fraud on the Internet takes advantage of a vast new medium that, on the one hand, could make it easier to perpetrate a deceptive scheme and get away with it, and turns that medium into a tool for warning potential scammers that they can't count on going undetected," said Jodie Bernstein, director of the FTC's Bureau of Consumer Protection. "Part of our goal is to inform marketers about the law, which says that a company making earnings claims must have hard evidence to back them up. We encourage consumers surfing the Web for a

*new business opportunity to insist on seeing substantia-
tion for every objective claim a company makes, as well
as a list of every person who has signed up for the business. While the Internet offers innovative, cutting-edge
opportunities, it is still old-fashioned legwork—poring
over the numbers, and telephoning and visiting in-
person the sites of other participants—that will best protect consumers from becoming the victims of fraud."*

FTC Takes Action—Again—and Again

The FTC charged nine companies that market their products
and services on the Internet with making false or unsubstantiated advertising claims. The FTC negotiated settlements to
halt the deceptive practices of eight of the companies and is
pursuing the ninth case in federal district court.

"Cyberspace is a new frontier for advertising and marketing," Bernstein pointed out in March 1997. "But," she added,
"the Internet will not achieve its commercial potential if this
new frontier becomes the "Wild West" of fraudulent schemes.
These FTC cases target deception in online marketing, and
our focus on this area makes clear that the laws prohibiting
fraud also apply to the information superhighway."

The nine cases involved online marketing for a range of
phony schemes including credit repair rip-offs, bogus income
opportunities, a phony grant assistance offer, and a computer
equipment supply scam. The FTC charged five of the companies and their principal officers with making false claims
about repairing consumers' credit records. Using ads that
made claims such as, "Guaranteed Credit Repair," and "How to
remove judgments, including bankruptcy from your credit
file," the companies urged consumers to send fees ranging
from $19.95 to $750 to get instructions or assistance on how
they could remove adverse items, such as reports of bankruptcy, from credit reports, even if the information was accurate and not obsolete. Two of the companies claimed that for a

---

* FTC press release, April 24, 1997.

fee, they could provide consumers with instructions to establish new credit identities and files. The statements made by the five companies were false, the FTC alleged, and the instructions for creating new credit files could violate federal criminal law.

The proposed consent agreements to settle the charges would enjoin the defendants from misrepresenting any remedy for credit history problems, including the ability to remove accurate but adverse information from credit reports. Settlements with the defendants who advertised programs to create new credit files also would bar them from misrepresenting the legality of any credit repair product and require them to disclose that consumers who follow their programs may violate federal criminal laws.

Four defendants were charged with making unsubstantiated earnings claims for the work-at-home businesses they advertised online. Touting earnings such as, "Earn up to $4,000 or More Each Month!" and "Our *Home Workers' First Year Income* averages $38,000 . . . ," they sold programs at prices ranging from $9.95 to $147. The FTC charged that by using such statements the defendants represented that the earnings were representative of what consumers could expect to achieve and that they had a reasonable basis to substantiate them. In fact, the challenged earnings representations are false and unsubstantiated, the FTC said.

The proposed agreements to settle the charges would prohibit these defendants from misrepresenting the income, earnings, or sales from any business opportunity and would prohibit any claims about past, present, or future earnings or income unless at the time of making the representation, they possess and rely on competent and reliable evidence that substantiates the claim.

Another FTC complaint targeted an advertiser who claimed to match consumers with private foundations with "billions of dollars" to give away to consumers. Advertising touted "*Free Cash Grants* by Mail . . . " and offered, for a fee, to match consumers with private foundations likely to give them money for business, travel, education, or debt consolidation.

The FTC complaint alleges that through statements like, "Most of our clients are approved for cash grants," the defendant represented that the majority of his clients receive a cash grant. The claim is false and unsubstantiated, the FTC alleged. The proposed agreement to settle these charges would prohibit the defendant from making similar false and unsubstantiated claims and from misrepresenting the services or assistance he provides for obtaining grants, loans, or other financial products or services.

"We want our message to be loud and clear," Bernstein said. "The Internet opens a world of opportunities for consumers. Unfortunately, it also presents opportunities for scam artists. . . . We intend to monitor the Internet rigorously and act decisively when we see deceptive and misleading marketing."

The final FTC case charged that a marketer of computer memory chips advertised online and promised that the chips would be shipped or ordered from an overseas supplier as soon as the consumer's check cleared the bank. In some cases, the FTC alleged, the company specified a delivery date of two weeks after the consumer paid for the order.

According to the FTC complaint, the company failed to deliver the chips and failed to comply with the FTC's Mail or Telephone Order Merchandise Rule, which requires companies offering goods through mail order, by fax, over the telephone, or via an online service either to deliver items when promised or to give consumers the option to cancel the order and receive a refund. Under this rule, these companies also must issue refunds automatically when these requirements are not met.

➤ Local Courts Attack Fraud

Local laws apply to merchants and to scam artists. Manhattan State Supreme Court Judge Diane Lebedeff ruled in May 1997, denying a plaintiff's claim that state laws don't apply to the Internet. She ordered Kevin Jay Lipsitz, the web-based operator/scammer of a magazine subscription business to discontinue his fraudulent practices.

New York State Attorney General Dennis Vacco said more than 50 consumers were victimized by Lipsitz's promotional devices, which were alleged to include spurious e-mail testimonials for his Krazy Kevin's Magazine Club, Magazine Club Inquiry Center, and Tempting Tear-Outs businesses.

➤ Achtung! Germany Blitzkriegs Online Schweinhunds

Germany passed the German Multimedia Legislation, a series of sweeping laws to prevent fraud, hate speech, and pornography on the Internet and other electronic media, including CompuServe and America Online. The laws are being studied by other members of the European Commission countries.

The law holds the supplier of the data guilty of the crime. It does not place the problem on the shoulders of the service provider. The law also calls for the introduction of digital signatures on transactional data, including e-mail. This will allow all messages to be traced to the original sources. Currently, people can easily hide behind anonymous IDs.

■ SOFTWARE PIRACY

Software piracy was an $11 billion worldwide crime in 1996—and the Internet is making matters worse, according to the Software Publishers Association (SPA), the principal trade group of the software industry. Many software publishers offer free downloads from their websites for sample software. If companies don't buy the software, but continue to use it, they are guilty of copyright violations and software piracy.

Another growing problem is pirate websites that offer full, working versions of software programs for anyone to copy and use. Copying software from these pirate sites is also illegal.

Peter Beruk, SPA director of domestic antipiracy, explained this problem: "The Internet is leading to more piracy, unfortunately. You can find any software program on the Internet and download it. You just have to know where to find it. Pirates put up a site for a few days and take it down. They put it up on another server a few days later. From an investigative standpoint, it is frustrating."*

The SPA actively fights software pirates. They get leads from former and current employees and consultants. SPA members who learn about piracy also contact the organization. Publishers learn about piracy when people call in for technical support. (For additional information on software piracy, see Chapters 7 and 9.)

➤ SPA Wins Judgment against Internet Software Pirate

The SPA has won hundreds of settlements against companies that have pirated software in the past decade.

Most recently, the U.S. District Court in Seattle entered a judgment against Max Butler in a lawsuit filed by the Software Publishers Association (SPA) as part of its Internet Anti-Piracy Campaign (IAPC). The judgment permanently enjoined Butler from infringing computer software copyrights, via Internet, using a File-Transfer Protocol (FTP) server or otherwise, and set recovery at $60,000. The action was filed on behalf of Cinco Networks, Inc., Symantec Corporation, and Traveling Software, Inc.

ABWAM, the Colorado-based Internet access provider (IAP) used by Butler, discovered the infringing material. Through routine maintenance of its site, ABWAM found exceedingly large file transfers, a significant volume of uploads and directory names containing filenames indicative of commercial software titles. Suspicious of the activity, an ABWAM representative contacted SPA's antipiracy

---

* Interview, July 1997.

hotline, 800-388-7478, and reported the IAP's concerns. With ABWAM's cooperation, SPA traced the activity to Butler, utilized FTP logs as evidence and filed suit on July 23, 1996, less than one month after receiving the initial report.

Beruk commented, "This judgment serves clear notice that Internet users who infringe computer software copyrights are subject to exposure and severe penalties under the law. Members of the Internet community need to respect copyright and intellectual property rights to protect the integrity and future development and application of the Internet" (SPA press release, February 20, 1997).

➤ Software Publishers Can Fight Piracy

Software publishers are taking steps to fight piracy. While most software publishers' sites require people to read the license and agree to its terms before downloading the software, few people wade through the dense legalese that warns users to not copy the software. Here are ways for software publishers to protect their intellectual property.

➤ Apply a "time lock" on the software so that after a certain number of days the program will cease to exist unless the user buys it.

➤ Require the user to call the company for a passcode to operate the program. Simply downloading the program won't make it work. With this method, the company knows exactly who is using the program.

➤ Require the use of a "dongle," a piece of hardware that fits onto the computer's serial or parallel port. When the user executes the program, it looks for the dongle. If the user makes a second copy of the software program and the dongle is not there, it will not work. Dongles are impossible to replicate.

➤ When you handle customer support calls, ask the caller to read the registration information. If the software is licensed to another company, you can ask the SPA to investigate the company.

➤ Software Piracy, Another View

McAfee Associates, Inc., publisher of several of the industry's leading virus protection programs, takes a slightly different view of piracy:

> *We pioneered the subscription pricing model that
> Netscape and others now use. It's simple: People down-
> load our software without paying for it—then they come
> back and pay us to get the technical support and two
> years of free upgrades. Last year, 8 million people did just
> that. Of course, some people do steal our software. But
> they end up spreading the word about McAfee's goodwill
> and top-rated products. All of which reinforces our posi-
> tion as the market leader. (according to a company ad-
> vertisement in a trade publication in July 1997)*

■ ORGANIZATIONS PROTECT CONSUMERS AND MERCHANTS AGAINST SCAMMERS

Organizations are springing up on the web to protect consumers from unscrupulous merchants, and to protect legitimate merchants from unscrupulous thieves. Here is a review
of the top organizations.

➤ Better Business Bureau Creates Seal of Approval

With all these abuses on the Internet, you would think consumers would relish a seal of approval from an undisputed
leader in consumer protection. In May 1997, the Better Business Bureau created its own seal of approval for its members'
websites. Members can display a seal on their site and be assured the same degree of protection as in the real world.

However, even the Better Business Bureau has been
plagued by a scam involving companies that claim to be
members of the BBB. By copying the BBB logo and placing

it on their page, these scammers trick people into believing their business is approved by the BBB. In reality, BBB members can display a logo that links them to a special Web page that confirms they are members. If a nonmember site displays the logo, the user will be linked to a BBB page saying the site has not been confirmed as a BBB member, whereupon you can send the page's information to the BBB for investigation.

➤ Filing a Complaint

Consumers with complaints about business opportunities advertised on the Internet should report them to the National Fraud Information Center (NFIC), a project of the National Consumers League, at 800-876-7060. Complaints about possible violations of the Canadian Competition Act may be filed by calling 800-348-5358.

The National Fraud Information Center is run by the National Consumers League, www.fraud.org, in cooperation with the National Association of Attorneys General and the Federal Trade Commission, to assist federal and state law enforcement agencies to gather complaints about online fraud and take appropriate enforcement action. "Our goal: a safe and crime-free Internet." You can file reports of fraud online, read daily and archived reports of frauds that have occurred online and other media, as well as follow links to government sites, http://www.fraud.org/nfic3.htm.

■ CHECK THE BUSINESS BACKGROUND OF THE COMPANY

American Business Information (ABI), www.lookupsusa.com, 800-274-5325, sells reports on the credit of the more than 10 million businesses in the United States for $3 each. Reports include company name, address, phone number, fax number, number of employees, type of business, Standard Industrial

RISKY BUSINESS' TIPS ON PROTECTING YOURSELF AGAINST ONLINE FRAUD

Here are tips to protect consumers and businesses from on-line fraud. The ideas have been collected from interviews, online areas, and other resources, including the Federal Trade Commission, NASAA, the National Fraud Information Center, CyberSource, and several lawyers.

1. Beware of "shills" or phony references. Don't accept a list of references selected by the company offering the business opportunity as a substitute for a complete list of franchise or business opportunity owners.

2. Investigate all earnings claims. Ask others who have purchased the opportunity if their experience verifies the claims. Demand to see the company's basis for its claims in writing. Be skeptical in judging whether the claims are backed up.

3. Avoid any plan that includes commissions for recruit-ing additional distributors, because it may be an illegal pyramid scheme that ultimately must collapse for lack of new recruits. Many state laws prohibit pyramiding by allowing commissions to be paid only for retail sales of goods or services, not for recruiting new distributors.

4. Ask for the disclosure document if you're investing in a franchise. This document, required by law, should pro-vide detailed information to help you compare one business with another. If the company has no disclosure document, beware!

5. For work-at-home plans, get specific information about the tasks you will perform, how you will be paid, by whom and when; make sure you know the total costs and fees and what you get for your money.

(continued)

ONLINE FRAUD (Continued)

6. Get all promises in writing, including any refund policy, in any contract you sign.

7. Check out the company with the state securities agency, attorney general's office, or other consumer protection agency not only in the state where you live, but also in the state where the company is headquartered. The Better Business Bureau is another good resource. These organizations can tell you if they have any consumer complaints about the company on file.

8. Never disclose checking account numbers, credit card numbers, or other personal financial data at any website or online service location unless you are sure where this information will be directed. Call NFIC's toll-free number or send e-mail to get assistance, advice, or further information.

9. Use the same common sense you would exercise with any off-line, personal, or telephone credit card purchase. Always know the merchant you are dealing with. A flashy professional Internet website does not guarantee that the sponsor is legitimate.

10. On your website, make it very clear you are serious about preventing fraud and that you will prosecute fraud. Warn users that credit card fraud is a felony.

11. Understand that banks are not your friends in the fraud effort. They charge you. If the chargeback rate gets significant, they will pull your merchant status. They hate chargebacks more than anything else. They will get rid of you very quickly. This is the bane of their existence. If you are an online merchant and can't accept credit cards, you will be out of business.

12. Paper never refused ink. Don't believe anything you see in print. Verify everything.

(continued)

ONLINE FRAUD (Continued)

13. Ask people to sign applications under penalty of perjury.

14. For large transactions, run credit checks with organizations like TRW. Check the report against the application information.

15. If customers apply for credit with several companies at the same time, you won't know that they might be exceeding their credit limit. You must ask them if they are applying for other funding simultaneously.

16. Do the people who place the order have the authority to enter into the transaction for their businesses? For example, a secretary might order a product from you, but if she doesn't have the authority to buy products, you will have trouble collecting.

17. Verify signatures. Have signatures witnessed by a notary public, not a personal witness.

18. Send documents stating the information to the principals. You might find that they know nothing about the transactions made by corrupt employees.

19. Buying used equipment may involve fraud. The product might be stolen or still have financing left on it. You must trace ownership and leases.

20. Confirm delivery of any product. Use Fed Ex or other signed service.

21. Confirm the price and merchandise information with the seller, including brand, model, color, accessories, and rebates.

22. Confirm the seller's return and refund policies. Who pays for shipping? Is there a restocking fee?

23. Keep a copy of all correspondence, including the order form, canceled checks, credit card statements, and

(continued)

ONLINE FRAUD (Continued)

phone records, including the name of the company representative.

24. If the products are not sent within 30 days, you have the right to cancel the order and get a refund.

25. Pay for the merchandise with a credit card. If something goes wrong, the credit card companies will withhold payment and investigate your claim.

26. If you can't get satisfaction from the seller, contact the Post Office if the product was sent by mail. The USPS mail fraud unit handles such cases.

27. Before investing any money with a company that promises to help set you up a business, contact your state securities agency to find out what laws protect you and what you should watch out for—including unsubstantiated claims about income and earnings. As with any investment, take the time to do your homework.

28. Make sure merchants use SET or SSL. They should post a message on their order form saying they comply with secure transactions.

Classification (SIC) codes, estimated sales volume, names of competitors, branch and headquarter locations, Internet address, and credit rating. The rating is based on in-house research of public information conducted by ABI. ABI also sells a CD-ROM of Business Profiles, which can help companies that need to evaluate credit reports for hundreds of companies. The CD-ROM is updated quarterly and costs $595 for an annual license and 1,000 profiles.

Dun & Bradstreet sells in-depth credit reports via the Web. The Business Background report costs $20. The Supplier Evaluation sells for $85. These reports contain more detailed data than ABI's. (The addresses of the major credit checking companies are listed in Chapter 1.)

■ SUMMARY

Before investing in any online scheme, do your homework. Don't let a flashy website, or promises of untold profits lure you into a web of deceit. There are plenty of resources online to help you investigate before investing.

ONLINE RESOURCES

Federal Trade Commission, www.ftc.gov, contains a virtual library of information on how to spot frauds and take action. Very readable documents detail con games and how to protect yourself. If you are looking to enter into a new business, check out www.ftc.gov/opa/busops for tips, tricks, and traps.

Direct Marketing Association, 202-347-1222, www.the_dma.org, explains how to get off direct marketing mailing lists.

Better Business Bureau, www.bbb.org, posts news of scams online and in other areas. The site has step-by-step instructions for victims of scams, a business library of information about schemes that target business owners and listings of public and private organizations which assist consumers and business.

Chapter

Website and Computer System Security

Try to imagine these crises: You go to your home page and instead of seeing your company logo you see a picture of a naked woman. You go to your e-mail box and find it filled with messages saying "bomb threat." You get a message from a friendly hacker who says he can read the entire contents of your hard drive because of a bug in your browser.

These aren't pie-in-the-sky fears. They are real-life threats that are happening every day. This chapter explains:

➤ Why you should be concerned about security threats.

➤ How to develop a mind-set about security.

➤ How to apply risk assessment.

➤ Hackers versus Crackers.

➤ The threats that exist to your computer system and website and how to protect yourself and organization.

➤ Where you can find online resources.

■ WHY YOU SHOULD BE CONCERNED ABOUT SECURITY THREATS

When people think about problems with the Internet and computers, they probably first think of security break-ins and technology snafus. While stalking, impersonation, and identity theft are serious issues that everyone should be concerned about, security remains at the core of an organization's consciousness.

"No one is immune. Everyone is vulnerable. You don't know if it is a 10-year-old or a corporate espionage attack," says Gale Warshawsky, msgale@netcom.com, co-ordinator for computer security training, education, and awareness for Lawrence Livermore National Laboratory.

The Computer Security Institute, a San Francisco-based think tank, surveyed about 3,000 large corporations, universities, and government agencies in 1995 and found that 20 percent of the respondents had some Internet-related security problem. Thirty of the organizations said they suffered monetary loss from Internet interlopers. The number of organizations that experienced some form of intrusion or other unauthorized use of computer systems rose within 12 months from 42 percent in 1996 to 49 percent in 1997. These organizations blamed employees, electronic vandals, domestic competitors, international competitors, and foreign governments.

"I don't know of any other discipline where the machine can be turned against itself. Computers are idiot savants. Computers are just as happy executing evil commands as good commands," says Jim Duncan, manger of network and information systems at the applied research laboratory of the Pennsylvania State University.* "The Cold War is over. The new battleground will be information. Information has

---

* Interview, July 28, 1997.

taken on extreme value. Since it is intellectual property, it can be easily copied and stolen without knowing that it has been stolen. There will be more and more attacks. Industrial espionage is growing. There are buyers all over the world. Some are governments. There is a great deal of concern."

Several external threats to your computer systems are related to the Internet. It is beyond the scope of this book to address all details of computer security.

■ DEVELOPING A MIND-SET ABOUT SECURITY

Every security system has trade-offs. The tighter the security, the longer it takes for employees to sign on to the system, decrypt e-mail, and go through other clearance procedures. The lower the security, the greater chance for invasions and thefts to occur. The tighter the security, the more expensive it will be to implement and maintain the system, as well as to train employees. Every company needs to decide where it draws the line of comfort, convenience, and price.

"You can't make things perfect. You have to balance security with convenience, efficiency, and decide what that balance is and reevaluate it to see if it is still useful," says Duncan. "Laws, technology, and environment might have changed. You have to decide what is relevant." He looks at security as a never-ending process that requires a unique mind-set. "Security is not just about keeping secrets. Security is about making sure the system works as designed. Security is a Zen thing. It is about the journey, not the destination. Security is an ongoing effort. It is about a mind-set and a policy and a personal way of thinking and caring about these issues."

■ RISK ASSESSMENT ANALYSIS

Managers need to be aware that computers and information systems have changed the way we work, live, and play.

Companies should do a risk and threat assessment, says Warshawsky, who offers this analytical tool:

1. What are the risks? What are you trying to protect? Are you dealing with intellectual property, trade secrets, etc.? How much people costs and equipment costs are you willing to spend on this task? Should you have a firewall, not have a firewall, or not even connect our computers to the Internet?

2. What are you protecting your information from? The biggest threat we have is people. Careless end users. They get busy and don't think about what they are doing. You had better think about what you are doing before you send information on the Internet. Once it goes, it is gone. You can't get it back.

3. Outsiders are also a problem. One university student put a malicious software program (a worm) on the Internet to try to break into computers connected to the Internet. He succeeded in bringing down thousands of computers connected to the Internet. He was convicted of felony changes and placed on probation.

4. Environmental threats. We live in earthquake country in California. What happens when you have a power surge? Or you work in World War II barracks and the air conditioners are overloaded and you have a brownout? On the East Coast, they have breathtaking thunderstorms. You have to save your files often. If you do not save your files often, and you experience a power surge or power outage, it is possible to lose the information contained in your files.

5. You have to have a comprehensive employee training, education, and awareness program. If you don't get the word out to your workers, you have lost the opportunity to help them deal with these threats and vulnerabilities.

Warshawsky sums up her role: "That's my big challenge. There are approximately 8,000 employees where I work.

How can I make them aware of the threats and vulnerabilities? We use the laboratory's Intranet, internal to our employees, to share computer security information with them. I am responsible for maintaining our computer security website. We offer a variety of computer security training courses for our employees. We also make use of awareness materials, such as posters, awareness cards, and show awareness videos." (For other training procedures, see Chapter 7.)

■ HACKERS VERSUS CRACKERS

While many people first think that "hackers" are running amuck, you should be careful about the terms you use.

"Hacker is an honorific," says Duncan. Highly intelligent hackers can figure out the security behind any computer system and defeat it. But they do it to show the world how smart they are, not how destructive they can be. Kevin Mitnick broke into an ISPs back office and stole 20,000 credit card numbers, but he didn't try to sell the cards or use them; he wanted to show the company their system was flawed. He was sent to jail anyway.

Companies hire hackers to find weaknesses in their systems. This process is called a "white hat." At conventions of hackers, hackers wearing T-shirts mix freely with corporate security officers in suits.

Instead of using the term "hacker," let's call the thieves what they are. "I call them electronic vandals, information superhighwaymen, crackers, or loose moraled punks (although they might be 40 years old)," says Duncan.

The crackers meet on newsgroups and private chat rooms and trade secrets, passwords, and other tools of the trade. That's part of the problem. Whenever a security violation is found in Microsoft Internet Explorer or Netscape Communicator, the companies say the flaw is minor and you have to be a genius to figure it out. But security officials know that isn't true.

"Anyone can exploit a flaw," says Duncan. "When someone discovers a vulnerability, the companies time and time again will tell the public that there is a flaw, but it takes a security expert to figure it out. That is bull. It only takes a savvy programmer the first time. They create a program and post it where others can find it. Any fool can run a program. People who develop and tweak the code are smart, but few. People who commit the crimes are stupid. We don't catch the smart ones. We catch the stupid ones."

Can crackers be caught? "We catch the ones who are not knowledgeable," he says. "The ones are who are truly knowledgeable we will never catch. The really good ones come and go and we never know it." The real horror is that because data on computers can be copied, the organization might not even realize the material has been stolen.

■ THREATS TO YOUR SYSTEM

If vandals can break into the systems of the CIA, Justice Department, NASA, and the Air Force, they can break into your website too. *The New York Times* reported on December 31, 1996, that the hackers had changed the Air Force's website front page to include antigovernment rhetoric, obscenities, and an X-rated picture with the caption "this is what your gov't is doing to you every day." The new page contained links to a site for hackers, and another site detailing an alleged government cover-up of alien landings. The attack on the Justice Department site contained a critique of the Communications Decency Act. Swedish hackers hacked the CIA site in October 1996.

This section will look at the most common types of security breaches, including the number one problem: poor password protection by employees, as well as viruses and myriad snafus such as e-mail bombs and other attacks that can hang up your system. Firewalls (a software program that provides security to computers) and other security software systems will protect your computers. Dealing with this type of attack is beyond the scope of this book, as it involves a deep understanding of computers, networks, phone lines, and software. For detailed information on how to protect your company from technical break-ins, please read any of these books, or hire a computer consultant well versed in these matters.

■ HOW TO PROTECT YOURSELF AND YOUR ORGANIZATION

If you are looking outside your organization for threats to your system, that's fine, but realize that a great many threats come from inside your organization, either from disgruntled employees who want to wreak havoc, or from employees who simply don't understand the consequences of letting their guard down. They might disrupt your operations by giving out their passwords (knowingly or unknowingly) or downloading computer programs with viruses that destroy files and corrupt operating systems.

One of the best ways to protect your system from internal threats is to hire competent system administrators.

"The single best security tool that I have seen is a good system administrator," says Duncan. "People need to recognize that and bank on that. Get good people in. They need to work well with other people and document what they are doing. Most of the sites that get broken into are systems that are not managed by a professional system administrator. I would look for someone who knows the platform and knows TCP/IP (a computer communications protocol among computers on the Internet) very well. I would want someone with UNIX (a computer operating system) expertise who has a knowledge of computer security."

➤ Passwords

Duncan and Warshawsky agree that a key threat to computer systems is internal—employees don't safeguard their passwords.

"The first problem is poor passwords. That is how most crackers get into sites," says Duncan. Lawrence Livermore's Warshawsky agrees about the password issue. "Most companies are still using static passwords (the same password is used each time one logs in. Static passwords have some disadvantages to them," she says.

According to Warshawsky, users tend to create poor passwords. You cannot use personal information (your name, your hobbies, the kind of car you have, the name of your pet, etc.; anything that anyone could know about you constitutes personal information). You can't use any word in any dictionary spelled forward or backward in any language. A software program named crack will decrypt passwords. It is fast, accurate, and available for free. Companies could use crack to check against their own users' passwords.

Some users do not like to memorize their passwords. Sometimes people stick their password on their monitor, under the keyboard, in a Rolodex, a phone book, or in a desk drawer. These are prime places to hide a password. People need to memorize their password. If they forget their password, their system administrator can give them a new one.

How can you create a good password? You have to think of a word-fragment—a piece of one word, a piece of another word, and throw in a number or some special characters in between the two fragments. Even if users create good static passwords, there is still the problem of being attacked by a sniffer program. If someone puts a sniffer program on a company's computer (e.g., a computer running a UNIX operating system) the program will capture every keystroke when the user types in a user ID and the password. This is not apparent to the user at all. The attacker then retrieves the sniffer session, and he or she now has the passwords of all the users who logged onto that computer.

One-time passwords are an alternative to static passwords. Each time a user wished to log on, a new password would be machine generated for that session. However, some companies do not want to use one-time passwords, as they are inconvenient. It adds an extra step to the log-in procedure.

RISKY BUSINESS' ADVICE FROM THE
FIELD ON PROTECTING YOUR PASSWORD

1. Pronounceable passwords are poor choices. Use a number or punctuation mark in the password. The longer the password, the better it will be.

2. Create a password from the first letters of the words in a phrase. "Mares eat oats and does eat oats" would create the password "meoade," which is easy for users to remember.

3. Change the password once or twice a year (more if highly sensitive material is involved or if employee turnover is rapid). However, don't change it so often that people can't remember it or are forced to write it down and put it on their desks where anyone can see it.

4. Don't use a password-generating program. They are awful. Anytime someone shows me a password program, I cringe. They are shortsighted. These programs might use a sequence that crackers can figure out quickly.

5. Passwords should never be shared.

6. Organizations must establish systems that prevent the exchange of password credentials over the network in plain text. Encrypting passwords that go across the network is a way to stay ahead of the game. A major problem is that people choose poor passwords and transmit them in the clear (where they can be grabbed). This is one of the primary sources of attacks on the Internet. Electronic vandals use sniffer programs like Root Kit. These devious packages are easy to install and disguise themselves so well that system administrators might not be aware they have been attacked. They grab log files and see people's names and addresses. They use the connection to launder stuff or steal information.

(continued)

PROTECTING YOUR PASSWORD (Continued)

7. Instruct employees to watch out for "shoulder surfers" who look over your shoulder to read your password as you type it.

8. Be careful not to point computer monitors toward windows, as people in adjoining buildings could use video cameras to see you type your password.

9. Remind workers not to divulge their passwords over telephone lines, or even the microphones on their multimedia computers.

10. Don't send your password in plain text over the Internet. This is a code breaker's dream.

➤ Viruses

Situation. Viruses are computer programs that destroy the files on your computer. There are more than 8,000 known viruses and more are being created every day. The Internet, with thousands of websites offering free software, is a breeding ground of viruses. Java and Active-X can carry viruses from the Internet into your computer system. Viruses can piggyback onto e-mail as well. While it has been impossible to catch a virus from an e-mail, it is possible to get a virus that affects Microsoft Word documents. Microsoft has created a fix for this virus that can be obtained from its website, www.microsoft.com.

No one is immune from viruses. Even a major software publisher transmitted a virus on their software program because they didn't check the disk for viruses before duplicating it. An embarrassing recall did little to help the victims of the virus.

"It is not a matter of if you will get a virus, it is a matter of when," says Warshawsky. "Unless you regularly obtain the

latest versions of virus definitions from the vendor's websites, you can be vulnerable to virus attacks."

In addition to destroying your files, a virus can have severe economic consequences on the company as well. "A
virus can kill a whole day. If you get a virus, your computer
may not work. Someone from a company's MIS department
has to come in and figure out what is wrong, eradicate the
virus, and determine what has been destroyed on the computer. Then it takes time to repair that damage," she says. "A
new operating system may need to be installed. Damaged
files may need to be replaced from backups."

To determine the economic consequences of a virus attack, add the cost of a network administrator's time to fix the
problem, the cost of the employee's downtime and multiply
that by the number of employees' computers affected by the
spread of the virus.

Solution. To protect yourself against viruses:

➤ Download only software programs from well-known
   companies.

➤ Run every software program through a virus checker.

➤ Install a virus checker program on each computer.

➤ Instruct employees to use the virus checker. Make it a
   company policy.

➤ Don't open attachments to e-mails from people you
   don't know.

➤ Update the virus scanning software each month, because new viruses come along regularly.

➤ Back up your files regularly.

Here is a list of the most popular virus protection software
programs and their websites, where you can get trial versions along with information on obtaining site licenses for
your organization or purchasing copies for individual use:

➤ Virus Scan, McAfee Associates, www.mcafee.com.

➤ Norton Anti-Virus, Symantec, www.symantec.com.

➤ Dr. Solomon's Anti-Virus Toolkit for Windows 95, www.drsolomon.com.

➤ Interscan Virus Wall, Trend Micro, www.antivirus.com.

➤ Anti Virus, IBM Corp., www.ibm.com.

➤ VirusWeb, Full Circle Technologies, www.virusweb.

➤ Browser Bugs

Situation. Netscape's browser has a serious bug that allows website operators to peek in to your hard disk and read its contents. The problem has been corrected in version 4.01. Teams of university students and others regularly report bugs in the major browsers. The browser publishers have been paying rewards for bug reports.

Solution. Install the latest version of Netscape. In fact, always install the latest version of any software program to remove the possibility of dealing with yesterday's bugs.

➤ SYN Floods

Situation. An upset customer with a very good computer background decides to tie up your computer system. He unleashes a SYN Flood, which confuses your computer into thinking that it is receiving a lot of network traffic from a false Internet Protocol address. Your computer attempts to connect with the incoming traffic, but it can't because it is impossible for the host on the receiving end of the message to receive an acknowledgment from the sender. The computer becomes so overburdened that it can't answer calls from your clients. Although your computer is sending out "SYN" signals to the incoming calls, it appears to be asleep.

"A SYN Flood forces the receiving machine to deal with the incoming traffic. It is a fundamental feature of TCP/IP," says Duncan. "It starves the network connection so that other services can't happen. The server is an idiot savant. All it sees is that lots of people want to connect. Your legitimate clients can't connect. It is not due to saturation of traffic. It will look like your machine has gone to sleep. It chokes the machine and affects its ability to make network connections."

Solution. Change the length of the time-out signals, so that your server can dismiss the intruder faster, free up the lines, and accept new incoming traffic. Software programs can also attack this problem.

➤ Internet Protocol Spoofing

Situation. A cyber vandal wants to wreak havoc with your company. He devises a system that fools your computer into thinking his computer is part of your network; your incoming traffic is rerouted to his website. He posts misleading or damaging information on his site for your clients to read. The cracker could create a phony site that has the same look and feel as the real site. The crooks can then ask for consumers to order products and obtain their credit card information, or other personal data such as passwords.

"Let's say inside a corporate network you have a client machine called C and a server machine called S," says Duncan. "Outside the network you have a cracker machine called X. The cracker machine sends a packet to initiate a connection with the server machine, pretending to be the client machine. There is a three-way handshake and acknowledgment. The cracker machine pretends to be the C machine. The server thinks it is connecting to C. It sends the password to C, which it doesn't understand. The cracker machine guesses the 'Internet Protocol sequence number' of the machine."

Solution 1. A well-designed system will have a way for the C machine to communicate with the server. Usually, it is being attacked with the SYN Flood.

Solution 2. Configure the router to reject packets that come in from outside the organization.

➤ Rogue Bots

Situation. These robots are programmed to overload servers.

Solution. It depends on how they overload a server. One way is with a SYN Flood, the other is with a mail bombing. You would set up a mail filter to block material from that one address, according to Brian Johnson, senior public relations manager for 3Com.

➤ Mail Bombs

Situation. You get a sugary letter saying that a company will donate funds to a charity each time you send this e-mail to the charity (the charities have ranged from Easter Seals to local hospitals). You are urged to copy this letter to your friends and have them do the same: copy the letter to their friends and urge them to send mail to the charity. In reality, the charity knows nothing about this. The effect, however, is that the charity gets flooded with e-mail. If there is enough mail, the charity's computer crashes or slows down to an intolerable level.

In another scenario, a person who hates your organization can create a program that sends hundreds of thousands of pieces of mail to your computer system, causing it to crash.

Solution. Filter the mail, says Johnson.

➤ Chain Letters

Situation. Employees receive chain letters via e-mail and forward the letters to other employees. Each time the message is forwarded, the file size gets larger and larger. Since computer systems at organizations keep e-mail on file for documentation and legal reasons, these messages are kept as well. This means that valuable computer storage space and technical time are wasted on these trivial matters.

Solution. If it looks like you are getting chain letters from a consistent address, filter the mail. You can also contact the ISP where the mail originated and ask them to put the user on notice, says Johnson. ISPs have created "cancelbots" that will erase mail originating from a particular source.

➤ Impersonation

Situation. Bill sits at Jane's computer and types an offensive e-mail to the entire company. Everyone gets the e-mail and thinks it came from Jane. "That results in an amazing loss of productivity. People talk about this all day instead of doing work," says Johnson.

Solution. Ask employees to log off their computers when they leave their desks.

➤ Verification Forms Are Messed Up

Situation. Your organization processes transactions on the Internet. Through a technical snafu, the customer gets misleading responses saying the order has not been received. He places the order again. He later finds out that he ordered the product twice. This actually happened to someone ordering airplane tickets. Since not all tickets carry the same price, he was billed for two sets of tickets at different prices!

Solution. Fully test your system and its response messages. Have backup systems in place in case your main server goes down.

■ SUMMARY

Your computer system and documents could be damaged by numerous internal and external threats. Proper policies, software programs, and personnel can make sure your potential for damages is minimized.

ONLINE RESOURCES AND RECOMMENDED BOOKS

FIRST, www.first.org, a worldwide clearinghouse for finding out about system vulnerabilities.

RFC1244, "Site Security Handbook," http://ds.internic.net /rfc/rfc1244.txt.

CMP Publications, www.cmp.com, one of the largest publishers in the technology industry, has many articles about security. Use their search engine to find new articles.

Recommended Books

Network Security: Private Communication in a Public World, by Charlie Kaufman, Radia Perlman, Mike Speciner, and Charles Kaufman. Englewood Cliffs, NJ: Prentice Hall, 1995. ISBN 0130614661.

Practical UNIX and Internet Security, by Simpson Garfinkel and Gene Spafford. Sebastopol, CA: O'Reilly & Associates, April 1996, ISBN: 1565921488. Available through Amazon.com.

Part Three
Security Issues

Chapter

Internet Access Policies: How to Fight Employee Theft of Services and Protect against Lawsuits

What's happening in your office while your back is turned?

➤ Bob is downloading pictures of naked women.
➤ Gary is seeking advice on a newsgroup on how to beat a computer game.
➤ Sam is catching up on the latest sporting news.
➤ Jennifer is following her stocks.
➤ Bill is downloading software that he has no intention of paying for.
➤ Gail is loading a new software program without checking to see whether it has viruses.

These situations have three elements in common. These employees are:

1. Wasting your company's time.
2. Wasting your computer resources, including disk space and time to retrieve information.
3. Exposing your company to legal and financial threats in terms of sexual harassment cases, copyright violations, and threats to computer system resources and data.

Before the electronic age, business owners and managers had a lot less to be worried about. The Internet opens up a whole new field of headaches and concerns that can cost the company big time.

One way to ensure your company won't be attacked from the inside by employees who steal resources or put the company into shaky legal situations is to create policies. Nearly every internal threat to your organization can be solved or mitigated by a policy.

A survey conducted by CIO Communications in March 1997 (www.cio.com/CIO/survey.html, 800-788-4605) shows business leaders are concerned about workers surfing for sports scores, stock market reports, and pornography. Less than 33 percent have official Internet use policies. Approximately 45 percent have informal guidelines. Of the companies with written policies, 42 percent say workers ignore them.

This chapter explores the legal ramifications of employee access to the Internet and suggests policies to help companies protect themselves from renegades. Sample policies are provided that you can show to your lawyer as a starting point to create your company policies. With the help of experts in the field, this chapter covers:

➤ Internet access policies.
➤ Rights to privacy.

➤ Confidentiality of company information.

➤ Trade secrets.

➤ E-mail policies.

➤ Legal and court uses of e-mail and company records.

➤ Libel and defamation.

➤ Employee use of newsgroups.

➤ Pornography.

➤ Verification of information received.

➤ Measures to ensure downloaded software is virus-free.

➤ Software piracy.

➤ Education of employees about Internet access policies.

■ THE CAST OF EXPERTS

An information security policy expert and several attorneys contributed to the research and writing of this chapter:

> The expert for this chapter is Charles Cresson Wood, the author of *Information Security Policies Made Easy*, a highly recommended book containing 840 already written policies in computer-readable form along with extensive instructions and explanations (1996, Sausalito, CA: Baseline Software, 415-332-7763, info@baselinesoft.com, www.baselinesoft.com). Many of the policies in this book are taken from his works and are noted as "Wood's Policy" or "Wood's Commentary."*
>
> Mark Grossman leads the Computer and Internet Law Department of Becker & Poliakoff, P.A. He is also the Computer and Internet Law columnist for the *South Florida Daily Business Reviews* and a regular contributor to the *Legal Times, San Francisco Recorder, PC World Magazine,*

---

* Wood's material is adopted from his book. All other comments are from interviews.

PC World Online, and other publications. He can be reached at CLTW@MGrossmanLaw.Com. His home pages are: http://www.becker-poliakoff.com and http://www.mgrossmanlaw.com.

Michael D. Scott is editor of *Computer Law Report,* a monthly print publication and an attorney in private practice, Scott Technology Law Offices. He can be reached at 310-545-3411 or mmlaw@ix.netcom.com.

Jonathan Hudis is an attorney with the intellectual property law firm Oblon, Spivak, McClelland, Maier and Neustadt PC in Arlington, Virginia. He can be reached at 703-412-7047, Jhudis@oblon.com.

■ THE NEED FOR POLICIES: A LEGAL VIEW

Many employee-related problems can be solved if the company has policies in place detailing Internet usage, according to attorney Michael D. Scott. Here are his views:

While many organizations carefully monitor what documents and other materials employees seek to remove from the workplace, far fewer monitor what information is sent from or received by the company electronically. However, a growing body of case law indicates that there are a number of areas in which an organization may face potentially enormous liability for the online activities of its employees.

It can take reasonable steps to lower the risk that the company will be held liable for the improper and sometime illegal conduct of its employees. These steps include the development of a comprehensive written corporate policy on proper Internet usage and an educational program to train employees in what conduct is permissible and what conduct is impermissible.

A comprehensive corporate policy concerning the use of online services and e-mail is an important first step in protecting the company from potential liability. However, a written policy is of limited value unless it is accompanied by an educational program to instill the corporate values relating to confidentiality, mutual respect, and appropriate conduct on its employees. Finally, the company needs a specific policy on monitoring online activities of employees and strong procedures to deal with any violations of the corporate policy. *

While the tone of a written Internet usage policy should reflect the corporate culture of the organization, the policy statement should contain at least the following:

➤ Limit the personal use of corporate accounts.

➤ Limit discussions of the employer and its business.

➤ Limit the disclosure or transmission of confidential materials.

➤ Affirm the employer's right to monitor e-mail and online usage.

➤ Prohibit access to or the display of illegal or objectionable materials.

➤ Prohibit any communications online that would be illegal if communicated orally or in written form.

➤ Prohibit downloading of copyrighted materials (particularly computer software).

➤ Encourage reporting of improper conduct.

The next step is to create an education program to train managers and employees and to monitor Internet use.

For an organization to defend itself against a claim, it is important to show that the organization made a reasonable effort to police its employees' conduct. Certainly if the company does no monitoring and makes no effort to enforce its written Internet use policy, it will have no defense to a claim that an employee violated a third party's rights.

---

* Interview, June 1997.

■ THE NEED FOR COMPANY POLICIES: MANAGEMENT'S VIEW

Policies can help organizations in many ways. This section provides information security policy expert Charles Cresson Wood's views:

Policies are management instructions indicating how an organization is to be run. They are high-level statements intended to provide guidance to those who must make present and future decisions. Some people prefer to think of policies as generalized requirements. Although they vary considerably from organization to organization, information security policies typically include general statements of goals, objectives, beliefs, ethics, and responsibilities. Such policies are often accompanied by the general means for obtaining these things, such as procedures.

Policies are mandatory; special approval is required when a worker wishes to take a different course of action. They are distinct from, but similar to "guidelines," which are optional and recommended. In fact, the policies can be easily transformed into guidelines simply by replacing the word "must" with the word "should."

In setting up policies, avoid the word "shall" which has a specific legal meaning. Use of this word may inadvertently create additional obligations and responsibilities for the policy-issuing organization. Creating policies can fulfill these company needs:

➤ Establish top management communication path.

➤ Avoid disputes and related internal politics.

➤ Achieve economies of scale.

➤ Avoid cart-before-the-horse problems.

➤ Avoid reinventing-the-wheel problem.

➤ Establish reference points for future audits.

➤ Guide security product selection and implementation.

➤ Assure consistent implementation of controls.

➤ Arrange contractual obligations needed for prosecution.

➤ Establish basis for disciplinary actions.

➤ Maintain trade secret protection for information assets.

➤ Avoid liability for negligence or breach of fiduciary duty.

➤ Document law and regulation compliance.

■ THE NEED FOR POLICIES: A NETWORK INFORMATION MANAGER'S VIEW

Jim Duncan is the manager of network and information systems at the Applied Research Laboratory of the Pennsylvania State University. Here are his views on the needs for company polices regarding the Internet:

> *Incident handling is becoming an important buzzword. What is an incident? An incident is anything from theft of information and theft of services, which can be major felonies, to electronic mail harassment. I've seen harassment, threats, sexual harassment, from younger to older from older to younger, male to female, male to male. It can happen anywhere. To define an incident, you have to have a policy. One of the best things upper management can do is develop a policy and guidelines.*

"A policy sets the tone. Guidelines set the details and implementation, such as how and when the policy will be revised. It is important to keep policies up to date because laws change, technology changes, and the goals of the organization change. A good policy is cognizant of state and federal law," Duncan adds.

When investigating an incident, Duncan advises taking these steps:

1. Collect information.
2. Document activity.
3. Remain impartial. Protect the user and the organization and myself to make sure I've done everything properly.
4. Consider whether the policy be amended.

■ INTERNET ACCESS POLICY

Question: *What issues should be addressed in an Internet Access Policy?*

Grossman: Your Internet Access Policy (IAP) should prohibit all unlawful and offensive communication. It should prohibit defamation, copyright infringement, inaccurate claims about your company and limit communications to publicly available information that you don't mind your competition viewing. An employee posting information to your website could potentially expose sensitive information to the competition's prying eyes.

Just because you intend certain information to be viewed only by customers doesn't mean that your competition will be unable to view otherwise difficult-to-obtain information about you. For example, you might want to consider just how easy you want to make it for your competition to have your latest price list.

To prevent disastrous blunders, you may want to set up a series of checks before any employee posts any content to your website. The potential for countless viewers to your website magnifies any potential mistake immeasurably.

While the Internet's omnipresence at the workplace may be inevitable, it is not without its potential for problems. The

**SOFTWARE PUBLISHERS ASSOCIATION'S
RECOMMENDED EMPLOYEE INTERNET USAGE POLICY***

Employee Internet Usage Policy

As part of this organization's commitment to the utilization of new technologies, many/all of our employees have access to the Internet. In order to ensure compliance with the copyright law, and protect ourselves from being victimized by the threat of viruses or hacking into our server, the following is effective immediately:

1. It is [organization's] policy to limit Internet access to official business. Employees are authorized to access the Internet, for personal business, after-hours, in strict compliance with the other terms of this policy. The introduction of viruses, or malicious tampering with any computer system, is expressly prohibited. Any such activity will immediately result in termination of employment.

2. Employees using [organization's] accounts are acting as representatives of the [organization]. As such, employees should act accordingly so as not to damage the reputation of the organization.

3. Files which are downloaded from the Internet must be scanned with virus detection software before installation or execution. All appropriate precautions should be taken to detect for a virus and, if necessary, to prevent its spread.

4. The truth or accuracy of information on the Internet and in e-mail should be considered suspect until confirmed by a separate (reliable) source.

5. Employees shall not place company material (copyrighted software, internal correspondence, etc.) on any

---

*Published by the Software Publishers Association.

(continued)

EMPLOYEE INTERNET USAGE POLICY (Continued)

publicly accessible Internet computer without prior permission.

6. Alternate Internet Service Provider connections to [Organization's] internal network are not permitted unless expressly authorized and properly protected by a firewall or other appropriate security device(s).

7. The Internet does not guarantee the privacy and confidentiality of information. Sensitive material transferred over the Internet may be at risk of detection by a third party. Employees must exercise caution and care when transferring such material in any form.

8. Unless otherwise noted, all software on the Internet should be considered copyrighted work. Therefore, employees are prohibited from downloading software and/or modifying any such files without permission from the copyright holder.

9. Any infringing activity by an employee may be the responsibility of the organization. Therefore, this organization may choose to hold the employee liable for his or her actions.

10. This organization reserves the right to inspect an employee's computer system for violations of this policy.

I have read [organization's] anti-piracy statement and agree to abide by it as consideration for my continued employment by [organization]. I understand that violation of any above policies may result in my termination.

_____

User Signature

_____

Date

Internet, like any revolutionary tool, can help your business, but only if you use it correctly.

An absolutely essential part of correct use is a skillfully drawn IAP written by an attorney who specializes in the unique new issues created by the Internet. A form out of the legal form book won't be adequate here. There is no one, correct-for-everyone, cookie cutter IAP. Each business has a different culture and different needs. Your IAP should be as unique as your business. Properly written, it can help make the Internet the wondrous tool that it should be.

■ INTERNET USAGE POLICIES

Please feel free to adapt and include this policy in employee manuals and utilize the principles in daily business operations.

A sample corporate policy for Internet use appears on pages 102–106. It is reprinted with permission by Tom Fischer, 100703.2023@compuserve.com, a forum host on CompuServe. Copies of this document in digital format can be viewed at the Intranet Forum (GO INTRANET), data library. It is reprinted with permission of the author.

■ RIGHTS TO PRIVACY

Question: *An American Management Association survey released in May 1997 shows nearly two-thirds of employers record employee voice mail, e-mail, and phone calls, review computer files or videotape workers. As little as 25 percent of the employers actually tell employees they are under surveillance. Is this legal?*

Hudis: There is no right of privacy in anything done or kept at work. Network administrators can automatically copy every message to the server and the company can read them all.

SAMPLE CORPORATE POLICY FOR
THE USE OF THE INTERNET

1.0 Introduction

Internet is a collection of worldwide interconnected computer systems providing access to information.

The network with an architecture based on UNIX operating systems and TCP/IP protocol today is about 25 years old.

Based on the board decision from < date > and this policy, < your company Name > is going to provide the Internet to the employees as an integrated extension to the existing < company name > private global Intranet.

The decision makers are aware that the Internet today still has the following limitations:

➤ Security,

➤ Reliability, and

➤ Performance.

2.0 Purpose

(1) The Internet is a powerful information acquisition and dissemination tool that provides access to unique resources. < company name > is providing access to the Internet for the sole purpose of facilitating business activities. Use of the Internet is encouraged to improve the quality of work and productivity.

Use of the Internet for nonbusiness purposes is not permitted and is considered a misuse of company's assets. Misuse can cause penalties.

(2) This policy establishes employee responsibility and < company name > rights regarding but not limited to e-mail, World Wide Web access, transfer of files, and information retrieval.

(continued)

SAMPLE CORPORATE POLICY (Continued)

3.0 Objectives

The common objectives are:

➤ Identify proper use of the Internet and
➤ Ensure employees are aware of proper conduct on the Internet.

4.0 Policy

(1) Like other company-provided tools, access to the Internet is for business purpose only.

(2) To prevent misuse of the Internet, a firewall will be installed. This firewall should avoid attacks from outside and violation of the fixed access rights from inside users. The job specific access rights for every user regarding on-/offline access are included as an attachment to this document.

(3) The use of the Internet is a privilege, not a right. Inappropriate use, including any violation of this policy, may result in cancellation of the privilege, disciplinary action including termination, or notification to proper authorities for criminal/civil proceedings, depending on the level of violation.

(4) Transmission of material in violation of any customer, country, state or local regulation is prohibited. This includes, but is not limited to, copyrighted, threatening, or obscene material.

(5) Information obtained through the Internet may not be accurate, and the user must check the accuracy, adequacy, or completeness of any such information.

Furthermore, it is the responsibility of the user when using information obtained from the Internet to be

(continued)

SAMPLE CORPORATE POLICY (Continued)

aware of copyrighted material in accordance with the permission granted by the publisher.

Users may encounter material on the Internet that is not business related. It is the user's sole responsibility to control access and dissemination of such material.

(6) < company name > reserves the right to restrict access to materials on the Internet where deemed appropriate. Any restriction to Internet material by < company name > shall not be deemed to impose any duty on < company name > to regulate the content of material on the Internet. Lack of such restrictions does not mean that access to such material is authorized; only materials to be used for business purpose may be accessed.

(7) Use of Internet access for commercial activities other than required for the conduct of < company name > business, including, for example, political lobbying, is prohibited.

(8) < company name > reserves the right, consistent with federal and state laws and regulations or customer agreements, to monitor all Internet accesses, including but not limited to e-mail and World Wide Web (WWW). No employee should consider information sent or received through the Internet his/her private information.

(9) Due to the nonsecure nature of the Internet mail, users must consider Internet e-mail to be public information. No trade secret, company confidential, or governmental classified information of any type should be transmitted over the Internet.

(10) No private or company confidential information should be transmitted over the Internet or stored on company or

(continued)

SAMPLE CORPORATE POLICY (Continued)

external computers that are available to the public access via Internet.

(11) <company name> and its employees are responsible for the full compliance with German, European, and additional export control regulations. Use of the Internet does not eliminate the need for compliance with these regulations.

(12) <company name> will not condone nor tolerate deliberate attempts to damage or degrade the performance or to derive authorized personnel of resources or access to any Internet computer system. This includes, but is not limited to, taking advantage of the breached security of computer systems to cause damage, obtain extra resources, take resources from another user, gain access to systems, or to use systems for which proper authorization has not been given.

(13) The most serious threat posed by the use of the Internet is from viruses, security breaches, or other forms of reckless mischief. Users of the Internet must be aware that information and programs downloaded from the Internet may contain hidden code capable of making the entire local and wide network unusable or destroying data. It is the user's responsibility to help secure the network from such attacks. As such, any data or programs acquired from the Internet must be downloaded in compliance with company guidelines.

(14) <company name> reserves the rights to define the job specific access needs of every Internet user in conjunction with the appropriate manager. These access rules every time can be changed if company interests are concerned.

(continued)

SAMPLE CORPORATE POLICY (Continued)

(15) <company name> reserves the rights to establish an accounting system for the Internet usage for cost control purposes.

(16) Every change of this policy will be sent to all authorized Internet users and their managers.

(17) Before getting the authorization for an access to the Internet, the appropriate users and their managers have to sign this policy, which automatically becomes part of the personnel file.

Date:

_____   _____

(User)   (Manager)

Scott: When you talk about monitoring someone's e-mail or Internet use, the immediate reaction is "Isn't that an invasion of privacy?" There are both federal and state laws which criminalize wiretapping or eavesdropping on electronic communications. However, the laws generally exempt the owner of private computer networks from liability for communications taking place on that network. Therefore, while it might be illegal for an employer or for America Online to gain access to an employee's e-mail account on a commercial service like America Online, it is not illegal for an employer to review employee e-mails stored on or transmitted from the employer's computer system.

There are a number of cases relating to the monitoring of telephone calls. They generally hold that where the employer informs the employees that it might monitor employee telephone calls, there is no reasonable expectation of privacy in such conversations, and therefore, no privacy rights exist in such communications. The same rules should apply to online communications as well. The cases emphasize the importance of fully disclosing that monitoring may occur in the written policy described earlier. Indeed, it would be prudent to have the employee specifically sign a document at the commencement of employment which acknowledges that employer's right to monitor all electronic communications using the employer's computer system to avoid a later claim that the employee did not receive sufficient warning.

RISKY BUSINESS IN THE NEWS

U.S. District Court in Pennsylvania ruled in January 1995 that Pillsbury Company has the right to read e-mail if it is sent over company systems, even if is done without employees' knowledge. (*The Wall Street Journal,* November 25, 1995, page B5).

Wood's Recommended Policy: Management reserves the right to censor any data posted to Company X computers or networks. These facilities are private business systems and not public forums, and as such do not provide First Amendment free speech guarantees.

Wood's Commentary: The intention behind the policy is that organizational systems not turn into mechanisms to damage the company. It could happen whenever members of a labor union, a group of dissatisfied customers, a minority stockholder faction, or another group of individuals disenchanted with the current management gets together online. Another intention is to be able to stop certain uses of the system if they are contrary to Company X policy or contrary to law. For example, if a system is being used to exchange stolen credit card numbers, management will want to censor messages dealing with this activity.

■ CONFIDENTIALITY OF COMPANY INFORMATION

Question: Wired *magazine was dealt a serious blow when an employee posted a sensitive company document on the Internet. The ramifications of this publication led to the company's postponing its Initial Public Offering. How can we prevent employees from disclosing information on newsgroups or through e-mail?*

Wood's Recommended Policy: Unless the information owner/originator agrees in advance, or unless the information is clearly public in nature, workers must not forward electronic mail to any address outside the company's network. Blanket forwarding of e-mail messages to any outside address is prohibited unless written permission from the Information Security Manager has first been obtained.

Wood's Commentary: This policy is intended to make sure that confidential internal information does not inadvertently go astray.

Wood's Recommended Policy: Care must be taken to properly structure comments and questions posted to electronic bulletin boards, electronic mailing lists, online news groups, and related forums on public networks like the Internet. If workers aren't careful, they may tip off the competition that certain Company X projects are underway. If a user is working on an unannounced software product, a research and development project, or related confidential Company X matter, all related posting must be cleared with one's manager prior to being posted to any public network.

Wood's Commentary: This policy is intended to sensitize Company X workers about postings on public electronic systems. While at first the policy may seem to be a restatement of common sense, by explicitly putting workers on notice Company X gains several advantages: the ability to discipline or terminate workers who do not abide by it, and the ability to successfully defend against wrongful termination lawsuits brought by those who have been terminated for offenses of this nature.

Wood's Recommended Policy: Consider e-mail to be the electronic equivalent of a postcard. Unless the material is encrypted, users must refrain from sending credit card numbers, passwords, research and development information, and other sensitive data via e-mail.

Wood's Commentary: E-mail communications are not protected the way an ordinary letter going through the postal service is. Unknown parties can readily intercept e-mail and use the contents as they please, without either the sender's or the recipient's knowledge.

■ TRADE SECRETS

Question: *A hostile employee leaves the company. The company has taken extraordinary measures to keep its process as a secret. The employee takes the information, puts it on a disk, takes it with him and publishes it on his website. What do you do?*

Hudis: If the employee and company are in the same state, the company can sue in state court under trade secret law of that state. If the employee has moved to another state and the damages are greater than $75,000, the company can sue in federal court.

Question: *The employee leaves the company and now wants to compete with you. He uses the company's trade secrets and advertises them on his website. What then?*

Hudis: Download the website as evidence of trade secret theft. When you get to court, you must be able to prove that what the ex-employee stole is a secret and that your company took steps to keep it secret.

RISKY BUSINESS' TIPS FOR PROTECTING YOUR TRADE SECRETS

Here are Hudis' practical methods to make sure your company's trade secrets stay a secret:

1. When any of your employees begin service, make them sign a confidentiality agreement and a "narrowly tailored" noncompete agreement. (If it is too broad, i.e., "five years" or "never in this industry," courts rule against that type of agreement as unreasonable restraint of trade. It can nullify the agreement.)

2. Make them read a detailed office manual that describes what you consider secret.

3. Tell them it is company policy to guard trade secrets. That would include telling employees which category of information is secret, physically restraining access to information except to those who need to know (i.e., firewall protection, password protection, and physically locking up of media disk and manuals).

4. Conduct an exit interview. Find out if the employee has an axe to grind. Ask what the employee is taking with him. Immediately cut off his password access, which prevents him from getting Internet access outside the firm.

If the former employee posts a website, copy the site as evidence of trade secret theft. When you get to court, you must be able to prove that it is a secret and that you took steps to keep it secret.

■ E-MAIL POLICIES

Question: *Can organizations create policies to cover employees' use of e-mail? Why would they want to?*

Wood's Recommended Policy: E-mail messages are company records. E-mail is to be used only for business purposes. All messages sent by e-mail are Company X records. The company reserves the right to access and disclose all messages sent over its e-mail system for any purpose. Supervisors may review the e-mail communications of workers they supervise to determine whether they have breached security, violated Company policy, or taken other unauthorized actions. The company may also disclose e-mail messages to law enforcement officials without prior notice to the workers who may have sent or received such messages.

Wood's Commentary: This policy is very employer-rights-oriented, placing more importance on the ability to monitor e-mail than on the rights of workers to communicate privately. The policy seeks to put workers on notice that their communications can be monitored without prior consent.

Question: *I thought e-mail was supposed to make our employees more productive, but it seems they spend a lot of company time writing letters to their friends, forwarding joke lists, and trying to sell Girl Scout cookies. Can I stop this time-waster?*

Wood's Recommended Policy: Broadcast facilities found in e-mail systems may only be used by top management or with top management approval.

Wood's Commentary: This policy is intended to reduce junk mail.

Question: *Employees send chain letters to one another. These letters grow large, larger, and huge as each person adds more information to the letter! While the content is usually harmless, the size of the files can affect a company's hard disk, which stores all e-mail messages. If employees send the chain letters to other employees, the company's computers can be overburdened. What can we do?*

Wood's Recommended Policy: E-mail systems are intended to be used primarily for business purposes. Any personal use must not interfere with normal business activities, must not involve solicitation, must not be associated with any for-profit outside business activity, and must not potentially embarrass Company X.

Wood's Commentary: The intention of this policy is to clearly specify what type of personal use an e-mail system is permissible.

Question: *It is important for our organization to read e-mail addressed to employees who are away from the office for vacations. That way we can answer mail from customers. Are we violating privacy by doing this?*

Wood's Recommended Policy: Workers must not use an e-mail account assigned to another individual to either send or receive messages. If there is a need to read another's e-mail, while they are away on vacation, for instance, message forwarding and other facilities must be used.

Wood's Commentary: This policy will help maintain the veracity and usefulness of electronic system logs, while at the same time reducing the confusion that might come about when someone uses another's account. A written policy also establishes e-mail masquerading as a prohibited act, making termination and less severe forms of punishment justifiable responses.

RISK BUSINESS IN THE NEWS

E-Mail Might Violate Open Meetings Laws

Elected officials who send e-mail to each other might violate state laws requiring all communication to be conducted in public. Public officials in Maryland, Sarasota and Phoenix have had to deal with this issue. (*USA TODAY,* July 3, 1997)

■ LEGAL AND COURT USES OF E-MAIL AND COMPANY RECORDS

Question: *Are online agreements really contracts?*

Grossman: Assume that every agreement you consummate online is enforceable. This is true whether it's a business deal done by e-mail, an order form for goods in a cybermall, or any other type of agreement. It still surprises me, but many people think that it doesn't count if you do it online. Wrong! Sure, there may be some open legal issues about online contracting, but that doesn't mean that an online contract isn't a real one. Watch your kids on this one. When they're using your account and your password, arguably they're you. Conceivably, you could be stuck if they contract online for something. At the least, you'll have another problem that you'll need to solve. You probably don't need any more problems.

Question: *Can e-mail be used in court cases?*

Scott: Yes. A claim for discrimination can also be founded on the content of e-mail messages. As many employers have found out, its own documents may be used against it in a discrimination case. A memo, which may appear innocuous on its face, could become incriminating when juxtaposed with numerous other documents. The same is true for e-mail messages. A strict policy must be implemented prohibiting the use of the Internet for receiving and or transmitting any language or messages that the employee could not say in person, on paper, or that is otherwise prohibited by federal, state, or local law. Sheer volume may make this practice impractical. However, a software program could create a word list (concordance) of the entire database of e-mails, which could then be sorted on such keywords as resume, comments on corporate policies, or comments on individual employees and managers.

Grossman: Civil litigants, police, and others can subpoena information stored on computers. If I can force you to produce a written document, I can force you to produce computer data. There's no legal distinction between the two.

In some ways, computers can be a nightmare when it comes to controlling the dissemination of information. It's easier to control copies of documents, old drafts, and other records when they're on paper than when they're computerized. Between backup tapes, copies on floppy disks, and recycle bins, copies of "destroyed" documents have a way of turning up at the most inopportune time for those trying to hide information. For a lawyer with expertise in electronic discovery, it's gold-mine time.

Wood's Recommended Policy: Company X must establish and maintain a systematic process for the recording, retention, and destruction of e-mail messages and accompanying logs. The destruction of both logs and the referenced e-mail messages must be postponed whenever a subpoena, discovery motion, or other legal notice is received. Such destruction should also be postponed if the material might be needed for imminent legal action.

Wood's Commentary: E-mail provides a new and more effective way to chronicle the internal communications within an organization and even between organizations. For this reason, e-mail messages and logs are often sought as part of discovery proceedings accompanying a legal action. For a historical perspective about the need for this policy, consider that the improper handling of e-mail logs played an important part of the investigation of the Iran Contra scandal perpetrated by Oliver North and others in the U.S. National Security Council.

Question: *Is an employer liable for employee's e-mail?*

Grossman: There's no doubt that an employee's improper use of e-mail can lead to employer liability. E-mail is no different from a letter. Again, just because it's an electronic rather than traditional written communication makes no difference. If an employer would be responsible for a letter, the employer would be responsible for an e-mail.

RISKY BUSINESS IN THE NEWS

Attorneys for plaintiffs charging racial discrimination against R.R. Donnelley & Sons Co., showed racist e-mail containing 165 racial, ethnic, and sexual jokes that were allegedly passed through the printing company's e-mail system. Donnelley officials say senior management did not know about the documents. "If such lists did in fact exist, it would be a clear violation of explicit company policy," said Jonathan P. Ward, executive vice president of Donnelley. "We encourage employees throughout the company to come forward if they see any type of this activity or behavior." (*The Wall Street Journal,* January 17, 1997)

The list of things employees can do wrong in e-mail is the same as the list for paper correspondence. Employees can violate copyrights, divulge trade secrets, commit libel, send obscene material, bind a company to a contract, harass people, and more. In some ways, e-mail can be worse than a letter. E-mail is easier to disseminate and harder to destroy.

I'm not suggesting that a business not use e-mail; that would be insane. E-mail is the best thing to happen to corporate communication since the telephone. What I am suggesting is that management educate itself about the risks, implement a fair and detailed corporate e-mail policy, and then enforce it.

■ LIBEL AND DEFAMATION

Question: *I got carried away and wrote a nasty message that would be considered libelous in the real world and sent it via e-mail to the person's boss and posted it on a newsgroup. Can I be held liable for libel?*

RISKY BUSINESS ASKS THE EXPERT

If I Have a Subpoena Giving Me Access to an Adversary's Computer, Where Do I Look for Hidden Information?

Your computer may contain evidence that can be used to protect and defend your company from legal attacks—or might contain the very evidence that could wreck your case. Attorney Mark Grossman presents a comprehensive approach to exploring your computer system from a legal point of view.

If you know where to look, you can find hidden information throughout a computer system. If you're a lawyer seeking discovery, the computer is where you may just find your smoking gun. The key is to know what to request and where to look. I'm going to write this column as a "how-to" for lawyers and criminal investigators, but it will also help others identify the weaknesses in their computer security.

Remember, prying eyes come in many forms with disgruntled employees and industrial spies being two obvious examples. First, the good news for lawyers and criminal investigators—if you can get access to the computer and things associated with the computer (disks, backup tapes, printers, external storage devices and related media, etc.) through a search warrant, subpoena or other discovery device, you'll probably find a gold mine of information. Even

This article originally appeared on Mark Grossman's website on April 25, 1997 as "Searching a Computer System" and May, 2, 1997 "Finding and Hiding Secret Information on a Computer." Reprinted with permission.

Mark Grossman leads the Computer and Internet Law Department of Becker & Poliakoff, P.A. He is also the Computer and Internet Law columnist for the *South Florida Daily Business Reviews* and a regular contributor to the *Legal Times, San Francisco Recorder, PC World Magazine, PC World Online,* and other publications. He can be reached at CLTW@MGrossmanLaw .Com. His home pages are: http://www.becker-poliakoff.com and http://www.mgrossmanlaw.com.

(continued)

RISKY BUSINESS ASKS (Continued)

if someone has tried to hide information, a skilled computer lawyer guiding a search can still probably find it. After all, computers are information storage devices. That's what they do best. Redundancy is part of what makes them reliable storage devices and this redundancy is also the weak link in computer security. It all starts with the language used in your subpoena or search warrant. You must involve the experts early so that your request is as comprehensive as possible.

Where to Look

The starting point is the primary information storage device which on most systems is a hard drive. Even here, be careful.

Don't just turn on the computer and search your merry way. A savvy user could set up a trip-wire, which could run a self-destruct program. For example, a person could write a program that requests a password periodically. If you fail to provide it within let's say 30 seconds, file destruction begins. One thing that an expert may do is not start the computer the normal way. He may choose to boot the system from a "clean" system diskette thus preventing any programs, including a self-destruct program, from automatically loading on system startup. Once you're into the hard drive, you should examine the computer's folder and file structure to see if they provide any hints as to where to look for the juicy stuff. Caution: don't rely too heavily on folder and file names. It's not too hard to put the good stuff in a folder named "Children's Games and Hobbies."

Encryption

A knowledgeable adversary will encrypt files. By employing inexpensive and easily used encryption software, a computer

(continued)

RISKY BUSINESS ASKS (Continued)

user can turn a computer file into a series of nonsensical and seemingly random characters. The available encryption software, using what's called RSA encryption, is so good that many believe that not even the CIA can break it. Even if they could, it would be a highly classified national security secret that they're not likely to reveal to help you with your civil theft action. Sorry.

So, how do you get to encrypted data?

First, don't assume that they've encrypted everything that's passworded. On some systems, the password is a bad joke where security should be. For example, on some Windows 95 systems, you "beat" the startup password by clicking "cancel" instead of "okay." REALLY!

Even if it's not quite that easy, often a password is nothing more than a minor and easily circumvented barrier to access. A password may stop you from directly reading a file using the application that created it, but you may find that it's completely readable using a utility program designed to read files written in many formats (a "utility program" is to a computer what a hammer is to carpentry—a tool). It may not look as pretty, but the data may just be intact. If that won't work, you might try a low-tech method like searching paper files, notes, etc., which might reveal the password. An expert may use programs designed to break passwords or might contact the software manufacturer. The manufacturer may have a utility to break the password or know a backdoor to the data. If the data is RSA encrypted and you can't get the password from somewhere, you probably can't access the file—at least not directly.

Recycle Bin

Although a file may be encrypted, the data it holds may reside somewhere else in an unencrypted form. Often that

(continued)

RISKY BUSINESS ASKS (Continued)

somewhere else is the "recycle bin." On many computers, you'll find what may be called a "recycle bin." It may go by many other names, but what it does is hold deleted files. On many systems, a deleted file moves itself to the recycle bin before it's truly deleted. The "recycle bin" is the "oops' emergency-recovery system." It allows you to easily, quickly and reliably undelete files. That ability to undelete files is the key. You may find that the recycle bin holds an unencrypted version of a file which they encrypted in its final form.

If the computer is using a common program like Norton Navigator or other similar utility program, you may find even a second level of the recycle bin which may hold files not caught by the recycle bin (it doesn't catch everything) and multiple versions of the same file. With this, you can actually see the evolution of a file which in its final form was so sensitive that they encrypted it. What a coup!

After the Recycle Bin

The recycle bin only holds files for a limited time. Usually, the user can configure it to automatically purge files after a set amount of time or after a certain percentage of the hard disk is full. Usually, it purges files on a first-in, first-out basis. After files leave the recycle bin and even on systems without a recycle bin, you can often still recover deleted files.

On many systems, when the computer purges a file from the recycle bin or otherwise deletes it, all that really happens is that the computer acts like the information doesn't exist. However, it does exist! Since the computer doesn't recognize the existence of "deleted" files that are not in the recycle bin, it will eventually allow a new file to physically place its new information on that same physical spot on the hard disk. At that point, you cannot retrieve the old information from the hard disk. Nonetheless, until the computer physically writes new

(continued)

RISKY BUSINESS ASKS (Continued)

information to that particular spot on the hard drive (when that will happen is mostly random), you can still recover the data. At this stage and with the right utility, it may be as easy as supplying the first letter of the file name and the file is back. Even after new data has truly wiped part of a file's information from the hard drive, you still can possibly recover part of the information that was previously contained in the file.

Now, you're getting into more sophisticated utilities (get rid of the hammer and bring in the jackhammer). An expert can search the parts of the hard drive that don't contain any files now. Those seemingly empty parts may contain fragments of previously existing files. It may be possible to zero in on relevant fragments by using utilities to search for key words like names, places, or dates. Once you find the physical location of key word on the hard drive, a utility can read the surrounding empty areas of the hard drive to see if they contain useful information.

This is just a hint of the many ways that computers can inadvertently drip information to those who know how to get to it.

Now I'll continue this "how-to" and discuss how to protect your sensitive information from industrial spies and other prying eyes.

If I Have a Subpoena Giving Me Access to an Adversary's Computer, What Can an Expert Do to Find Hidden Information?

I'll take you a bit deeper into the world of computer forensics by talking about extracting information from parts of a computer system that no one thinks of as storing information. Finally, I'll conclude with some suggestions for securing your computer from prying eyes.

(continued)

RISKY BUSINESS ASKS (Continued)

Input and Output Devices

Generally, you don't think of input and output devices like monitors, keyboards, and printers as storing information and generally you're right. Nonetheless, they may hold secrets and you shouldn't overlook them as part of a thorough search. For example, a monitor could have a burned-in image of some picture commonly left on the screen. (When you leave a single unmoving image on some older computer monitors for a long time, the image can actually burn itself into the screen.) So, when your adversary denies that Ripoff Incorporated even exists, a burned-in image of that company's corporate logo on their monitor might put you in the position to ask: "So then, tell me how the corporate logo of that nonexistent corporation came to be burned into your computer screen?"

Keyboards generally don't store information, but some unusual keyboards do contain a disk drive. Although a keyboard is unlikely to bear fruit, don't overlook it. Laser printers too can hold some interesting and unexpected secrets. Let's start with the low-tech here. Is there a paper jam that's holding anything interesting?

More high-tech is that an expert may be able to duplicate the image of the last printed page. This one is probably only feasible in a criminal case where you can seize the printer without warning, but be careful here. This must be done before you move the printer. Although it's not well known and is usually overlooked, be aware that some printers have their own hard drives. Printers use these hard drives to store images before they print. An expert could search the hard drive for information sent to, and stored by, that printer. There are also some unusual looking storage devices to consider.

(continued)

RISKY BUSINESS ASKS (Continued)

One example is a "hard card" which looks like something that wouldn't hold data, but in fact functions like a hard drive and stores information.

Backups

Backups are a wonderful source of discoverable information. Oliver North learned this the hard way when he deleted damaging documents, but failed to take into account the routine backups of the White House computers. It was there that investigators found documents which haunted Mr. North. Backups can take many forms. A computer user may backup his data to tapes or other devices. A thorough subpoena requests all backups of every kind and nature. There may be daily, weekly and even archival backups that are often stored off-site. Make sure that you clarify what the backup routine is and make sure that you get all of the backups.

Backups can also take the form of individual file copies. Many programs routinely and automatically create copies of data files. They often get automatically assigned extensions like "bak." For example, I might call this file "column.doc" and WordPerfect might automatically create a file called "column.bak" as a backup in case this file gets corrupted. These "bak" files can hold wonderful tidbits and may be unencrypted although the file, in its final form, is encrypted and therefore unreadable.

Swap Files

Some operating systems such as Windows automatically create what are called "swap files" on the hard disk. It's an automatic part of the operation of the computer and has nothing to do with the individual application software that the computer is running.

(continued)

RISKY BUSINESS ASKS (Continued)

(Quicken is an example of application software.) These swap files may contain information which your adversary never meant to be permanently saved or they later saved in encrypted form. What goes into a swap file is completely unpredictable and so is your result in checking it. Nevertheless, don't overlook it. An expert scanning it may just strike gold. Virtually nobody considers the swap file in terms of computer security and privacy.

Networks

Networks of interconnected computers are becoming increasingly common. With a network, computers in different locations may communicate by telephone or other means. Conceivably, one location could have only "dumb terminals," with no storage capability, that manipulate data sent to them by a distant networked computer.

These dumb terminals may rely on the network which has a file server which stores the important data many miles away. You need to insure that your subpoena is broad enough to cover all parts of a computer network no matter where these parts are found. If you limit your scope, you may find that you missed the good stuff.

Keeping Prying Eyes Out of Your System

We're entitled to protect our private information from getting into the hands of disgruntled employees, industrial spies, and others. The sobering fact is that the only perfectly secure computer is one secretly locked away in a vault with all of its backups. The problem is that locked away, it's not a very useful computer. There are ways to strike a balance between perfect and reasonable security.

(continued)

RISKY BUSINESS ASKS (Continued)

A computer lawyer can help you set up effective and legal ways to control your data and maintain your privacy. While it's certainly improper to start erasing data after you're served with a subpoena, it's not generally illegal nor improper to control the dissemination of sensitive information. When it's legal to shred a paper document, doing the same to a computer file is likewise legal. The problem with the computer file is that it's not as easy as hitting the delete key. It takes a higher level of computer expertise to insure true destruction of the private data.

Your company should have a policy statement concerning the dissemination and control of sensitive computer data. It should define what data you can legally destroy, when you should destroy it, set up effective procedures for its destruction and clearly define what data you should encrypt to keep prying eyes out. You must consider everything in these procedures including the law which may limit what you can destroy and when.

You must take into account things like the recycle bin which lets you easily undelete a file and utility programs (a utility program is to computers what a wrench is to plumbing—a tool) which allow you to irretrievably shred a file (assuming that it's not on a backup or elsewhere). You must set up procedures requiring effective encryption, proper use of passwords, and file shredding rather than deleting. You must consider your backup routines which should only archive information intended for long-term storage. It doesn't help to shred a file if I can get it from your backup tape. And, if I'm doing the subpoena, I promise you that I'll get it from that tape.

I've given you only a primer on how to search someone's computer system and how to protect yours. My advice is bring in the experts. He who has the best one will win this little game of measure and countermeasure.

Grossman: Cyberspace is a place where you can destroy personal and business reputations. A statement on a website or posted to a newsgroup can cause immeasurable damage because of the Internet's ability to disseminate information widely and quickly. It's absolutely clear that the law will hold you legally responsible for defamatory online statements. Statements made in websites, e-mails and newsgroups can and will get you sued. For some reason, people think that online doesn't count. Wrong!

Be careful about making statements that can harm a person's or company's reputation. You're as responsible for your false or misleading words online as elsewhere. Disparaging facts on a website, or in an online forum or Internet newsgroup (forums and newsgroups are like electronic bulletin boards where potentially millions of people can read what you've posted) can get you sued just like they can in a newspaper. In fact, you can cause more damage on the Internet because of the potential for widespread distribution. So, if you post a disparaging fact about a person or company, just be sure that you're right. Truth is an absolute defense to a libel or slander action.

■ EMPLOYEE USE OF NEWSGROUPS

Question: *Your employee, Bob, seems like a level-headed guy, but when he goes into newsgroups, he spouts his opinions, which are anything but mainstream. Let's say he goes into a newsgroup on abortion or gun control, two very volatile issues, and gives his views. Now tens of thousands of people—including your clients and prospects—see your company name associated with his views. What strategies and policies can a company use to prevent exposure?*

Grossman: Every company should consider a few basic tactics to reduce its exposure to liability. First, look at your employees' e-mail addresses. An address like EmployeeName@CompanyName.Com may create the implication that the employee is an official spokesperson for the company. You might want to consider e-mail addresses without the company name for unofficial e-mail and newsgroup postings.

Next, you might consider mandating that all unapproved and unofficial e-mail have a tag line at the end disclaiming corporate responsibility for the message. Any good e-mail software can easily automate this message.

Finally, you must educate your employees. They too are ignorant of the cultural norms and laws in Cyberspace. You should have a formal written corporate Internet Access Policy which should be put in place along with a formal training program about Cyberspace. Only then have you begun to adequately protect your company from potential liability.

The way your company is perceived in the real world has traditionally come from public relations executives who make and distribute strategic messages to the media and key communities, such as employees and shareholders. At some companies, employees were told never to speak to the media and to refer all calls from reporters to the public relations office. However, the Internet is affecting this process—whether companies like it or not.

"The net effect of a wired society is that you have a free flow of information through many channels," says Charles Pizzo, cpizzo@prprnet.com, www.prprnet.com, principal of P.R. PR, Inc., a public relations agency in New Orleans. "Apple Computer has a policy of not letting employees speak to the media. The have a company policy forbidding employees from going on camera. However, they don't have a company policy against e-mail. Reporters at *USA Today* reported in the paper that, while Apple did not return calls, employees they were able to reach by e-mail sounded upbeat (about losses). Increasingly reporters have the employees and management e-mail addresses and they circumvent the public relations department. In the real world secretaries screen mail and phones, but they don't screen e-mail! Reporters are smart. They are getting access to their sources."

Companies must have policies clearly spelling out who can and can't talk to reporters. Before creating an iron-clad policy prohibiting all employees from speaking to the media, realize that employees can be very good ambassadors for the company if they are told the facts and how to present the case. Consider the case studies and information about this topic in Chapter 14.

➤ Usenet Newsgroups

Employees will use newsgroups to find information. They do this by reading messages and by posting questions.

"By and large that is constructive," says Pizzo. "But there can be a downside. If a person uses the company e-mail address (dan@yourcompany.com) and posts a question like 'Has anyone ever mixed compound a and compound b?' they could be alerting the competition and reporters to new products the company is working on. This actually happened to a pharmaceutical company. A scientist unwittingly spilled the beans on a new product under development because, and it's not intuitive, newsgroup discussions are searchable."

One way around this is for the company to create what Pizzo calls "stealth e-mail accounts" which can't be traced to the company (joel123@prodigy.com). Using that address, the scientist could go into a newsgroup and ask the questions he likes without revealing the company's name inadvertently through the e-mail account address.

Another potential problem for companies is that many people put signature files or business card information at the end of their e-mail messages and newsgroup postings. While these are useful tools for marketers, they also make every user a spokesperson. Your company does not want this to happen because employees could post off-color remarks or make disparaging comments that reflect badly on the company. You need to have a policy that forbids the use of the company e-mail account in newsgroup postings, which leaves the employee free to get his own account with the nebulous title of joel123@prodigy.com. Another strategy would be to maintain a policy that requires the insertion of a line at the bottom of the message saying "The views of the writer do not necessarily reflect those of XYZ Company."

Wood's Recommended Policy: When engaged in bulletin board discussion, chat sessions, and other Internet offerings, only those workers who are authorized by management to provide official support for Company X products and services may indicate their affiliation with Company X. This may be accomplished by explicitly adding certain words to their messages, or implicitly via an e-mail address. In either case, unless they have received instructions to the contrary, whenever workers disclose an affiliation with Company X, they must clearly indicate that "The opinions expressed are my own, and not necessarily those of Company X."

Wood's Commentary: The intention of this policy is to strictly limit the number of official representations on the Internet coming from Company X. This will help reduce the chances of libel, defamation, misrepresentation, and similar legal problems. Organizations adopting this policy may additionally wish to put those authorized to represent them on the Internet through a public relations training class.

Question: *We did a search on Deja News and found employees posting to game newsgroups during the middle of the day. Can an employer restrict access to portions of the Internet, such as pornography, sports, and other areas not related to business?*

Wood's Recommended Policy: News feeds from the Internet must be restricted to those which are clearly related to Company X business.

Wood's Commentary: The purpose of this policy is to put systems administrators on notice that they should screen news feeds from the Internet such that only business-oriented material gets through. In some cases, the policy can also be issued to users, in effect acting as a response to their requests for certain news feeds. The policy will prevent news feed discussions about sexual fetishes, bizarre hobbies, and other irrelevant things from distracting internal staff. It will also help conserve disk space.

■ PORNOGRAPHY

Pornography. Supreme Court Justice Oliver Wendell Holmes once said he couldn't define it, but he knew it when he saw it. For many years, the definition of pornography was left open to community standards, which varied from community to community.

In 1996, the U.S. Congress passed the Communications Decency Act, making it a crime to display sexual and other adult-oriented material on the Internet to children. The CDA attempted to protect children from "indecent" communications and pornography on the Internet. Civil liberties organizations and First-Amendment advocates rallied quickly, but the most important action occurred in June 1997, when the U.S. Supreme Court overturned the CDA and ruled that there can be no censorship on the Internet. In fact *The New York Times* called the ruling "a sweeping endorsement of free speech on the Internet" (June 27, 1997). The Supreme Court held that the law signed by President Clinton would have a "chilling effect on free speech." Although most commentary on this decision centers on children, the ruling has implications for adults as well. Here are several scenarios and opinions from lawyers and human resource specialists.

Scenario 1: Instead of revising the accounting figures, Bob downloads porn from the Internet on company time. Do you have the right to stop him and put his nose to the grindstone?

Scenario 2: Bob is so proud of himself for downloading the latest pictures of Pamela Lee Anderson that he uses company resources to send the pictures to his buddies via the e-mail. Can you stop him?

Scenario 3: *Bob is a complete jerk. He invites Betty, his female coworker to review his work but as they discuss his findings, his screensaver pops up and displays the Pamela Lee Anderson photos on the monitor. Betty claims this is sexual harassment and not only sues Bob, but sues the company as well. Is the company liable?*

Scott: Just as the display of *Playboy* centerfolds or similar photographs in the workplace can create a hostile workplace environment, the display of similar images downloaded from the Internet or accessing online sex sites from company computers may create similar liability. There is no question that the employee would be liable for any violations of state or federal obscenity laws. There is no case law on whether a corporation would also be liable for its employees' actions.

Wood's Recommended Policy: Company X retains the right to remove from its information system any material it views as offensive or potentially illegal.

Wood's Commentary: This policy is intended to put users on notice that management has no obligation to retain information stored in its system if it considers this information to be either offensive (harassing, pornographic, etc.) or otherwise questionable.

➤ Software to the Rescue

In addition to issuing employee policies, companies can install software programs that prevent their computers from reaching sites that contain pornography. The programs can help organizations manage and control employees' access to the World Wide Web, newsgroups, chat rooms, and FTP sites. The sophisticated filtering technology gives employers the ability to control access to specific parts of the Web and specify the hours of the day when the controls are operative.

Sexually explicit websites are accessed by employees at nearly three-quarters of organizations surveyed, according

---

SOFTWARE THAT CONTROLS INTERNET ACCESS

Cyber Patrol Corporate, Microsystems Software, 800-828-2608. www.cyberpatrol.com.

CYBERsitter, Solid Oak Software, 800-388-2761. www.solidoak .com.

Microsoft Plus! For Kids, Microsoft. www.microsoft.com.

Net Nanny, Net Nanny Ltd., 800-340-7177. www.netnanny .com.

On Guard, ON TECHNOLOGY, 617-374-1400, www.on.com.

Little Brother, Kansmen, Corp. www.kansmen.com. This product also shows managers where employees go on the Internet and what they do there (i.e., chat, or play games), as well as blocks sites.

---

to On Technology Corporation, which publishes software that tracks Internet usage for corporate network managers. The results come from companies using its product. Other nonbusiness-related sites are also popular, including sports (16 percent of organizations) and music (14 percent of organizations). "For many organizations, simply announcing that a product such as the Internet Manager will be used is sufficient to curb inappropriate usage," said Phil Neray, Director of Product Marketing for On Technology Corporation.

■ VERIFICATION OF INFORMATION RECEIVED

Question: *I can basically trust a newspaper because reporters try to verify information. However, nothing on the Web goes through that process. Information posted on newsgroups could be wrong or misleading and could go unchallenged because* *there is no independent verification. How can we protect our company from misinformation?*

Wood's Recommended Policy: All information taken off the Internet should be considered suspect until confirmed by another source. There is no quality control process on the Internet, and a considerable amount of Internet information is outdated, inaccurate, or deliberately misleading.

Wood's Commentary: The intention of this policy is to make workers aware that much of the information on the Internet is not reliable. Workers often naively believe that what they read on the Internet is trustworthy. The Internet is, for the most part, unregulated and unsupervised. As a result, con games and other scams are now being perpetrated via the Internet.

Question: *We received an e-mail from President Clinton, but we don't think it is really from him. Can people fake their identities using e-mail?*

Wood's Recommended Policy: It is relatively easy to spoof the identity of another user on public networks. Before workers release any internal Company X information, enter into any contracts, or order any products via public networks, the identity of the individual and organization contracted must be confirmed. Identity confirmation is ideally performed via digital signatures, but in cases where these are not yet available, other means such as letters of credit, third-party references, and telephone conversations may be used.

Wood's Commentary: There have been a number of cases where individuals have represented that they were somebody else, such as the president of the United States. This policy is intended to put workers on notice that they need to perform a due diligence process before they rely on the alleged identity of those they correspond with over public networks. Identity confirmation is not built into the Internet and must be achieved via controls added by user organizations (such as this policy). Over the next 10 years, the most prevalent and most expedient way to confirm the identity of other users will be via digital signatures, a sequence of bits appended to a message. Digital signatures not only indicate that a message came from the person it is alleged to have come from, they also indicate that a message has not been altered in transit.

■ MEASURES TO ENSURE DOWNLOADED SOFTWARE IS VIRUS-FREE

Question: *I hear a lot about computer viruses that can mess up our entire network. What can we do to make sure that our systems don't get infected?*

Wood's Recommended Policy: All software and files downloaded from the Internet or any public network must be screened with virus-detection software.

Wood's Commentary: The intention of this policy is to clearly define the process that users must go through before they execute software or open data files. While viruses, Trojan horses, and worms used to be threats only with software, they are now increasingly being included with data files (such as macros that come along with applications software). Dealing with the unauthorized programs after they have spread is expensive. This policy helps to reduce the negative side-effects occasioned by viruses and related programs. (See also Chapter 6.)

■ SOFTWARE PIRACY

Bob surfs the Internet and reads a banner ad for a new software program. He goes to the software publisher's website and downloads a copy. Instead of reading the license material, which says he must pay for the software, he uses it freely. He tells everyone what a great program it is and makes copies for everyone in the office. Bob has just opened your company to an expensive legal nightmare.

Not only does software piracy cost software publishers a small fortune, piracy can also cost your company big bucks. Companies that allow software piracy to occur can face fines of up to $100,000 for each infringing copy, plus court costs, attorney fees, and negative publicity, according to Peter Beruk, director of domestic antipiracy for the Software Publishers Association, the largest trade group of software publishers, www.spa.org.

"A company that doesn't have a policy against software piracy is much more likely to have a piracy problem," he says. "If employees are told to get the job done, and they don't know what the company's position is on piracy, they will do what they have to do get their jobs done, including copying software from a colleague."

Many Fortune 500 companies police software use.

"It is a much smaller problem today than in the past," says Beruk. "Many if not all Fortune 500 have a policy against software piracy and view this as an issue that they have to think about. They don't want to get caught with their pants down by having unauthorized software in their organization. They will have an MIS department who will monitor software use."

The problem comes with smaller businesses. "The smaller companies use an ad hoc person who sometimes monitors software use, but also does other things. It is not a full-time job. The smaller companies don't think about this until there is a problem."

The SPA actively fights software pirates. They get leads from former and current employees and consultants. SPA members who learn about piracy also contact the organization. Publishers learn about piracy when people call in for technical support.

Here are two policies approved by the SPA that can help your organization eliminate software piracy.

➤ SPA Recommended Software Policy and Employee Usage Guidelines

The following is SPA's Recommended Software Policy and Employee Usage Guidelines. Please feel free to adapt and include the policy in employee manuals and utilize the principles in daily business operations.

SOFTWARE POLICY FOR [ORGANIZATION]

1. *General Statement of Policy.* Appointment of a Software Manager. It is the policy of [organization] to respect all computer software copyrights and to adhere to the terms of all software licenses to which [organization] is a party. [Name] is [organization's] Software Manager, and is charged with the responsibility for enforcing these guidelines.

    [Organization] users may not duplicate any licensed software or related documentation for use either on [organization] premises or elsewhere unless [organization] is expressly authorized to do so by agreement with the licenser. Unauthorized duplication of software may subject users and/or [organization] to both civil and criminal penalties under the United States Copyright Act.

    Users may not give software to any outsiders including clients, contractors, customers, and others. [Organization] users may use software on local area networks or on multiple machines only in accordance with applicable license agreements.

Published by the Software Publishers Association.

(continued)

SOFTWARE POLICY FOR [ORGANIZATION] (Continued)

2. *User Education.* Each [organization] user must complete the software education program (to be crafted by the software manager). Upon completion of the education-program, users are required to sign this anti-piracy statement. New users will be provided the same education program within 10 days of the commencement of their employment.

3. *Budgeting for Software.* When acquiring computer hardware, software and training must be budgeted at the same time. When purchasing software for existing computers, such purchases will be charged to the department's budget for information technology or an appropriate budget set aside for tracking software purchases.

4. *Approval for Purchase of Software.* To purchase software, users must obtain the approval of their supervisor or area manager and then follow the same procedures [organization] for the acquisition of other [organization] assets. (Note: Specify which applications and versions [organization] will support address the purchasing of non-organization-standard software.)

5. *Acquisition of Software.* All software acquired by [organization] must be purchased through the [MIS, purchasing, or other appropriate] department. Software may not be purchased through user corporate credit cards, petty cash, travel or entertainment budgets. Software acquisition channels are restricted to ensure that [organization] has a complete record of all software that has been purchased for [organization] computers and can register, support, and upgrade such software accordingly.

6. *Registration of Software.* When software is delivered, it must first be delivered to the software manager so he/she can complete registration and inventory requirements.

(continued)

SOFTWARE POLICY FOR [ORGANIZATION] (Continued)

The software manager is responsible for completing the registration card and returning it to the software publisher. Software must be registered in the name of [organization] and job title or department in which it will be used. Due to personnel turnover, software will never be registered in the name of the individual user. The software manager m aintains a register of all [organization's] software and will keep a library of software licenses. The register must contain:

(a) the title and publisher of the software;

(b) the date and source of software acquisition;

(c) the location of each installation as well as the serial number of the hardware on which each copy of the software is installed;

(d) the name of the authorized user;

(e) the existence and location of back-up copies;

(f) the software product's serial number.

7. *Installation of Software.* After the registration requirements above have been met, the software will be installed by the software manager. Manuals, tutorials, and other user materials will be provided to the user. A copy of the applicable license agreement will be provided to the user. Once installed on the hard drive, the original diskettes will be kept in a safe storage area maintained by the software manager.

8. *Home Computers.* [Organization's] computers are organization-owned assets and must be kept both software legal and virus free. Only software purchased through the procedures outlined above may be used on [organization's] machines. Users are not permitted to bring software from home and load it onto [organization's] computers. Generally, organization-owned software cannot be taken

(continued)

SOFTWARE POLICY FOR [ORGANIZATION] (Continued)

home and loaded on an user's home computer if it also resides on [organization's] computer. If a user is to use software at home, [organization] will purchase a separate package and record it as an organization-owned asset in the software register. However, some software companies provide in their license agreements that home use is permitted under certain circumstances. If a user needs to use software at home, he/she should consult with the software manager to determine if appropriate licenses allow for home use.

9. *Shareware.* Shareware software is copyrighted software that is distributed freely through bulletin boards and online services. It is the policy of [organization] to pay shareware authors the fee they specify for use of their products. Registration of shareware products will be handled the same way as for commercial software products.

10. *Quarterly Audits.* The software manager will conduct a quarterly audit of all [organization's] PCs, including portables, to ensure that [organization] is in compliance with all software licenses. Surprise audits may be conducted as well. Audits will be conducted using an auditing software product. Also, during the quarterly audit, [organization] will search for computer viruses and eliminate any that are found. The full cooperation of all users is required during audits.

11. *Penalties and Reprimands.* According to the U.S. Copyright Act, illegal reproduction of software is subject to civil damages of as much as US$100,000 per title infringed, and criminal penalties, including fines of as much as US$250,000 per title infringed and imprisonment of up to five years. An [organization] user who

(continued)

SOFTWARE POLICY FOR [ORGANIZATION] (Continued)

makes, acquires, or uses unauthorized copies of software will be disciplined as appropriate under the circumstance. Such discipline may include termination of employment. [Organization] does not condone the illegal duplication of software and will not tolerate it.

12. *User Agreement.* If you have any add.itional questions about the above policies, address them to [software manager] at ext. [xxx] before signing this agreement.

I have read [organization's] anti-piracy statement and agree to abide by it as consideration for my continued employment by [organization]. I understand that violation of any above policies may result in my termination.

_____

User Signature

_____

Date

■ EDUCATION AND TRAINING

There is no shortage of ways your employees can mess up your organization and expose it to legal situations or security breaches. However, creating policies that spell out what employees can and cannot do diminishes the threat of crises and assures that legal protections for the company are in place. Finally, a policy that is not communicated to employees is

SPA'S EMPLOYEE SOFTWARE USAGE GUIDELINES FOR [ORGANIZATION]

Purpose

All users will use software only in accordance with its license agreement. Unless otherwise provided in the license, any duplication of copyrighted software, except for backup and archival purposes, is a violation of copyright law. In addition to violating copyright law, unauthorized duplication of software is contrary to [organization's] standards of conduct. The following points are to be followed to comply with software license agreements:

1. We will use all software in accordance with its license agreements.

2. Legitimate software will promptly be provided to all users who need it. No [organization] user will make any unauthorized copies of any software under any circumstances. Anyone found copying software other than for backup purposes is subject to termination.

3. We will not tolerate the use of any unauthorized copies of software in our organization. Any person illegally reproducing software can be subject to civil and criminal penalties including fines and imprisonment. We do not condone illegal copying of software under any circumstances and anyone who makes, uses, or otherwise acquires unauthorized software will be appropriately disciplined.

4. No user will give software to any outsiders including clients, customers, and others.

5. Any user who determines that there may be a misuse of software within the organization will notify the software manager, department manager, or legal counsel.

6. All software used by the organization on organization-owned computers will be purchased through appropriate procedures.

Published by the Software Publishers Association.

(continued)

**SPA'S EMPLOYEE SOFTWARE USAGE GUIDELINES
FOR [ORGANIZATION] (Continued)**

I have read [organization's] software code of ethics. I am fully aware of our software compliance policies and agree to abide by those policies. I understand that violation of any above policies may result in my termination.

_____

User Signature

_____

Date

---

a danger waiting to happen. Organizations need to establish training programs or job aids to ensure every employee knows the policy.

"It is important to have a computer use policy and to ensure that the employees have access to that policy. It is a good idea to give the computer use policy to all new employees as part of their new employee orientation," says Gale Warshawsky, msgale@netcom.com, coordinator for computer security training, education, and awareness for Lawrence Livermore National Laboratory. "The most important part of creating company policies is sharing them via a training, education and awareness program. Without such a program, you have no way to reach employees and tell them what they need to know to protect the company's information."*

The way you begin to design a training course is to consider these questions:

➤ Who is my audience?
➤ What do they need to learn?

---

*Interview, July 28, 1997.

➤ Why do they need to learn it?

➤ Why would they care about it?

➤ What compliance regulations do you have to work with (government agencies, board of directors, etc.)?

Next, you need to outline the areas employees need to understand.

Research the topic by reading books, going online and conducting searches, and reading manuals. Brainstorm with your organization and colleagues to identify ways to reach this audience: Should it be live in a classroom, a distance learning class over the Internet, a videotape with an instructor briefing students? If a course is videotaped, then people who missed the live presentation with an instructor could borrow the videotape at a later date. Does this need to be a formal training course, or could it be a poster with information?

Warshawsky created a poster with information, sent it to information systems security officers and asked them to copy and post it everywhere: bulletin boards, bathrooms, company vehicles. "No matter where you went for a couple of months, it hit you. It was all over. It wasn't a formal training course. It was a job aid. All it took was a laser printer and copying machine."

Second idea: awareness cards. "We used sheets of business card stock and printed awareness information on them. All work was done in house by computer security's training, education, and awareness coordinator. The card stock was printed on a laser printer. The card had contact Information for the computer security organization: phone number, e-mail address, and the computer security website's Intranet URL. It also had a space for employees to write in the name and phone number of their Information systems security officer. This awareness card was given to all employees as part of every training course offered live," Warshawsky said.

"It is a good idea to beta test the information security courses, website, job aids. Ask a selected group of information systems security officers to look at these things and ask them to give you their opinion. Consider their suggestions carefully. Sometimes you will make use of them, or of parts of them. Programmers beta test software. As a trainer, it is important to beta test courses, your website, and job aids. It is a team effort and everyone wins," she says.

"Finally, you need to evaluate what they've learned. This can be done with tests or by having a question-and-answer session. You may need to change some of your training materials if the desired information is not being understood. For example, if many students miss the same test question, that tells a trainer that they need to cover that material in a slightly different way to make it clearer to the students."

■ OTHER JOB AIDS

To remind employees, some companies post the policies on the computer sign-on screens. As the computer warms up, the screen flashes the important company policies such as: "The computer belongs to the company and is subject to auditing and monitoring by the company." or "Computers are to be used only for company business."

■ SUMMARY

Many problems regarding the Internet could be solved by having clearly defined policies. This chapter presented most types of potential employee abuse of the Internet and showed how these actions could affect the company. Easy-to-read and understand policies were shown as an illustrative guide for companies to begin creating their own policies. However, the best policies won't mean a thing if the employees are not told about these rules and regulations.

Virtual Nemeses: E-Mail and Spam

E-mail is one of the primary tools that make the Internet interactive. By encouraging customers and prospects to contact the company, one-to-one relations can be developed for mutual gain. If companies don't process e-mail efficiently, many serious problems can occur with customer service and sales that can damage a company's reputation. This chapter explores various real-life scenarios and marketing strategies that can help turn e-mail into the online benefit it was meant to be. (E-mail is also covered in Chapters 6 and 7.)

This chapter looks at several widely different uses of e-mail in companies:

➤ Netiquette: The ins and outs of writing and using e-mail.

➤ Strategies and policies for handling and responding to e-mail from the public.

➤ Spamming and the unsolicited sending of advertisements via e-mail.

■ NETIQUETTE: THE INS AND OUTS OF E-MAIL

E-mail might be one of the greatest communication tools ever created. It is fast, effective, and inexpensive. You can get your message across to one person or dozens. No more phone tag. No more messages lost in the mail. What a life!

However, e-mail must be treated as a new type of communication, not just a simple conversion of your plain text writing. For example, the tone of e-mail is much harsher than regular writing. Comedy and sarcasm don't come across as well in e-mail. You might risk alienating people by being cute, witty, or smart. To even out your communications, use pleasant words, such as please and thank-you, and ask questions instead of giving orders.

There is etiquette used in writing e-mail. Online aficionados call it "Netiquette."

Don't write in all capital letters. IT LOOKS LIKE SHOUTING. Doesn't it?

Next, you don't need to put To: and From: in the message; it will be carried over from your e-mail header.

Length is a tricky problem. For most general business correspondence, keep messages limited to one screen length, which is about 24 lines. People don't seem to want to read more than that, especially reporters who are being sent press releases and pitch letters. An exception can be made for requested information, such as FAQs (Frequently Asked Questions). These can be as long as you feel is necessary.

Two other online conventions are abbreviations and emoticons. Abbreviations are letters that stand for groups of words. IMHO, which stand for In My Humble Opinion, and IANAL, which stands for I am not a lawyer (usually followed by advice on a legal matter!). They are used frequently in messages on newsgroups and mailing lists. Emoticons are punctuation symbols arranged in a certain way to convey emotions. Tilt your head toward the left and look at these symbols and their meanings:

Happy: -)
Sad: - (

These, too, are used widely in newsgroups and mailing lists. However, they should be used sparingly, if at all, in business correspondence because the recipient may not understand this secret language, or may think the idea of using punctuation symbols to represent emotions is silly.

E-mail programs are now capable of including hyperlinks. That means you can write a message that includes a hyperlink to a website. The practical applications include:

➤ Sending a pitch letter to reporters with a hyperlink to the full press release.

➤ Sending a letter to employees with the latest changes in the health plan, with a hyperlink to those changes.

➤ Sending a notice to registered software owner of new patches, with a hyperlink to the page where they can download the files.

With hyperlinks, you can send short e-mail notes that capture attention, and then direct the people who truly want to read the information to your website.

■ COMPANIES MUST MANAGE THE FLOOD OF E-MAIL

A funny thing will happen when you post your e-mail address on your website, or in your ads: people will send you messages!

Companies can find hundreds and thousands of new prospects by posting their e-mail addresses online or in

---

RISKY BUSINESS ASKS THE EXPERTS

What Not to Do by E-Mail

Attorney Mark Grossman, mdg@mgrossmanlaw.com, www
.mgrossmanlaw.com, advises people to NOT send these types
of messages via e-mail:

1. Never, ever give bad news by e-mail. Bad news always de-
   serves a real human voice, whether in person or over
   the telephone.

2. Never use e-mail to criticize people. It stings more in
   writing and doesn't heal with time. All day long, the recipient gets to reopen that e-mail and feel bad all over
   again. Critical e-mail inevitably eats at the craw of the
   recipient.

3. Never discuss personal issues over the office e-mail system. It's truly bad office etiquette. It's also asking for
   trouble, because there's no guarantee that private e-mail
   will remain private. Carbon copies being what they are,
   you may just find your personal e-mail posted on the
   lunchroom bulletin board. Ouch.

4. If there is even the slightest possibility that what you
   are going to say could be taken wrong, don't use e-mail
   to say it. Sorry, but sometimes there's no substitute for
   that human touch.

Occasionally, you must leave your seat, you must walk down
the hall, and you must personally deliver a message.

---

print publications and encouraging these people to ask
questions, request information, or begin a relationship with
the company. However, if this resource is not managed properly, these hot prospects may turn into cold fish or even
worse—they may think negatively about the company. In all
too many cases, companies are receiving far more e-mail

than they ever thought possible and they are drowning in the inquiries.

Don't think you can take the easy way out and refuse to respond to e-mail. While you might not care whether you have personal relationships with 30,000 customers, *The Wall Street Journal* does. An investigation showed that many companies did not respond at all to e-mail. The embarrassed companies received lots of free publicity on the front page of the second section of the newspaper.

You also risk alienating prospects who ask intelligent questions about your product, as well as customers who want to know how to use your product more efficiently. Many computer hardware and software companies have long used online services and the Internet to handle customer support questions in a timely manner (usually within 24 hours). Surprisingly, companies that use electronic bulletin boards, which post e-mail queries that can be read by other customers, have found that many other customers provide answers before the customer support representatives first read the query! The online environment fosters a spirit of community and helpfulness.

Here's a strategy that can save you time and boost your credibility. If you can't answer e-mails immediately or within a 24-hour period, people might think you are ignoring them. Since people sign on for e-mail several times a day, they might grow frustrated if they don't see a response after the third or fourth sign-on, even though they posted the initial message a relatively short time earlier. People wouldn't necessarily expect such a fast response from a telephone message, but for some unknown reason, they really do expect quick answers from e-mail. Despite this leap of logic, the negative perception must be dealt with. Consider creating an infobot that responds to each e-mail message with a simple acknowledgment of the original correspondence and a statement of corporate policy on answering mail:

> *Thank you for sending a message to My Company's Customer Support Service Center. Our company promises to*

respond to each question within 72 hours, as we need time to research each question.

While one might think that most of the questions are duplicative and can be answered with a form letter, the opposite is true: Most people who post questions have a slightly different need from the next one or the previous. If you mention that your ski resort has a day care center for children, someone will send e-mail asking you whether special services for children with learning disorders are provided. Each e-mail that fits outside the norm requires personal human interaction from your company to answer the question.

Here are a few more ideas that might help.

➤ Use auto-responders to respond to the generic questions and requests for information. An auto-responder works like a fax-on-demand system. The customer sends a request to you via e-mail to a predesignated mailbox. That mailbox is instructed to send a reply message via e-mail that contains a prewritten text file that answers their initial request for information. For example, a prospect sees an ad for your product, which contains the call to action statement: "For free information, send e-mail to info@mycompany.com." When their e-mail reaches your computer, your computer immediately sends the response via e-mail to the prospect's e-mail account. The benefit for companies is obvious. They can write a message once and send it to hundreds or thousands of prospects who specifically request that information. The beauty of this system is that the system runs itself without human intervention. You save a fortune on human resources, as well as printing and postage. Plus, you are reaching customers when they are most interested in reading about your product.

➤ If you have numerous products, you can sent up an unlimited number of infobots and label them for each product, i.e., seminar-ny@mycompany.com; seminar-sf@mycompany.com, product-1@mycompany

.com, product-2@mycompany.com. By keying the e-mail address, you can even see which source generated the request and send more highly targeted information. For example, if you are producing seminars in 10 cities, you can have 10 different infobots that each contain the generic information about the event, agenda, and registration information, but customize the message to include hotels where seminar attendees might like to stay. By individualizing the messages to that limited extent, the message is targeted to a specific audience that can find information quickly. If you put all the hotel information for 10 cities in one message, prospects might find it hard to find information in a long message.

➤ You can even acknowledge that the prospect came from a given source, or send targeted information to a particular audience. For example, if you place an ad in *Rolling Stone* for Product 2, the infobot e-mail address could be product2-rs@mycompany.com. Your response could begin, "As a reader of *Rolling Stone* . . ." These strategies can help you deal with many requests for information, the first step in building a business relationship.

➤ Overstuffed E-Mail Boxes

Many companies post a notice on their website saying: for information or comments, please send e-mail to info@mycompany.com. While this tactic is inviting, the trouble comes when that one mailbox is flooded with e-mail. Suddenly, your Webmaster turns from techie into mailroom manager! Here are strategies to alleviate this problem:

➤ Create targeted mailboxes for specific job functions. This will ensure that mail is delivered to the current job holder. For example, if you have people send resumes to Mary Williams at mary_williams@mycompany.com and she leaves the company, the mail might sit unattended. If her account is closed, the e-mail from prospective employees will be bounced back to the sender. If employees take on different job responsibilities or leave the company, Mary now has to sift through misdirected mail and forward it to the person who has her old job. Finally, any time an employee changes positions, the webmaster would have to revise that information on the online directory. As you can see, this can create a lot of needless work.

➤ To avoid having one person or job title inundated with e-mail, create numerous mailboxes for different job functions and applications. For example, if you ask people to respond to a job vacancy, you could have them send e-mail to jobtitle1@mycompany.com, or jobtitle2@mycompany.com. The employment counselor who is in charge of recruiting for each position will be able to sort through the responses for that specific job. If all resumes and inquiries went to a generic mailbox (i.e., alljobs@mycomany.com), someone would have to read each letter and forward it to the proper counselor and the specific job. For a sales response, consider using targeted e-mail addresses that highlight sales territory, product1-ny@mycompany.com. Your salespeople can sort through these leads knowing that the senders are in their sales territory and follow up appropriately. (One company that had been inundated with e-mails from headhunters used this method to hide names of salespeople from recruiters.)

➤ Your company should have an internal policy spelling out who is responsible for answering e-mail before making the e-mail address public. This rule sounds basic, but it is surprising to find how many marketing departments that are swamped with e-mail suddenly want to dump responsibilities for answering e-mail to people outside their department. Sticky questions of policy arise when the marketing department receives a question about investor relations that they are not prepared to answer. If the IR department is swamped handling deadlines for the Securities and Exchange Commission, they might not take kindly to answering e-mail from a person considering buying 100 shares of stock.

■ CAN SPAM!

The bane of online marketing has been—and will always be—spam. "Spam" is the word used to describe the sending of unsolicited e-mail. It is the online version of junk mail. While few people violently object to finding direct mail in their mailbox on their front porch, people react quite differently to spam. That practice could land your organization in trouble.

Some people have organized boycotts against spammers. People with a fair bit of technical knowledge have flooded the junk e-mailer with thousands of pieces of mail—so much that their computer connections shut down—or their ISP decides to cut them off. Spam recipients have threatened ISPs with computer damage and boycotts. In fact the president of a Dearborn, Michigan, based ISP known for working with spammers, received daily death threats after sending out numerous spams. Phillip Lawlor, the president and chief executive of Apex Global Internet Services, even moved out of his house after his address and telephone number were posted on the Internet by anti-spam crusaders. Lawlor said he routinely gets more than 200 e-mail messages a day from people complaining about spam (*Detroit News*, July 2, 1997).

America Online and CompuServe have waged a legal battle against the largest spammers and have won huge settlements in court, as the spammer violated the "terms of service" policies of these private networks. There is no such provision on the Internet, since there is no central governing body. However, this action should tell you that the marketplace really hates this form of junk mail—so don't send spam!

This section explains:

➤ Why you should think twice—and a third time—before incorporating spam into your marketing plan.

➤ Legal steps to outlaw or restrict spam.

The debate—and lawsuits—over spamming never seem to end. Spamming—the unsolicited sending of e-mail advertisements to consumers—is universally despised by consumers, yet even the august Direct Marketing Association can't get its members to agree on this matter. And recent court rulings have flipped and flopped on the issue of privacy versus censorship versus free speech in cyberspace.

While marketers debate the ethics of the issue, I would like to put this ugly practice out of its misery by pointing out three factors that touch the heart of every marketer: the bottom line. Spamming fails in three key areas: the economic factor, the effectiveness factor, and the embarrassment factor.

➤ The Economic Factor

Buying a list gathered from online address books and mailing lists is one step better than picking names from a telephone book. But only a baby step.

I recently attended a seminar given by a marketing guru who has made millions selling products direct through catalogs. He knows the ins and outs of magalog marketing the way Isaac Stern knows how to play a violin.

He brought up several points about buying lists in the real world that make so much sense, I can't believe no one else thought of relating them to the online world:

1. When you buy a list, the people on it must have first been qualified as people *who have bought by mail order*. It doesn't matter whether they are identified as people interested in your product category if they have a fear of buying on the web or prefer to buy in retail stores.

2. The people on the list who have bought by mail order must be buyers in the price range of your products. It doesn't make sense to sell a $500 product to people who have a threshold of $50.

3. Are they on a "hot list" showing they've bought in a specified period of time?

4. Have they bought repeatedly?

5. Do they buy from several companies, or are they loyal to only one?

Which e-mail list brokers have added these important, profit-ensuring variables to their e-mail lists? If you are buying a first-pass list, you could be wasting your money on unqualified prospects.

► The Effectiveness Factor

Is spamming effective? For all the misery this horrible practice places on consumers, can any marketer actually show that spamming has provided a significant return on investment?

I can't tell you how many new business meetings I've attended where publishers of software utilities base their business plan on what I call "spreadsheet-omics." You've heard it too. "There are 10 bazillion people who use widgets. If we can capture one-tenth-of-one-percent of that market, we'll be rich." I've never seen any of those companies in business a year later.

The same pitch is being used by the spammers. "If we rent 10 million names, and one percent respond and one percent of those buy the product, we'll be rich."

Well, the IRS and I would love to find those people!

➤ The Embarrassment Factor

If those last two factors don't get you to examine your marketing plan, then beware of irate consumers who use cyber tools to exact revenge by:

- ➤ Flooding your e-mail box with nasty messages that slow delivery of orders and regular correspondence.
- ➤ Blocking your 800 number with crank calls that prevent your customers from getting through.
- ➤ Organizing a boycott over the Net, as has been done to dozens of companies. While the effect of these boycotts is not well known, it probably doesn't make any sense to be on the lists.

So what does this mean for you? Spamming is an ineffective means for producing sales, but a tremendously effective tool to annoy the hell out of your potential market. It doesn't make any sense to spam.

■ GOVERNMENT SOUGHT TO ACT ON SPAM

Complaints about spam are being heard in the halls of Congress, and elected officials are taking those messages seriously. People want their legislators to protect them from spam. Here are bills that have been introduced to the House and Senate.

- ➤ Representative Christopher H. Smith (R-New Jersey). introduced House Resolution 1748, the Netizens Protection Act of 1997, which calls for prohibiting transmission of unsolicited advertisements by electronic mail.
- ➤ The legislation could serve to extend the Telephone Consumer Protection Act's ban on unsolicited faxes.

The U.S. 9th Circuit of Appeals in 1995 held that advertisers don't have the right to turn consumers into a "captive audience." It also ruled the government has a legitimate right to protect consumers from having to pay for unsolicited ads.

➤ U.S. Senator Frank Murkowski (R-Alaska) introduced the Unsolicted Commercial Electronic Mail Choice Act of 1997, which would allow spamming if the senders include the word "Advertisement" as the first word in the subject line. Violators would face civil penalties of up to $11,000 per incident.

Spamming legislation is being considered in California, Colorado, Connecticut, Nevada, New York, Pennsylvania, and Virginia.

■ CONSUMERS FIGHT SPAM

While you will probably never be able to remove spam from your daily life, here are a few tips to at least cut down on the number you receive.

1. Create a secondary e-mail account on a free service like Rocketmail. Use that address for all your public postings on newsgroups. Bulk e-mail collection programs read the newsgroup messages and strip out the e-mail addresses and then sell the names to spammers. If you have a secondary mailbox, the spam will go there. You use your primary e-mail account for your business colleagues and friends, but never use that address on public messages. Since the new e-mail account is free (these services make money by selling advertising), you don't pay a penny to protect your privacy.

2. Filter your mail. (You might not be able to eliminate spam completely from your mailbox, but this strategy will help cut it down.)

3. Spam list makers capture e-mail addresses from news-groups. If you post a message on the gardening news-group, chances are you will receive spam from a company that wants to sell you rakes, hoses, and seeds. To prevent getting on these lists, you have two options:

RISKY BUSINESS' STEPS TO
FILTERING YOUR E-MAIL

You won't even see spam if you use Netscape 4.0 to kill spam automatically. You can do this by setting up a mail filter. Here are the simple steps:

1. Look at the command bar and select "edit."
2. Choose "mail filters."
3. A mail filter dialog box will appear on the screen.
4. Select "new" and give it a name.
5. Fill out the dialog box form. It reads: "If the (sender, sub-ject, body) contains BLANK then move to folder (NAME)
6. You will want to take these steps:
7. Select "sender" and type the spam sender's e-mail address or name. Change the folder name to "trash." All mail from this sender will go to trash.
8. Save the filter by pressing the "OK" button.
9. Select a new mail filter and name it.
10. Select "subject." You will now be able to send spam that contains certain words or phrases directly to the trash can. Here's how: type "Make money," "Get rich," "$$$," "!!!" or any other generic message you see in the subject box. Save the filter.
11. Repeat this step for all the obnoxious ruses you've seen. Be careful not to use generic words such as "Important" or "Read this now" as these notes might be from your boss!

> Don't post messages to newsgroups (not a good option
> since you want to participate in the discussions and
> ask questions), or create a second e-mail account to fil-
> ter your mail.

A list of hundreds of domain names used by spammers
has been created by the Multimedia Marketing Group,
www.mmgco.com, and is available for free from their site.
You can use this list to filter out many of the spams you
are being sent. However, remember that spammers create
new domains every day so the list needs to be updated
frequently.

■ SPAM SCAMS AGAINST BUSINESSES AND INDIVIDUALS

➤ "Remove Me" from This List Scam

Mailing list operators are clever. They are constantly looking
for new e-mail addresses to collect and sell to businesses.
There are two scams you should be aware of.

Marketers are finding themselves conned by a spammer
who offers to sell them an advertisement in an e-mail magazine or e-mail joke collection. One in particular is called
humor@powertips.com. The trouble is, there is no magazine; it is just a spam list. The unsuspecting marketer finds
that his message has been sent to several thousand irate people who then might retaliate against him (not the "publisher" of the "magazine").

Many spams seem to offer the reader a way to get off the
e-mailing list. Simply hit the "reply" button and write "cancel" or "remove" and your name will be taken off the list,
they promise. However, this is really a signal to the spammer
that you actually open your e-mail and begin to read it.
While this is not a great buying signal, it places you one step
above people who kill the message as soon as they realize

they are reading junk mail. They then send more spams to you hoping you will open all of them and read some of them. They never take your name off the list.

➤ Solutions

➤ Use the mail filters to automatically handle these spams.

➤ Don't respond to any requests to be removed from the lists.

➤ This Spam Is Brought to You by Scam

In this scam, a spammer attaches your name as the sender of the spam. Now 40,000 people think the latest get-rich-quick scheme is coming from your company. There are two variations on this theme. In the first variation, an electronic villain wants to defame your company, so he attaches your name to the most hated piece of e-mail around—spam. You are left to explain that the mail did not come from you. In the second variation, the spammer actually wants to sell products, and he invites people to send in the order form via regular mail to a post office box. He uses your name to give credibility to his message, or to hide his company from being attacked by people who hate getting spam. After all, if his ISP gets thousands of messages complaining about the spam, the ISP might shut him down. Now if your ISP gets those complaints, he's still in business.

➤ Solutions

➤ Set up an autoresponder informing people that you had nothing to do with the spam and that you are a victim in this affair.

➤ Alert the Federal Trade Commission to this activity.

➤ If you can trace the source of the message, contact the ISP and warn them what is happening.

RISKY BUSINESS' 10 WAYS TO FIGHT SPAM

Everyone talks about how much they hate getting spam, but they feel powerless to do anything about it. Here are 10 simple steps people can take to protect themselves against spam:

1. Set up filters in your mail program that automatically send spam to your trashcan if the e-mail header contains the tell-tale signs of spam: XXX, sex, make money, get rich, lose weight, and !!! No real person every uses three exclamation points.

2. Read all your important mail first. Then route the mail to folders or delete it. Only the spam will remain in your inbox. Select all the messages at once and hit the delete key. They will disappear and you won't have to read them.

3. Don't respond to any spam—even if they say they'll take your name off the list. You might actually be placed on another list of people who open spam and take action.

4. Create a public e-mail account and a private e-mail account. Use the public account for postings on newsgroups. Spammers mine these newsgroups for e-mail accounts. If they get yours, spam will go to your public mailbox, which you don't have to read. Meanwhile, the important correspondence from your boss and family will go to your private account.

5. Take advantage of spam-blocking filters on AOL and CompuServe.

6. Don't fill out the member's profile on AOL. Spammers read those for leads.

7. Merchants on the net can send spam, or sell your name to spammers. They get your name when you fill out registration forms or order products. Don't fill out these

(continued)

WAYS TO FIGHT SPAM (Continued)

forms unless they promise they won't give out your name. Reputable companies will tell you their policies up front.

8. Don't complain about spam in newsgroups and on mailing lists. In many groups, it seems like there is more discussion about spam than about the group's main topic.

9. Don't encourage flooding the spammer's mailbox. Chances are they closed the account after they sent the mail. They encourage responses via mail, fax, or phone. If they closed the account, you'll get another message in your box saying the mail can't be delivered.

10. Tell your congressperson that you object to spam and want to outlaw spam the same way that federal law prohibits the sending of unsolicited faxes.

■ SUMMARY

E-mail can make or break your company's reputation. You can use e-mail as a lifeline to the world and create relationships with your customers and employees—or you can abuse e-mail and turn off your prospects and employees with spam, long messages, redundant messages, or no messages at all. Furthermore, people hate getting unsolicited e-mail and can take actions that can muddy your organization's name with the online community or actually cost spammers money or harm their computers. Consumers can take several actions to protect their time and resources by using mail filters to block spam. Congress is considering legislation to protect consumers against spam.

Chapter

9

Protecting Your Business' Intellectual Property

Imagine surfing the web and finding your specially commissioned artwork posted on another company's website, your articles appearing in political e-zines whose other content would rile your stockholders, your music serving as background to an advertisement, and your logo appearing majestically on a website that criticizes your company.

Sound far-fetched? It is happening every day as web authors routinely copy and print copyrighted materials. In fact, *Penthouse* magazine found more than 50,000 illegal uses of its name on web pages (*The New York Times,* June 8, 1997).

This chapter examines how to protect your company's intellectual property—and not trample on the rights of other companies' intellectual property. It covers:

➤ Copyrights.

➤ Linking.

➤ Work for hire.

➤ Defamation.

➤ International copyrights.

➤ Trademarks.

➤ Fan sites.

➤ Software piracy.

■ COPYRIGHT AND TRADEMARK PROTECTION IN CYBERSPACE

The laws of copyright and trademark are steeped in history and tradition, and upheld by centuries of precedents in court in the Western world. Our forefathers imposed these limits and boundaries long before computers or the Internet were invented. As the digital revolution evolves, one wonders if these laws will survive or evolve to a new form to handle the myriad new scenarios the framers of the Constitution could only dream about.

> "The Internet is the cyberworld where law and the computer engineers collide," says Jonathan Hudis, an attorney with the intellectual property law firm of Oblon, Spivak, McClelland, Maier & Neustadt, P.C. in Arlington, Virginia. "Engineers think all information is free for distribution. Lawyers want to protect rights."

To help in this quest are lawyers and legal experts who have helped numerous clients deal with intellectual property issues in cyberspace. They are:

Michael Scott, computer attorney and editor of *Cyberspace Lawyer* magazine, www.legalwrks.com, mmlaw@ix.netcom.com.

Lance Rose, elrose@well.com, www.netlaw.com, informational law and Internet attorney based in New York, author of *Netlaw.**

Jonathan Hudis, an attorney with the intellectual property law firm of Oblon, Spivak, McClelland, Maier & Neustadt, P.C. in Arlington, Virginia, jhudis@oblon.com.

Mark Grossman leads the Computer and Internet Law Department of Becker & Poliakoff, P.A. He can be reached at CLTW@MGrossmanLaw.Com. His home pages are: http://www.becker-poliakoff.com and http://www.mgrossmanlaw.com.

Neil A. Smith, partner at the intellectual property law firm Limbach & Limbach, in San Francisco and San Jose; 415-433-4150; nsmith@limbach.com; www.limbach.com.

■ COPYRIGHT

Question: *Can text be copied from one website to another?*

Grossman: This one never ceases to amaze me. Even reasonably astute people think that copyright law doesn't apply to digital data and particularly, the Internet. This has got to be the most common misconception about computer law.

Copyright law does apply in cyberspace. There is no "but copying was so easy" defense to copyright infringement. Just because you can readily copy digital data doesn't mean that it's legal to do so. The same copyright considerations exist whether you steal my work by retyping it, or by copying and pasting it in a computer file. Sorry, even on the Internet, you still need to get the author's permission.

---

* New York: Osborne McGraw-Hill, 1995.

You must not use somebody else's work on your web page or in your e-mail without permission. This admonition applies equally whether the work is written text, program code, clip art, or anything else that can be copyrighted. For some strange reason, people commonly believe that copyright law doesn't apply to the Internet. That's wrong! Copyrights are as real online as elsewhere.

Scott: You can't copy large portions of text. That would be a copyright infringement. There are certain exceptions:

➤ Documents that are in the public domain such as government documents like those from the Federal Trade Commission, Securities and Exchange Commission, and Federal Bureau of Investigation.

➤ Press releases. There is an implicit right to reprint.

➤ Small sections can be reprinted for criticism purposes.

Rose: Even if the work does not contain the copyright symbol or the word copyright, the work is still protected. You can presume there is a copyright somewhere. Any work copyrighted after March 1989 is protected in this manner. You can't publish it at your site. You can't copy words or structure. You need to rewrite it entirely.

Question: *A magazine gave my product a glowing review. Can I print the review on my website?*

Rose: You can't print the article unless you get permission. You can get away with a little bit of text. The "fair use" doctrine on copyright law says it is fine to take short quotes. It doesn't detract from the article itself.

Grossman: The "fair use" doctrine allows you to copy and distribute copyrighted material without permission under certain circumstances. The factors used to decide if a particular use is "fair use" include the purpose of the use (a school can copy more than a business), the amount of the original used (using a small part of the original helps), and the effect of the use on the potential market for the original. However, be careful with "fair use." The boundaries are murky and you can easily cross the line into copyright infringement. When in doubt, contact the author and get permission to use the material. Finally, always acknowledge the author's copyright when you copy material.

Question: *Is material posted in a newsgroup copyrighted?*

Rose: In an unmoderated newsgroup, the writer of the message owns the copyright. A newsgroup can't own anything, it is just a place to talk.

Question: *Is material posted to a mailing list copyrighted?*

Rose: A mailing list or moderated newsgroup can have their own rules that you agree to abide by when you enter it. There could be rules that say everything is public domain or you are assigning all rights to the list owner and the list owner can publish anything.

Question: *What are the penalties for copyright violations?*

All: First-time violators of the Copyright Act can get prison sentences for up to five years and fines of $250,000 for individuals or $500,000 for organizations.

➤ Artwork

Question: *Can someone copy a picture or animation from your site and print it at his site?*

Rose: Pictures are not free because you find them on the web. You must ask for permission. Every single image is protected. If the work is in the public domain, then you can print it.

Question: *How does a work become part of the public domain?*

Hudis: If copyright in the work is owned by an individual author, it falls into the public domain 50 years after her death. If owned by a company as a work made for hire, the work falls into the public domain 75 years after its first publication, or 100 years after its creation, whichever comes first.

Question: *What can artists do to protect their works?*

All: Artists can protect their works on the Internet by using a new process called "digital watermarks," which encode ownership information into the photograph. Copyright holders can track unauthorized copies, according to Digimark, the Portland-based company that created this process. The watermark is invisible to the eye and cannot be corrupted or erased. Previous attempts to trace pictures didn't work as the thief could easily crop the copyright information. If thieves download the picture and try to edit it with popular software programs, they will see only copyright and licensing information. *Playboy* magazine is among the first users of Digimark's products. Digimark's Markspider program will search the Internet for copies of copyrighted pictures.

Question: *What do you think of the use of a digital watermark?*

Smith: If it works, and truly stays with the work and there are no "black boxes" or programs available that strip it out, that is fine. What engineers can build, other engineers can build around, so unless they can't be removed, they will not be effective. The U.S. law will probably be effective to stop the sale of decoders and "black boxes" to defeat copyright management information in watermarks.

Question: *Some web designers have told me they think that if they copy a picture and change a pixel, it is a new work and is therefore free of copyright laws. Is that true?*

Rose: No. The test in copyright law is not how much did you change, but how much is left of the original picture. If a substantial portion remains, it is not a close case.

Question: *Can someone copy your company logo and print it at their site?*

Rose: No. You can't use a logo without the permission of the logo owner. That act would infringe on trademark law. If you don't use the logo, but use the words *"Fancy Magazine says our product is the best of the bunch,"* then it is okay. Truthful use of other companies' trademarks is fair use.

Question: *Can someone copy your website's look and feel and print it at their site? Even Netscape's instructions on how to create a web page suggest you copy a web page you like and edit it. Viewing the page source from the menu bar, select all, copy and paste into a Hyper Text Markup Language (HTML) editor can do this. What is the law?*

Rose: There is no law on this yet. I fully expect look-and-feel protection to be established in the law under trademark instead of copyright law. Trademark law protects the interior décor of fast food restaurants. That is trade dress infringement. This carries straight over to the web. If someone has consistent "motifs and themes" where the public is confused, there could be a problem.

Question: *My company is the victim of a website operator who stole our site's look and feel. It has our logos, our color ink, everything. A person who visited that site by mistake would think they were at our site. What can we do?*

Hudis: This is a violation of the laws of trade dress. Contact a trademark lawyer. Send a cease-and-desist letter. Say these are our rights, this is what you are doing. Stop it. If they don't heed the warning, you have no choice but to sue them.

Bring trademark, trade dress, and unfair competition claims against them in federal court.

➤ Work for Hire

Question: *If you hire a web design firm to create art, graphics, and a look and feel, do they own the rights to the work?*

Rose: If you don't sign a contract clarifying the rights up front, you can run into a big mess of property rights. The best approach to this is to write it down in a contract and specify who owns what. That way you won't have a problem later on. The problem comes when you don't write it down. That's when lawyers have their fun.

If you hire them and don't get a contract, they could own certain things and be joint owners in other things. A web page designer would want to own CGI scripts and give the company the right to use it. The designer can use these scripts for other clients. If the design firm and customer both contributed to the art and text, they could be joint owners. The design firm couldn't stop them from using it, neither could the customer! Both sides can use the work.

Question: *We didn't negotiate a contract with our web designer and our site has been up for a year. The issue of who owns the copyright was not addressed. Who owns the work?*

Hudis: Contact a copyright lawyer to determine whether the website qualifies as a work made-for-hire or a joint work under the copyright laws.

The Recording Industry Association of America has filed suit against website owners who copy music and allow listeners to make copies. Illegal duplications via cassette recorders have hampered the music industry for decades; those duplications always were of a slightly inferior quality than the original. However, with digital technology, every copy is identical to the original.

Question: *The Internet is the world's cheapest copy machine. With the press of a button, viewers can copy text, art, material. Can music be copied?*

Scott: No. If it is recognizable, it cannot be used. Copying one note is not a problem, but putting Michael Jackson's voice online is a problem. The Digital Transmission Act says you need a license from the copyright holder.

■ LINKING

Question: *Can someone link to my site without getting my permission?*

Rose: There are no laws against linking today. One law in Georgia had been struck down.

Question: *Do I have to get permission to link to someone's site?*

All: While most people would think that this is the ultimate compliment—and great for marketing—some web owners don't want people to link to their sites. Here are two cases that show why.

➤ Total News

The Washington Post and several other newspapers claimed an information provider, Total News, was stealing their "hot news" and diverting it to other audiences in a way that did not benefit the original news provider. Total News printed the articles, but also printed their own ads, not those sold by the newspaper. Since advertising revenue on the Internet is based on the number of ads shown to readers, the newspapers lost revenue. Readers of Total News saw *The Washington Post* articles and ads sold by Total News, not those ads sold by *The Washington Post*. The case was settled when Total News agreed to license the material.

➤ Ticketmaster

Ticketmaster accused Microsoft of copyright violations when the latter linked to the former's site. Ticketmaster claimed the link went directly to a subpage on their site, thus bypassing the front page, which contained information and ads that Ticketmaster wanted everyone to see. The case is still pending.

Rose: Regarding Total News, if you run a site and print news information that was taken from another site and has value when it is a day or two old, you could be subject to a claim by the original publisher.

Question: *What other types of linking could cause problems?*

Rose: Under trademark law, there is an implied endorsement theory. If someone links to your site and they make it look as if you endorse their site, that could give rise to a type of trademark claim.

For example, Goniff Company lists its business partners on a page and presents their logos. They also print the logo of a company that is not their business partner. A normal person would infer that the last company is a business partner as well and might accord that Goniff is a high-class company because it has a relationship with that company.

Question: *Some companies are creating sites that "frame" the editorial content of another site. Some sites acknowledge the copyright of the original company, some don't. In either case, the motivating factor for the framing company is to present the content in a frame and surround the content with ads. The framing company sells the ads and generates revenue. It does not share the ad revenue with the original creator of the content. Is framing legal or illegal?*

Smith: This raises very interesting issues of copyright and trademark infringement which have not been resolved yet. It will be important to understand what the user believes as to the source of the material displayed.

Question: *Can an ISP be liable for publishing works on the Internet?*

Smith: Yes, it can. Liability may come about under copyright law or trademark law, or both, depending on what the ISP permits to be used. The copyright law gives a copyright owner or author the right to prevent others from making copies or distributing copies of a copyrighted work. An ISP may be found to be a copyright infringer, if it makes available copyrighted works for copying by others or copies the works itself.

I represented Sega, (*Sega v. Maphia*), the computer game manufacturer, and helped them stop an online service provider who was making available for downloading numerous copies of Sega video games. In that case, we obtained a court order enjoining the service provider from continuing to make those copies available, and we actually obtained a secret court order allowing the U.S. marshals to enter the defendant's premises and remove the computer server so that the counterfeit copies of the Sega games could be removed.

Question: *What are the current standards under which the court might find liability?*

Smith: Currently there is a debate going on in the courts as to whether the liability would require that the ISP owner or operator be aware of the copying. Some courts have suggested that the ISP might be liable for even innocently making available copyrighted works. But the current trend of some courts in northern California, including a case I have been involved in, suggests the courts may require that the ISP be aware of the copying in order to be liable.

There may also be liability in the ISP if trademarks or brand names are used to misrepresent a product or services being sold or rendered. For example, if an ISP makes available for downloading unauthorized copies of software using a trademark owned by someone else, there may be liability under state and federal trademark laws for the unauthorized use of the name.

■ LIBEL

Question: *If a company has a chat room and someone says something libelous, is the company responsible?*

Rose: That is not something where we have an automatic yes or no. There is the risk that if someone says something in a chat room, the company could be sued.

However, you can reduce the risks if you have people agree by contract that they are not going to sue anyone for what they say in a chat room and they are not going to repeat what they read in a chat room. If you design your contract correctly, you will control your risk. If a libelous thing pops out before it can be caught, the law would hold the person who made the remarks responsible, but not the moderator. If someone on a call-in radio show said something libelous, the radio station would not be held responsible. It is the same principle for a chat room.

However, the risk can be greatly managed if:

1. You hire a moderator and have the moderator kick out people who say offensive things.
2. You can outsource a chat room. Let these companies manage the chat room and the risk.

Smith: There is less law on that, but there is certainly a potential for liability, particularly once the company is aware of the statements.

■ INTERNATIONAL COPYRIGHT CONCERNS

Question: *Which country's laws apply to the Internet?*

All: There are two questions. If you are in one country and there is a violation of your country's laws on the 'Net by a foreigner, can you sue the foreigner in your own country? In that situation, as is often the case, the law is not clear, but it seems that the laws of many countries will sometimes not allow you to reach out and get a court's power over nonresidents, just because the website is accessible in your home country.

The second part to your question is when the court acts, which laws apply? If you can get the court to act against a nonresident for violations in your home country, then your home country's laws apply, but it is not always clear. You can usually go to where the foreign website server is located and apply the local laws there. However, the law may or may not be favorable.

Question: *Assume France has a law saying all advertising must be in French. If you print an ad on your site and it is accessed by a French government official in Paris, could you be held liable for breaking French laws?*

Smith: France would have a great deal of difficulty enforcing its laws in that example, just because your material is accessible in France on the Internet.

Question: *Germany has strict laws against comparative advertising. Could I be sued for comparing my product to a competing product made in Germany?*

Smith: As usual, there is no easy answer, but I suspect the German courts would have a problem reaching you if you weren't physically located in Germany. I do not think the courts will reach out over two U.S. companies attacking each other for violating German law only on the Internet. However, this is one of the many examples of where the Internet may expose advertisers to different laws around the world.

■ TRADEMARKS

Question: *What is a trademark?*

Smith: A trademark is a brand name, a design, or a logo that is used by a company to identify its products or services.

Coca-Cola, Sega, and Apple are trademarks. Examples of trademarks for service businesses, sometimes also called "service marks," are McDonald's for restaurant services and Drycleanery USA for dry-cleaning services.

I represented Toys "R" Us in a case against Adults "R" Us, a website using the domain name "adultsrus.com" to sell "adult toys," that is, sexual devices. We were concerned about tarnishment to the trademark Toys "R" Us by such activities. We obtained an injunction against the website operator from using the domain name. The theory under which the court gave this injunction was that it diluted and tarnished the Toys "R" Us name.

Question: *If a website uses your company's trademark, what can you do about it?*

Smith: Depending on the aggressiveness of the company, you can start by putting the website webmaster or his or her company on notice of the infringement: this can be done by e-mail, but even today a certified letter is a good idea.

If the website refuses to discontinue the use of the trademark, it might be necessary to file a lawsuit and seek to obtain an injunction in the courts. If the website has an ISP, it may be helpful to put the ISP on notice of the infringement, and ask the ISP to discontinue access to the website. The law would suggest the ISP would have some liability once the ISP has awareness of the liability. If the infringement continues, you can go to court and gain an injunction order that requires the website to remove the infringing material or, in certain cases, even obtain a proactive order that allows the federal marshals to seize the server and delete the infringing work.

In the context of publicity, one always has to consider the negative publicity on the 'Net, of calling attention to the infringement, giving the defendant additional hits or attention that would be detrimental.

In the *Toys "R" Us* case, we were concerned the publicity would have given the adult site more visibility. A search engine would list all references to the adult site and kids could find it.

■ FAN SITES

Fan clubs and hobby clubs focus on movie stars, baseball players, and musicians as well as collectibles such as dolls, models, and stamps. With the Internet, fans can host their own personal pages that honor their heroes. *Star Wars,* Barbie, and Beanie Babies have dozens of sites in their honor. However, holders of trademarks and copyrights might find this offensive. Paramount and its parent company, Viacom Inc., sent letters to "unofficial" *Star Trek* sites alleging they used graphics without corporate permission, thereby claiming copyright infringement. Other companies do the same.

Question: *When you have concerns about others using your intellectual property on the Internet, when do you bring in the lawyers?*

Smith: Depending on the number of violations a copyright or trademark owner is faced with, it might make reasonable sense to try some self-help in putting the violating sites on notice. It is a good idea to touch base with a lawyer first to find out what rights you have and not overreach.

I have seen situations where people either overreach or scare infringers underground where they are harder to stop, so I am somewhat cautious in telling people not to use lawyers in an early stage. I am also conscious that lawyers cost money. However, I think it is a good idea to have at least some general knowledge about what legal rights you have and what claims can be made against an ISP or a website owner before you threaten them with civil or even criminal liability, which may not exist in many cases. The reader should have some basic knowledge of intellectual property subjects before beginning a campaign of threats, particularly on the 'Net, as your protest letters get spread around. It makes it harder for me as a lawyer to do it right.

There are situations where self-help can be effective. A cartoonist found websites were using his cartoons. He sent e-mails to the site owners saying the "characters were his children and they were taking his children out of their home." He appealed to their emotions to take the cartoons off. Many did; some did not.

■ The Public Relations Response

The PR response is different from the legal response. They feel the companies should support the sites—if they follow company rules.

"They are real fans. They did this out of love for our product," says Allan Wallace, chairman of the Interactive Agency, www.iagency.com, awall@iagency.com, 310-664-6710, a public relations agency. "My advice is to incorporate the fan into what you are trying to do. In the long run and short run, it will benefit you."

Wallace goes a step further. Not only should companies support the fan sites, they should create professionally designed graphics and encourage the fan sites to use that material. In this manner, the fan sites will look professionally designed and will reflect positively on the company. If the fan site owner creates his own art, it might be done badly and that would reflect poorly on the company.

"If he is promoting something on your behalf, enjoy it," he says. "If you do that, you need to give the fan preapproved artwork and descriptions so they don't do anything detrimental. Thank the fan sites. Send them a free product. Or say 'Do us a favor. Since we have worked so hard to build this brand up, just follow our guidelines so our legal department won't give us grief.' I can't imagine a fan in the world who wouldn't think this was inappropriate. If they don't abide, then close them down."

Shel Holtz, principal of Holtz Communication + Technology, of Concord, CA, shel@holtz.com, www.holtz.com, agrees: "This is a site they should be nurturing. They look worse than if they hadn't done anything."

At least one company is taking this enlightened approach. Acclaim Entertainment encourages websites to use its graphics, screen shots, Quick Time videos, and logos for its Turok Dinosaur Hunter game for Nintendo 64 as long as they also print the copyright and trademark acknowledgments. There are about 100 unofficial Nintendo websites. The move is aimed at gaining a broader acceptance for the characters, a company spokesman said. I also permit people to take the articles I've written for my website and reprint them on their websites and in their printed newsletters. My strategy is to gain as wide a following as possible. By allowing people to print my articles in their publications, people all over the world—literally—have been exposed to my writings and thoughts. The marketer in me says that some of those people will buy my books, hire me to speak at their conferences or retain me to handle their projects.

Enforcing the copyright can lead to a consumer backlash. A fan put up a site to honor Barbie, but received legal notices from the Mattel lawyers. The website owner retaliated by posting web pages in English, Spanish, German, and French. Now the world knows about the problem (see Chapters 13 and 14 to learn how companies can deal with sites that attack companies).

When do you bring in the lawyers?

"When the fans aren't listening to me, I toss it over to the lawyers," says Wallace who has handled similar cases for his clients. In the meantime, he advises clients to listen to PR first. "You hired us because we are experts. Please listen to our advice. Let us do what we have been doing for many clients so you are represented properly."

When would Wallace not hesitate to bring in the lawyers? When pornography is used.

Holtz agrees. "You need to educate the lawyers and show them that cyberspace is different. You need to defend your

THE SOFTWARE PUBLISHERS ASSOCIATION'S
THEORIES OF COPYRIGHT INFRINGEMENT

As part of its educational efforts, SPA is providing the following information to educate Internet users and server operators on how their actions may be in violation of federal copyright law. These definitions explain some of the different elements of copyright law and may be easily applied to situations on the Internet. Following each legal definition is a practical application in reference to Internet use.

Direct Infringement

➤ "Anyone who violates any of the exclusive rights of the copyright owner [reproduction, adaptation, distribution to the public, public performance, public display, rental for commercial advantage or importation] is an infringer of the copyright or the right of the author . . ." Section 501(a) of the Copyright Act. Examples include:

➤ Downloading software,

➤ Uploading software,

➤ Making software available for download, and

➤ Transmitting software files.

Indirect Infringement

Contributory Infringement: Anyone who knows or should have known that he or she is assisting, inducing or materially contributing to infringement of any of the exclusive rights by another person is liable for contributor infringement. Examples include:

➤ Posting of serial numbers,

➤ Posting of cracker utilities,

(continued)

THEORIES OF COPYRIGHT INFRINGEMENT
(Continued)

➤ Linking to FTP sites where software may be unlawfully obtained,

➤ Informing others of FTP sites where software may be unlawfully obtained,

➤ Aiding others in locating or using unauthorized software,

➤ Supporting sites on which the above information may be obtained, and

➤ Allowing sites where the above information may be obtained to exist on a server.

Vicarious Liability for Infringement by Another Person: Anyone who has the authority and ability to control another person who infringes any of the exclusive rights and who derives a financial benefit therefrom, is vicariously liable for the infringement of another person. Examples include:

➤ ISPs who have warez or pirate sites on their system,

➤ ISPs who have pirates for customers, and

➤ Sys admins for newsgroups or IRC where pirate activity takes place.

---

trademarks but it is a question of balance. Protecting your trademark isn't worth it if 10,000 people now know about this case. Lawyers aren't always right," he says.

➤ Recent Trademark Cases and the Web

Tandy, which owns the Radio Shack trademark, threatened the owners of Bianca's Smut Shack, alleging trademark violations. Protecting a common word like "shack" is a dangerous legal minefield for Tandy. The case has dragged on for more than two years as lawyers for each side send letters back and forth without resolution (*San Francisco Chronicle,* April 15, 1997).

As mentioned earlier, Toys "R" Us filed suit in federal court in San Francisco against the owners of the website Adults "R" Us claiming the latter was undermining their wholesome image. Adults "R" Us makes inflatable dolls and sexual devices and clothing.

■ COMMONLY ASKED QUESTIONS AND ANSWERS ABOUT SOFTWARE PIRACY

The following questions that people often ask about legal software use are divided into these categories:

➤ General.

➤ Software piracy.

➤ Internet piracy.

➤ Reporting a case of piracy.

➤ Liability for piracy.

➤ General

What is SPA? What do they do?

SPA stands for Software Publishers Association. It is a non-profit trade association for software publishers and related organizations. There are currently over 1,200 member companies of SPA. The SPA's mission is to provide information to the industry, protect the industry, and promote the industry. As part of their mission to protect the industry, SPA members give the SPA permission to enforce their software copyrights and trademarks.

➤ Software Piracy

Can you explain software piracy? What is it?

Software piracy is the unauthorized use of software. It includes:

➤ Purchasing a single user license and loading it onto multiple computers or a server ("softloading").

➤ Making, distributing, and/or selling copies that appear to be from an authorized source ("counterfeiting").

➤ Renting software without permission from the copyright holder.

➤ Distributing and/or selling software that has been "unbundled," or separated, from the products with which it was intended to have been "bundled."

➤ Downloading copyrighted software from the Internet or bulletin boards without permission from the copyright holder.

Question: *I saw cheap software at a weekend show at my local civic center. Is that legitimate software?*

Answer: It may be legitimate, such as shareware, but it may be illegal—counterfeit or unbundled (which often is labeled "not for resale"). Be careful and report it to the SPA if the deal is too good to be true.

Question: *Why shouldn't I use pirated software? Who am I hurting?*

Answer: There are several reasons to avoid pirated software. First, it's illegal. Second, it's risky; unless you are certain that your software is from an authorized source, you could be getting a program that is infected with a virus, that may be incompatible or not fully functioning, and that is without a manual or technical support. Sometimes "getting what you paid for" isn't such a good thing. Third, you may be hurting yourself or your organization by failing to take advantage of the economic benefits of many newer software licenses. Fourth, there won't be another version of your favorite software if there is no revenue to put back into research and development. Finally, it is an unethical thing to do. Put yourself into the shoes of the software author and ask yourself how you would feel about a year or more of your life's work being used without permission or compensation?

Question: *I have seen the same copy of a software package run on multiple computers; if there are no licenses or disks, is that piracy?*

Answer: Any single-user copy of software run on multiple PCs without licenses or disks is pirated. If the license states that the software can only be used on one PC or with one person, then using it multiple times is a violation of the license agreement.

Question: *I went to a store and I was sold a computer with a lot of software already on the hard drive. I don't have the license or disk for it; what should I do? Is that piracy?*

Answer: If you have purchased any software that does not come with a license or registration, then that is probably a case of piracy. It also puts you, the consumer, at risk for having an illegal product on your PC. Illegal software comes with no technical support and often has viruses that can crash your hard drive. If a dealer tries to sell software with no paperwork, take it back and report the dealer to the SPA. There are, however, times that software may be installed legally on the system. This is often called *bundled* software. Bundled software is specially licensed to the computer with which it came. If you have a question about the software's legality, please consult the reseller or publisher of the product.

Question: *I went to a store that was renting games and software. Is that piracy?*

Answer: It is illegal to rent software without written permission from the copyright holder. When in doubt, ask the rental store to see the permission (or "license") to rent the product. If they can't produce it, then they probably are not authorized to rent and are committing piracy.

Question: *I have a copy of a Shareware game. Does that mean it's free?*

Answer: Shareware is software that is passed out freely for evaluation purposes only. If you wish to keep the software program, then you must pay to keep your evaluation copy. The evaluation time is usually 30 days.

➤ Internet Piracy

Question: *If I find software available for download on the Internet, can I assume I can download it legally?*

Answer: Not always. There are generally three types of software: shareware, freeware, and commercial. You may legally download shareware or freeware; however, commercial software such as Norton Utilities, Corel WordPerfect, and Adobe Photoshop are not legally available for download on the Internet. If you have any questions, check with the publisher to determine whether the distributor (i.e., operator of the site) has a license to distribute these products.

Question: *My server operator allows me to download software free as part of my account. Is this legal?*

Answer: Sometimes. Many server operators have licenses with publishers to distribute software to their subscribers. Or, they may make shareware and freeware available for subscribers to try out and use. If you have concerns that pirated software may be available, please check with your server operator or the publisher to confirm appropriate licensing.

Question: *Is it illegal to link to pirated software?*

Answer: It may be. Under certain circumstances, links to illegal material such as pirated software may represent a contributory infringement under copyright law. In addition, aiding someone in committing an infringement, or crime, is unethical and violates the sanctity of the Internet community.

Question: *What are "warez"?*

Answer: Warez are most commonly defined as pirated software and should be avoided. Sites labeled as warez usually contain pirated software. In general, it has become accepted usage in the Internet community to pluralize words that describe illegal activity by using the letter "z" instead of an "s."

Question: *Is posting serial numbers and cracker utilities illegal?*

Answer: The provision of serial numbers and cracker utilities, which are intended to circumvent the copyright protections in software, when used by an individual to commit a direct infringement, may represent contributory infringement under copyright law.

➤ Reporting a Case of Piracy

Question: *If I make a piracy report, can I remain anonymous?*

Answer: All piracy reports are completely confidential. SPA understands the need for confidentiality among sources and maintains a policy of keeping source information confidential on its toll-free piracy hotline, via: netpiracy@spa.org. Anonymous reports are difficult to pursue because SPA has no means to contact the source should additional information be required.

Question: *I am currently employed with the company. Will they find out that I am a source if I give you my name?*

Answer: Often, sources who are current employees will leave their name and contact information in the event SPA needs to contact them for additional information. SPA will not voluntarily supply the pirate organization with any information pertaining to the identity of the source. All information is held strictly confidential.

Question: *What will happen after I report information to the SPA?*

Answer: A report is taken and investigated before the company is contacted. If the report is valid after the investigation, one of four actions will be taken:

1. Sending a cease-and-desist letter.
2. Conducting a cooperative audit.
3. Initiating litigation.
4. Gathering additional information.

Question: *I think that the company will try to destroy the evidence. What can you do to stop this?*

Answer: The SPA can file a lawsuit if there is strong reason to believe that the company may destroy software. If a lawsuit is filed, and the company then destroys the software, the company may be in contempt of court and thus subject to the court's disciplinary action in addition to the copyright infringement claim.

Question: *Is there a reward for reporting piracy?*

Answer: SPA does not offer monetary rewards. SPA feels that this practice would compromise its reports and negatively affect the credibility of the source. Reporting the wrongdoing creates a level playing field for all software users.

➤ Liability for Piracy

Question: *What are the fines for being caught with pirated software?*

Answer: If sued for civil copyright infringement, the penalty is up to $100,000 per title infringed. If charged with a criminal violation, the fine is up to $250,000 per title infringed and up to five years' imprisonment.

Question: *What proof does the company need to keep to show that we have purchased our software?*

Answer: SPA requires positive proof that all software has been purchased to demonstrate copyright compliance. The best documentation substantiating authorized purchases includes approved purchase orders and invoices.

Question: *I work with a company that is not compliant. To do my job, I have illegal software on my company-owned machine. Am I liable for that?*

Answer: Liability usually falls on the party that owns the PCs loaded with pirate software. In this case, the company itself is liable.

Question: *If the company has a software policy and even has its employees sign a policy statement on software usage, does the company shield itself from liability?*

Answer: The answer is no. While having all employees sign a policy statement is sound business practice, it does not eliminate the liability of the company if the company is found to be using illegal software.

Question: *Okay . . . if I know that a company is pirating software, and I work with them and have seen it on their machines, am I liable if I don't report it?*

Answer: SPA does not hold the individual liable for company piracy; however, it is the responsibility of the individual to report a crime that they know is happening. It is also the right thing to do.

Question: *I have some old software that I do not use anymore. I want to give it away. What do I need to do? Do I need special permission?*

Answer: It depends on what is meant by "old software." If, for example, you wish to give away old software that has been upgraded, the answer is generally no. Upgrade licenses supplant the license of the original, voiding the original license thereby making the original version legally unusable. On the other hand, if you bought a new, full copy of a higher version of the software, license permitting, you could sell or give away the older version.

Question: *I would like to use a software program, but the company has gone out of business. Is it okay for me to make a copy since they are not making any more copies of this software for purchase?*

Answer: Copyrights may be valid for 75 years or more, so they may continue to subsist long after a company has gone out of business. The copyrights may even have been transferred or assigned to someone else. To copy a software program, you need express permission from the copyright holder. The U.S. Copyright Office may be helpful in finding the current copyright holder to write for permission to copy the product.

Question: *When I am purchasing software, what paperwork should I expect to have with it?*

Answer: A reputable dealer will sell software providing the customer with the original disks, manuals, registration, and the license agreement. If these items are not made available, do not buy the product.

■ HUNTING FOR YOUR PIRATED MATERIAL

Since millions of printed web pages exist around the world, searching for your copyrighted material on the Internet presents a serious challenge. However, new tools, sophisticated search techniques, and dedicated companies that search for material are making this task easier. Search engines like Yahoo!, Alta Vista, and InfoSeek can be used to find references to your organization and its products on websites. Deja News can find similar references on newsgroups.

Here are several search strategies:

➤ Search for the company, organization, product, or term.

➤ Search for the term as part of a URL (uniform/universal resource locator), or web address.

➤ Search for misspellings of the name.

➤ Hire experts to find the infringements.

➤ Search Services

To find instances of copyright and trademark violations on the Internet, you might hire a company that specializes in search services. Infringatek Internet Division, www.infringatek.com, bose@infringatek.com, 703-256-2222, polices trademarks and copyrights on the websites, newsgroups, chat rooms, and other areas on the Internet. says Sudeep Bose, Director of Infringatek, Inc.* "Our mission is to protect the assets of our Fortune 1000 clients in cyberspace. We are looking for anything referencing our clients—company names and products. When we find someone using a client's trademark, we examine the context of the use and determine whether to report it to the attorneys."

"Commercial search engines are often used in an attempt to police marks but often thousands of hits delay efforts to locate damaging materials," remarks Robert Badgik, lead researcher. Many of the commercial search engines produce hit lists with nonexistent sites.

"By the time you get around to viewing all the sites, the damage is done. Also, chat rooms and posting areas within various Internet service providers like AOL are never indexed by the commercial search engines. This leaves a lot of room for infringement."

---

* Company press release, March 21, 1997.

The company offers a wide range of tools for the policing, protection, and maintenance of intellectual property rights. The staff includes former U.S. Patent examiners, computer research experts, and former U.S. law enforcement agents.

■ SUMMARY

The laws of copyright and trademark apply to the Internet. You can't simply take huge blocks of text, pictures, or music and publish them on your site without permission. New laws and situations are being developed as the Internet embraces the world, so contact your attorney before you publish anything from other sources on your website.

Competitive Intelligence

Today's the big day for your company. You're announcing new products, new pricing schedules, new distribution strategy. You're really going to give your competitors a heart attack when they find out.

In the good old days before computers, your competitors might have found out about the news a week or maybe a month later as word spread through the grapevine and rumors were verified by trade paper reports.

Now, with the Internet, your competitors know about your plans almost as fast as your customers, maybe sooner.

This chapter explores the ways competitors can find out about your company and its newsmaking events. You'll learn:

➤ What your competitors know about you.

➤ How they can find out even more about your company.

➤ What you can do about it—and what you can't.

■ WHAT YOUR COMPETITORS KNOW ABOUT YOU

One of the great things about the Internet is that your customers and prospects can read about your new products and services. Since you have unlimited printing capabilities, you can tell the world about your new features in much greater detail than would be possible for articles printed in a daily newspaper or even the most fact-oriented trade publication.

Unfortunately, so can your competitors. Any information you put on your website can and will be read by your competitors. Press releases announcing new products, earnings reports, personnel changes, and the like will be known by your competitors moments after you post the information on the Internet. This situation is similar to the real world, where any competitor could call your office, pose as a prospect, and ask you to send information, which you would do gladly. Also, at trade shows, any competitor could walk into your booth to see your products and talk to your salespeople and support staff to find new information—and milk them for private details!

A well-designed website usually has these items that inform your customers as well as your competitors:

> ➤ Press releases announcing new products, new alliances, new distributors, new customers, earnings reports, personnel announcements, white papers, and research reports.

> ➤ Product fact sheets that describe your new products in more detail than any newspaper or trade publication would print.

Armed with this information, your competitors now know about your new products and how their products compare; they know who your new distributors are and who to call to carry their products; they know your most recent hires—and who might make a good addition to their staffs.

Nevertheless, while one competitor finds this mineful of data, so do 20,000 prospects and customers. You need to determine the risk and benefits for each piece of information you reveal.

"If you don't want others to see it, don't put it out there. The way that the Internet technology operates presently, it is not a secure environment for trade secret material," says Alan S. Wernick, computer lawyer, copyright, trademark, trade secret and licensing, in private practice at Wernick & Associates, Co., L.P.A. in Columbus, Ohio, 614-463-1400, alan@wernick.com. "Encryption techniques can be used to protect sensitive materials. Trade secrets are very fragile in that they can be lost very easily."

■ HOW THEY CAN FIND OUT EVEN MORE ABOUT YOUR COMPANY

Your competitors can find out news about you while they sleep. By using software tools on the web, they can read about your company's news when convenient.

➤ Website Monitoring Programs

Your competitors use software programs (Web Whacker, Freeloader, Milk Truck, Web Ex), that monitor your website, copy entire pages to their hard disks and printers. These programs will even send warnings to their operators letting them know when you post a new page. Your competitors on-line might know more about your business than your employees or stockholders who don't have a computer.

➤ Search Engines

News about your company, analysts' commentaries, and stock market predictions can be found on many home pages, all of which are indexed by the major search engines like Alta

Vista, www.altavista.digital.com; Excite!, www.excite.com; and InfoSeek, www.infoseek.com. Try searching for your company's name or product names on any of these search engines. You'll be amazed at what you find.

➤ Online News Services

Your competitors can also use news services to monitor all the articles written about your company. They can also easily capture original press releases your company distributes via PR Newswire, www.prnewswire.com, or Business Wire, www.businesswire.com. Free news services monitoring several newswires can cull articles about your company and print them on a special news page for your competitors to read, or even send the articles to their mailboxes. Lexis-Nexis, www.lexis-nexis.com offers several services that find news articles from a much larger database of newspapers and magazines from the United States and around the world.

By the way, in the old days when you left a reporter's office on your press tour, you could plan on the story being in print in the next edition, a week or so later. Now, the Internet is ramping up those deadlines: Many publications have online versions and reporters have daily deadlines instead of weekly deadlines. In other words, as you leave the building after your interview, the reporter is writing the story. By the time the cab drops you off for your next interview, the story is on the Internet. As you reach the next reporter's desk, he already knows what you are going to say. And so do your competitors.

All these activities are perfectly legal. You can't do anything to stop your competitors from monitoring news services and press release services.

➤ Newsgroups

Are your employees posting notices about your company in newsgroups that can be read by anyone, anywhere? Apple Computer employees, on several occasions, have leaked internal memos to newsgroups. Other company employees might reveal company secrets unknowingly by asking questions that intelligent industry observers can use to deduce your new product line, sales activity, or company morale. Your company must have a policy that forbids employees from posting internal documents in a public forum. (See Chapter 7 for sample wording on such policies.)

■ WHAT YOU CAN DO ABOUT IT— AND WHAT YOU CAN'T MOVE TO TRADE SECRETS

Can you keep competitors out of your website?

"The short answer is no. The Internet's real value is its openness. You want your customers to come. You want to make it easy for them to get there," says Wernick.*

"If you wanted to spend the time and money, you could set up and monitor log files that could provide some information about those who visit your site. It would seem to be a wiser investment of time and money if you protect your intellectual property assets through properly protecting the intellectual property rights, not by limiting access to your publicly available material," he says.

Wernick says, "It is a dilemma. But it is no different than a company deciding to publish this type of information on a billboard or a flyer. The Internet is no different. You have to ask yourself if it is an appropriate medium for publishing this type of information?"

---

* Interview, August 8, 1997.

You can take the steps described in the next few sections to keep your website safe from prying eyes.

➤ Conduct an Intellectual Property Audit

An intellectual property audit needs to be done on a routine basis. An IP audit can discover many things including:

- ➤ What IP assets do they have?
- ➤ How do they claim to have ownership in them (ownership or licensing)?
- ➤ Have they registered the rights?
- ➤ Have they limited access?

"It gives a snapshot of the IP assets, like a financial audit. It helps a company see if they are in compliance with their license rights, and if they are protecting the rights adequately so they don't lose value in the IP," says Wernick.

➤ Accept Responsibility for Your Actions

Recognize that anything you put on a website should be considered open to the public. Your prospects and customers, as well as your competitors, will soak up everything you put on public display. Before you post anything on the Web, ask yourself if this is something you want your competitors to know. If it isn't, then don't put it up. If the value of informing your customers and prospects outweighs the consequences of your competitors knowing about the facts, then post the information.

➤ Registration

Make it difficult for competitors to have access to the information. Many business-to-business websites, for example, use a two-tiered website. That is, they post just enough information on the website to create interest and excitement in dealing with the company. Then the site asks the prospect to register by filling out a form online with such information as name, title, company, address, purchasing power, purchasing decision ability, company size, sales, and other qualifying information. The answers on this form can help a company decide whether the person should be allowed to read the more detailed information about the company and products, or if a salesperson should call the prospect to initiate a relationship. An assistant should call the person and verify the information, as competitors are likely to provide false information. Obviously, if a competitor lists correct information and acknowledges being a competitor, you can deny access.

This test is not foolproof and has significant pros and cons: A crafty competitor could use someone else's name and make the person sound like a qualified applicant. On the other hand, if a prospect passes the test, you can issue a password that allows access to the rest of the site; this helps you qualify customers and give them information targeted for their size company and buying motives.

➤ Company Policies

Create a company policy for deciding what type of information can and can't be posted to the website. Make sure each employee knows about this policy.

Create a company policy on who signs off for approving each document that appears on the website. Management Information System (MIS) or technology staffs run many company websites although they have inadequate background and training for this responsibility. I've crisscrossed the country talking to communications and PR managers who tell horror stories about their organizations' poorly run websites: Postings may include outdated material, violate company advertising procedures, and add misspellings to corporate documents (the word "mathematics" was misspelled on one school district's website). In addition to possessing writing, communication, and computer skills, people who decide which documents are posted should be familiar with public opinion, corporate relations, the intricacies of the regulations of the Securities and Exchange Commission, or laws of trademark and copyright. These tasks belong to the marketing, corporate communications, or legal departments. (See also, the section on trade secrets in Chapter 7 for a list of ways to restrict employees from revealing company information.)

These steps might be effective, but like any system, competitors can find workarounds that could subvert even the most clever safeguard.

■ SUMMARY

Information posted to your website can be sitting on your rival's desk within minutes of publication. Your competitors can monitor your site, your news feeds, and even newsgroups to find information about your company. All these methods are legal. Your main recourse is to control the unauthorized distribution of information by employees and to decide how much information you want to put online. You need to weigh the benefits of presenting information to your clients and prospects compared with the risks of having your competitors find out what you are up to.

Chapter

11

Protecting Your Online Alter Ego: Domain Names

Congratulations!

> *You've made the decision to put your organization on the Internet, and you've instructed your Internet Service Provider to hang your shingle on the Internet.*

> *A few minutes later, she returns with distressing news: Another company is using your company's name on the Internet.*

> *A few minutes later, a client calls and says he tried looking you up on the Internet, but although your company name was online, it presented information about buying prepaid telephone calling cards!*

> *Your lawyer calls the holder of that domain name and finds out they would be happy to sell you the rights to your own name—for $100,000!*

What can you do? A lot!

There are two important issues here:

1. Domain name registration.
2. Domain name theft and extortion.

There are numerous legal activities and creative guerrilla strategies to present and protect your name to the Internet public. This chapter explains:

➤ What a domain name is and why it is important.
➤ How to register your company's domain on the Internet.
➤ How to register your company's domain in other countries.
➤ What you can do—legally and strategically—if another company has registered your preferred domain name.
➤ How to deal with cybersquatters who register domain names with the intention of selling them.
➤ Interesting cases of domain name thefts.
➤ Online resources.

■ WHAT'S IN A NAME? WHY YOUR COMPANY NEEDS A DOMAIN NAME

A domain name is a company's name and identity on the Internet. Consumers, prospects, potential employees, dealers, distributors, and other people who are interested in your company find your site by typing the domain name in the browser.

You've seen domain names, even if you didn't know that was their actual name. If you watch TV, read a newspaper, or listen to news radio, you've seen dozens of ads with contact information that includes the address or phone number and

---

RISKY BUSINESS IN THE FIELD

Procter & Gamble, manufacturer of such popular house-hold products as Tide, Pampers, Safeguard, Pepto-Bismol, Old Spice, and Clearasil registered 52 domain names including pimples.com, underarms.com, toiletpaper.com, and diarrhea.com.

---

the domain name, www.mycompany.com. Almost all business cards and letterheads now include a domain name.

■ SO THAT'S WHAT THOSE FUNNY SYMBOLS ARE!

The format of a domain name is the company name followed by a period followed by an extension. Most businesses use this format: mycompany.com. It is pronounced "My Company dot com." The first part is the name of the company and can also be called the second-level domain name. The extension, also known as a top-level domain, describes the company's main activity. The other extensions and meanings are:

.edu—education, e.g., berkeley.edu (University of California at Berkeley).

.mil—military, e.g., army.mil (U.S. Army).

.org—nonprofit organization, e.g., prsa.org (Public Relations Society of America).

.gov—government agency, e.g., whitehouse.gov (The White House).

.net—network providers and network-related companies, e.g., ccnet.net (CCNET).

.int—organizations established by international treaties, e.g., reliefweb.int (Relief Web, a division of the United Nations).

In addition, seven new top-level domains were created in 1997.

.firm—business or firm.

.store—businesses offering goods to purchase.

.web—entities emphasizing activities related to the World Wide Web.

.arts—entities emphasizing cultural and entertainment activities.

.rec—entities emphasizing recreational and entertainment activities.

.info—entities providing information services.

.nom—personal nomenclature.

Domain names can have subdomain levels as well (e.g., altavista.digita.com). This can be helpful to marketers who want to direct prospects to a certain part of their website. For example, Toshiba prints the domain name computers.toshiba.com to lead people directly to their website dealing with computers.

The domain name does not have to be the exact same as the company's full legal name; for example, Janal Communications can be simply janal.com because a shorter name is easier to type. Variants, and the reasons for using them, are discussed later in this chapter.

The domain name identifies your business to the world. If your domain name is easy to remember, people will find your website intuitively. If another company has your domain name, your customers might go to that website by mistake. Therefore, it is in your best interests to protect your company name by registering it with the proper authorities in the United States and other countries (because the Internet is truly a worldwide media, a company with a similar name in another country might have used your company's name).

Register your domain name as soon as possible to prevent someone else from getting the name first and causing confusion. For example, the National Speakers Association uses nsaspeaks.org because nsa.org was already registered—legitimately—by some other organization. However, NSA members and prospects would type nsa.org first, thinking this would be the logical domain name for the organization.

Although many domain names typically identify companies, you can also protect your intellectual property by registering domains for:

➤ Acronyms

➤ Aliases, nicknames

➤ Association names

➤ Assumed (dba) names

➤ Book titles

➤ Brand names

➤ Common and similar variations of names

➤ Common misspellings of company names

➤ Company initials

➤ Convention/ tradeshow names

➤ Copyrighted titles

➤ Descriptive terms

➤ Event names, festivals

➤ FCC call letters

➤ Franchise names

➤ Industry names

➤ Legal names

➤ Licensed properties

➤ Mascot names

➤ Packaged goods

➤ Parodies of names

➤ Patent names

➤ Person's name

➤ Phone numbers

➤ Phonetic spellings of names

➤ Product names

➤ Service marks

➤ Slang terms

➤ Slogans

➤ Software names

➤ Song titles

➤ Stock symbols

➤ Trademarks

The source of this list was idNames.com. If you register domains for your company and its intellectual products, you can be assured that no other company can take them and attempt to extort money from you for the rightful use of your name.

■ MARKETING USES OF DOMAIN NAMES

Why should you register a domain name?

You are not required to register a domain name, but any serious organization should. Any Internet service provider will let you use its domain name for your website or e-mail. Your address would look like this:

    www.bellsouth.com/companies
    /smallinsignificantcompanies/yourcompanyname

and an e-mail address like this:

    joe@bellsouth.com

Those aren't very personal names and don't do a thing to build brand-name recognition. Instead, you look like a small, insignificant company. Who would want to do business with you?

If you register your own domain name with the company name, your audience will be able to find you easily by typing:

    www.yourcompany.com

or sending e-mail to:

    info@mycompany.com

There is a great deal of brand awareness for the "dot com" domain names. People who don't know much about the Internet still know that "dot.com" signifies an Internet address. "Dot.Com" has entered the vernacular.

"Our society treats 'dot com' as a household name. It has become part of the language," says Pinkard Brand, vice president of idNames.Com, a Houston-based company that registers domain names for companies around the world.*

Network Solutions, Inc. (NSI) the entity responsible for administering the assignment of domain names in the United States and Canada, likens the domain name to a vanity license plate. If someone sees the plate, they remember the name of the car.

■ MAKING A NAME YOUR OWN

The Domain Name Registration Process in the United States NSI registers all company domain names in the United States through a company called InterNIC. They assign names on a first-come, first-served basis and they do not check for trademark infringements so it is important for companies to register the names of their companies and products as soon as possible to prevent other companies from getting rights to those names first. The registration process is straightforward and involves several steps.

First, your company must decide on the name it wants to register. The best name is your company name or product name. However, typing the entire name might be

---

* Interview, July 1997.

cumbersome or awkward. For example, Law Offices of Smith, Jones, Brown, Green and Partners contains more letters than InterNIC allows. The limit is 22 characters plus the dot and the extension. It is also very long to type. The more letters, the more chance for introducing typos. A better choice might be smithjones.com.

Names that contain hyphens are also hard to type and hard to explain to people over the phone. They always ask "Is that a hyphen or a dash?" Invariably, they will type the wrong character! smith-jones.com could be written as smith—jones.com, which would not lead the customer to your site.

The only valid characters are letters, numbers, and a hyphen. Punctuation symbols like ampersand, exclamation point, asterisk, parentheses, equal sign, plus sign, percentage sign, underscore, and caret cannot be used. If these symbols are part of your company name, they must be deleted. AT&T can't use the ampersand in its domain name. Instead, it uses: att.com. Kinko's can't use the apostrophe, so it uses kinkos.com. An underscore can be used in an e-mail address (e.g., john_smith@mycompany.com).

Now that you have decided on a name, you need to make sure that it is available and that no other company has registered it. You can do this by searching NSI's WhoIs database, which contains records for all the domains that have been registered. You will find an easy-to-use search tool for the WhoIs database at http://rs.internic.net/cgi-bin/whois. (Notice, there isn't a "www" in that URL.)

If the search comes up empty, no one has registered the name and you can begin the registration process. If the name is taken, you will see who owns the name, along with the phone numbers, e-mail addresses, and mailing addresses of the technical and administrative contacts. There are a number of creative marketing ideas or legal avenues to explore.

To continue with the registration process, the easiest way to register the domain name is to call your Internet service provider, who might charge an extra fee. This is a necessary step because each domain name needs to be linked to a computer address, which is a long string of numbers that is difficult to remember. This string is also called the IP (Internet Protocol) address. That's why domain names are used: they are aliases for those numbers. It's like saying the president lives at 1600 Pennsylvania Avenue, Washington, DC, or the much easier to remember "The White House." Since computers understand only numbers, they must attach a numerical address to your company domain name. When a consumer uses a browser to type in your company domain name, the computer translates the name into the IP number. This process is called "resolution." You'll probably never need to know this term, but you can impress your geek friends by dropping it in conversations. The ISP is integral in this process because it provides the IP address. Without that address, your domain name cannot be registered. For example, my domain name is "janal.com" but the IP address is a series of nine numbers.

"Without domain name service, the InterNIC will not process your registration request, you will not be able to use your domain name, and other people will not be able to use your domain name to find you on the Internet," according to InterNIC literature.

The registration form can be found at http://rs.internic.net/cgi-bin/itts/domain. NSI's policy statements and payment procedures can be found at: http://rs.internic.net/help/index.html.

After the IP address is obtained, you or the ISP need to fill out the application form, which asks for contact information and the IP address, and e-mail it to hostmaster@InterNIC. (Paper mail and fax are not accepted.) NSI assigns a tracking number, checks for errors, and if the form is filled in properly, sends a bill to you. You must pay NSI $100 (US) which covers the initial registration updates to the domain name's record for two years.

That's it. Your domain is registered in as little as 10 minutes or as much as 24 hours, according to NSI.

By the way, if payment is not received by the due date, the name is subject to deactivation and deletion. If a domain name holder doesn't pay the renewal fee by the due date, that name can then be reassigned. This is important to note if your name has been taken.

Once a domain is registered, your company owns the domain name, not the ISP or marketing company who helped you register it.

➤ Geek Stuff

Is the "www" part of a domain name? Many people are used to seeing the following string of letters: http://www.example .com

This is an example of a uniform resource locator, also known as a URL and pronounced "earl" or "your'll." The command "http://www" issued by consumers to their Web browsers to find documents and resources on the WWW is not a domain name. However the example.com is the domain name and is a vital part of the URL.

➤ Competition Might Change Everything

NSI's exclusive contract to control domain names expires at the end of March 1998. At this writing, there is no clear understanding of whether NSI will continue to have a monopoly on this service, or if other companies will be allowed to do this as well. There is also confusion as to which company or companies will operate the new top-level domains. With a great deal of money at stake in licensing and regulating this growing industry, it is not surprising that organizations around the world are lobbying to get a piece of this action.

For latest developments, read *WebWeek,* www.webweek.com, or *Interactive Week,* www.interactive-week.com.

■ PARLEZ VOUZ DOMAIN? HOW TO REGISTER YOUR DOMAIN NAME INTERNATIONALLY

Registering your domain name in the United States is the first step to creating a worldwide presence on the Internet. This makes sense because the Internet is a worldwide medium. Large companies should register their domain names on other countries' domain registration procedures.

Why?

You might find that another company in that country is using your company name.

The holder of that name might be:

➤ A "cybersquatter" whose only purpose is to sell the name to your company at extortionist prices.

➤ A legitimate company that has been conducting business in that country for generations and has as much right to use that name (or more) than your company does.

➤ A political group that wants to damage your reputation.

"The legal community is about to be shocked because it still doesn't understand that these domain names are like trademarks, if they have any value to a firm, they must be protected and registered in every country around the world where they, or their competitors, may do business in the future," said Pinkard Brand, president of idNames.com, a Houston-based company that registers domain names worldwide and conducts worldwide searches of domain names (idNames, phone 713-974-0069, 888-436-2637, fax 713-974-5459, info@idNames.com).

"Not protecting each and every name that has a value is a 'pay now or pay later game.' It's just not prudent business to not have a strategy to deal with this." (Pinkard Brand idNames.)

AT&T and MCI are two companies that have seen their names registered in different countries—and there is little they can do about it.

"If you've registered your company name in a dot com, you are not protected in another country," says Brand. "If you have brand names or properties you want to protect, it won't protect you from other companies registering and using your mark."

As of 1997, 190 countries accept domain name registrations. Each has its own policy for registering companies. Of those, 51 countries accept registrations on a first-come, first-served basis. That means that anyone can register your company's name in that country. A business prospect in that country could type in your company name and find herself at the website of a local company that has absolutely no relationship to your company.

idNames.com has spent a year learning the legal, regulatory, and technical parameters in registering domains in those countries. The results are daunting for companies that want to do the registration process themselves.

According to Brand, Taiwan requires companies to register in the native language. In Belgium, individuals cannot register domain names. In France, a company must use a French Internet service provider to host data.

"We specialize in knowing what these policies are, currency calculations, foreign language translations, and the rest," said Brand, who notes there can be 100 technical and regulatory questions that have to be answered to register a domain name in each country. Each of these questions must be addressed and accurately completed when registering a

---

RISKY BUSINESS IN THE FIELD

Tonga, an island country in the South Pacific, has the rights to the "TO" extension, or second level domain. They began selling domain names like love.to, go.to, how.to in June 1997 from their San Francisco embassy. The fee is $100 US, the same as that charged by NSI.

The registry does not require a physical presence in Tonga and no proof that registrants hold the copyright to the name.

"These names are the property of the kingdom of Tonga, and the names are granted in accordance with Tongan trademark law, of which there is essentially none," a spokesperson said.

So, if you want.to, you can go.to a registrar who is happy.to sell.to you a domain name that is sure.to give.to your competitors anxiety attacks.

---

domain name in any country. "If any person tried to do this, it would take a long time. We are a one-stop solution to registering domains world wide."

Although he won't disclose who his clients are, citing attorney-client privilege, he notes that his office has been flooded with companies seeking help. "In the short time we have been marketing, we have been approached by many companies."

"The value of an Internet domain name will grow over time in proportion to the amount of information kept on a website. Those names MUST be protected in the United States and internationally," he said. "Someone, anyone, with a connection to the Internet can register your company's name, without your knowledge or approval. If you register first with idNames.com, you won't have to worry later."

■ HELP! SOMEONE'S USING MY COMPANY NAME ON THE INTERNET

So now we get to the basic question that is causing all this concern. You decide it is time to put your company online. You ask your ISP to register your company name. A few minutes later, she tells you that the name is taken by another company. What can you do?

Jonathan Hudis, jhudis@oblon.com, is an attorney specializing in intellectual property rights with the firm of Oblon, Spivak, McClelland, Maier and Neustadt PC in Arlington, Virginia, 703-412-7047. We ran several scenarios by him to get a firm, legal opinion.*

■ ASK THE EXPERTS

Question: *A company has taken my name. We both have registered these names with the county clerks in our own states. Neither of us has a federal registration.*

Hudis: The first person to get there has the legitimate right to use the name. If you are the second guy, there is nothing you can do. "My advice is to get a federal registration for your name. Considering NSI's current domain name dispute resolution policies, there is immense value in having a federal trademark registration from any country. This is because federal trademark registration gives the owner priority over the domain name holder, who is the newcomer.

Trademark laws can divide up trademark rights geographically. You can't do that on the Internet because you are everywhere and nowhere at the same time. Hudis also advises registering your trademark, product, or company with all permitted top-level domains (such as .com, .org, etc. and also to

---

* Interview, May 9, 1997.

RISKY BUSINESS IN THE FIELD AND AT COURT!

In one of the first disputes over a domain name, Adam Curry, an MTV employee, created a website and registered the domain mtv.com. When he left the station, he took the domain with him, claiming he was the registered owner, according to NSI records. MTV cited its trademark and forced Curry to relinquish the name.

---

register these names with spaces and without spaces. For example, 1-800-dentists.com and 1800dentists.com are two websites owned by two different companies. The likelihood of confusion is enormous.

Question: *A company has taken my name. We have a federal registration. What can we do?*

Hudis: Write to the domain name holder. Tell them they are infringing on your trademark. Ask them to transfer the domain name. If they don't comply, shut them down. Go to NSI. Give them a certified copy of your federal registration and ask them to place the domain on hold. Now neither company can do business on the Internet until the dispute is resolved. If they still refuse to give up the name, sue in federal court to get a judge to make them assign the name.

Question: *A company has taken my name. They have the federal registration.*

Hudis: You are out of luck.

Question: *If another company holds a generic name, like shoestore, but the site isn't being used, can we force them to give us the name?*

Hudis: NSI policy mandates that every domain name be assigned to an IP address, but there is no rule that a company must actually post information on that site. In other words, they own the domain name.

Question: *My company owns a federal trademark to our name and a company that had registered our name wants to sell us the name. What can we do?*

Hudis: If you have a trademark, the second they ask you for money, you can sue them in federal court for dilution. There is a qualification before the dilution statute can apply. It only is applicable when someone is doing something in commerce. If all you do is register a domain name and do nothing with and don't hold it out for sale, you are not engaging in commerce and the statute would not apply. If you want to shut him down, the seller must make the offer.

Question: *I want to register a domain name to prevent competition or let someone else get it.*

Hudis: A prolife group registered planned parenthood.com (and wanted to post antiabortion material on the site). A federal judge forced the group to give up the name. They were preventing another company from engaging in commerce. That is a violation of dilution law.

Question: *Could the prolife group register Plannedparenthood .com while the actual group register Planned-parenthood .com?*

NOTE THIS!

Princeton Review registered kaplan.com, the name of its competitor, Stanley H. Kaplan Educational Center Ltd. Kaplan got the rights to the name.

Hudis: In computerese, these are two different names, so they could both be registered. However, this would be dilution.

Question: *You want to check your website and instead of typing "mycompany.com," you type "mycompany.org." Surprisingly, you see a site that belongs to another company. You are concerned people might make the same mistake and find that company instead of yours. What can you do?*

Hudis: Ask the owner of mycompany.org to transfer the domain name to your company. If they refuse, and if your company has a federal trademark registration, use the current NSI dispute resolution policy to put mycompany.org on hold.

Question: *You do further research and find that the "org" version of your site has been registered by a competitor. Furthermore, the information displayed on the opening screen says, "Welcome users of Your Company products. To see the next generation of products. Click here." You do so and find yourself at your rival's home page, which addresses each key product feature between the two companies. What can you do?*

Hudis: Sue the competitor in federal court for trademark infringement, dilution, and unfair competition.

■ PUBLIC RELATIONS POINT OF VIEW ON DOMAIN NAME DUPLICATIONS

That's the legal point of view. There are other ways of handling these sticky matters. Here's what professional communications people would do if their companies or clients found their preferred names are being used.

"The first thing I like to do is pick up the phone and call the person who has it," says Allan Wallace, chairman of the Interactive Agency, www.iagency.com, awall@iagency.com, 310-664-6710, a public relations agency handling many entertainment companies on the Internet, and say, "Look you are going against HBO. How much do you want this to cost you in court? You are going against monsters that have huge public relations and legal departments. You are going to be in the category of someone who is not doing legitimate business on the Internet. You are not making a good name for yourself no matter what you think you are doing."

Smaller companies, especially those that don't hold the trademark for the domain, must look elsewhere for solutions.

"My first thought is, 'What else can I use.' I don't know that I would try to take it away. I suppose I could call him and come up with alternatives for him," says Shel Holtz, www.holtz.com, principal of Holtz Communication + Technology.

■ GEURRILLA MARKETING METHODS AND DOMAIN NAMES

Just because your name has been taken doesn't mean you have to resort to being smallandinsignificant.com. Here are my suggestions for getting around the problem—all legally sanctioned.

> ➤ *Full company name.* Instead of MyCompany, use My-CompanyInc.com.
>
> ➤ *Initials.* Mail Boxes Etc. uses mbe.com. GE Information Services uses geis.com, Northwest Airlines uses nwa.com.
>
> ➤ *Part of the company name and product.* Mitsubishi uses mitsucars.com.
>
> ➤ *Modification of full company name.* Delta Airlines use delta-air.com. Sun Microsystems uses sun.com. Bell Atlantic uses bell-atl.com.

➤ *A specific company division.* Fujitsu, which makes many electronics products, uses fujitsu-pc.com.

➤ *Slogan.* Southwest Airlines uses their slogan iflyswa .com, which is also their 800 number.

➤ *Modifier.* Thisisnorman.com; welcometomycompany .com; finditatmycompany.com.

➤ *Vanity phone number.* 1-800-mycompany.com.

➤ *Action verb.* Sugar Bowl Ski Area uses ski-sugarbowl .com. Continental Airlines uses, flycontinental.com.

➤ *Made in the USA.* Lexus uses lexususa.com. Sharp uses sharp-usa.com.

➤ *Planet.* Reebok uses planetreebok.com.

■ SELECT A NAME WITH GREAT CARE

In addition to the great marketing reasons to select a domain name, you should take great care in choosing a name because you are going to use it for a long time. If you change the name, you will have to change your letterhead and business cards as well. Just as important, you'll have to change hundreds or thousands of links to your website from search engines, complementary websites, and other sites that have chosen to link to your site and print your web address on their pages.

A woman who attended one of my seminars asked for my opinion on her marketing consultant's choice of using the domain name "xtownprinting.com" to stand for "Crosstown Printing." I told her that no one would think that "x" meant "cross" and that this was a bad decision. She agreed and said she thought it was a bad idea when the consultant made the suggestion, but she figured he must know what he was talking about. He was wrong. Go with your gut instinct.

NSI maintains a list of domain names that are on hold because the owner has not paid to renew the name or the name is involved in a trademark dispute. Check the WhoIs database (http://rs.internic.net/cgi-bin/whois) to see if your name is on hold for nonpayment. If so, you might be able to persuade the owner to sell it to you.

■ DOMAIN NAMES FOR SALE

If your company name has already been registered, it might be in the hands of a profiteer (cybersquatter) who hopes to make money by reselling domain names. Cybersquatters have registered domain names for the purpose of selling those names to companies. There are legendary stories of these cyber entrepreneurs who register company names or common words (television, TV) and find companies to buy them, sometimes for tens of thousands of dollars. Microsoft paid $10,000 for the domain slate.com as the name for its political magazine. An undisclosed business paid $150,000 for the domain business.com. That's a nice return on an investment of the $100 to register a domain name! There is nothing illegal about registering a common word, like tissue. However, it is against the law for anyone to register a registered trademark, like Kleenex, except, of course, for the legal holder.

There are two types of cybersquatters:

1. Companies that register domains with the express purpose of selling the names to other companies.

2. Companies that register domain names with the original purpose of using those domains. However, in the course of time, they decide not to use the name for one reason or another. For example, a company might decide to create a new product and list three possible names. They register each name. They finally decide to use one name and have no use for the other two names. Since they have a valuable piece of intellectual property, they try to sell it.

Companies in the first case are looked on as vermin. In the second case, these companies are perceived as legitimate businesses selling a product acquired through ethical means.

"If your entire business model is buying domain names, like Calvin Klein or McDonald's, then you are one step below child porn sites on the Internet," said Wallace. "However, if you are a legitimate developer or a company that owns prime real estate because your sole intention was to use the name on your behalf or your client's behalf and you now no longer see the need for those domains, it makes sense to sell them. Then I think you should sell them."

The Trademark Dilution Statute of 1996 is being used in court to force cybersquatters to give up their domain names, says attorney Hudis. He cites cases in which Dennis Toeppen, an engineer, was sued by Intermatic Corporation, of Chicago, and Panavision in California. An Illinois court ruled that he had registered 200 domain names with the "intention to arbitrage," which constituted a commercial use. He was ordered to forfeit the domain names. The court held that Panavision was injured because consumers would have found it difficult to locate the true Panavision site.

Hudis' advice: Threaten cybersquatters with a lawsuit. They usually give up when they realize they are not going to win.

In a landmark case, *Porsche Cars North America, Inc. v. Chen,* the German auto manufacturer sued to get the rights to its trademark after Chen offered to transfer the domain if Porsche paid a $35,100 fee and ongoing monthly payments of $2,400. Porsche sued for infringement under the Lanham Act (the federal trademark statute), dilution under the Lanham Act, and common law unfair competition under Virginia law. The court issued a preliminary injunction.

If a cybersquatter registers a generic name, like television or computer, he would not be violating any law. If he attempts to register someone else's trademark as a domain name, he'll be sorry.

■ TELEVISION.COM

One of the first instances of a person selling a domain name came from Mike O'Connor, who registered the domain "television.com."

"With the emerging possibilities of entertainment delivery through the Internet, the value of easily remembered domain names has increased. I acquired this domain name with a different purpose in mind. Now I find myself in possession of an asset which would be considerably more useful to other organizations than it is to me," he says.*

"C|Net made a $50,000 cash offer for this domain. I turned them down and sponsored an Internet bidding war to which nobody came. They eventually bought and developed tv.com instead. That $50,000 bid doesn't reflect what I believe to be the ultimate value of this domain name. So this domain remains for sale. If you're interested in putting forward an offer, feel free to contact me (mike@gofast.com). Think of the PR opportunity!"

He is still waiting for a bidder.

■ HEY BUDDY! WANT TO BUY A DOMAIN NAME?

Many high-visibility domain names are not being used by the companies that registered them, and are now available for sale. The Internet Company was the first company dedicated to helping business understand the Internet as a commercial resource and acquired some of the choicest addresses on the World Wide Web, destinations like finance.com and wealth .com.

"Addresses like magazine.com and sweepstakes.com will give the right companies important boosts, making it easy

---

* Interview, June 1997.

for established clients to remember their address and for new customers to find the way to their doors," according to Wallace of the Interactive Agency written in a press release. For information on buying these domain names, contact the Internet Company's Joyce Dostale at 617-547-3600, x104, jdostale@world.std.com.

Here is the list of available domain names from the Internet Company:

- alpha-page.com
- boomtube.com
- caddyshack.com
- coin.org
- ear.com
- etech.com
- federalsearch.com
- finance.com
- fw.com
- gig.com
- healthcenter.com
- healthi.com
- magazine.com
- market.com
- messenger.com
- metanews.com
- navigator.com
- netkeno.com
- newsspace.com
- reason.com
- risks.com
- sweepstakes.com
- wealth.com

■ INTERESTING CASES IN DOMAIN NAME DUPLICITY

➤ Gateway 2000

Computer manufacturer Gateway 2000 lost its fight to gain gateway.com as its domain name when Federal Judge W. Earl Britt denied its motion. The judge said Alan B. Clegg is the rightful owner of the site for his company, called Gateway, which had registered the name in 1988, long before the rush to get domain names. The judge said Gateway 2000 did not make any attempt to get the name until 1994.

This case shows how dangerous it is to try to trademark a common word. It also shows how important it is for companies to protect their marks as soon as they become aware of the conflict.

➤ Microsoft Takes Action against College Student

A California college student registered "microsoftnetwork .com" and more than a dozen other domains containing Microsoft products and names. A Microsoft spokesman says the student "is clearly involved in copyright infringement, trademark infringement and unfair trade practices. We will try to contact him and request him to stop. Failing that, we'll send a cease-and-desist letter requesting he stop infringing upon our name" (*The New York Times,* June 3, 1997).

➤ Microsoft Swaps for MSNBC.Com

The day after Microsoft and NBC announced their MSNBC television network, a company with those initials registered msnbc.com. Microsoft agreed to give the company an undetermined amount of software in exchange for the domain name.

➤ McDonald's

McDonald's had a big Internet attack when it realized a reporter from *Wired* magazine had registered www.McDonalds.com. The reporter gave up the name when asked. He wrote the article to show that corporate America was ignoring an important new medium in 1994.

➤ President Clinton's Domain

President Clinton used a website with the URL www.clinton96.com during the 1996 election. After the election, the site was taken down. However, today if you typed that address, you would find yourself staring at a screen for an ISP based in Switzerland. By hijacking the president's URL, the Swiss company was hoping to find new customers who stumbled onto the site by accident. The message here is that if you change your company URL or product URL, you should still try to maintain the rights to that URL so your customers don't type it and find they are seeing a page hosted by a competitor or a company that does not reflect positively on your business.

If you decide to abandon a URL for marketing purposes but don't want it to fall into the wrong hands, consider this tactic: Turn the page into a referring page. This type of page is a live page, but when people type the address, they are transported to a page that is hyperlinked. So if people type the address for last year's product, they will see the page for this year's updated version. With proper programming, customers won't even realize they are at a different page than the one they requested.

➤ Candyland

Toymaker Hasbro, Inc., was shocked to see that its generations-old game "Candyland" was the name used by the Internet Entertainment Group to host an adult site. Hasbro sued and won after a costly endeavor. Hasbro has registered almost 40 domain names since then.

However, Hasbro has its hands full trying to gain clue.com for its board game Clue. The domain had been registered by Clue Consulting. While the lawyers argue this case, Hasbro registered clue.net, a perfect choice for the consulting group.

■ SUMMARY

Domain names are vital pieces of intellectual property that can mean the difference between a prospect finding you online easily, or finding a competitor. You must act quickly to register your domain name in the United States and in other countries to protect your company against others who would like to use the same name. If your name has been taken and you have no legal right to obtain it, there are many creative ways to invent a new name with tremendous marketing power and name recognition. Use lawyers and marketers wisely to protect your turf.

· ONLINE RESOURCES

NSI, Internic, http://rs.internic.com, lists all the procedures to apply for domain names, rates, and renewal information. Thomson & Thomson, www.thomson-thomson.com, a trademark and copyright search firm, has a free database to search for embedded words and phrases.

Part Four
External Threats

Chapter

Attack Sites, Rogue Sites, and Spoof Sites: The New Language of Crisis Communications

You decide to use a search engine to find references to your organization. As soon as you type "My Organization," the search engine responds with two choices:

The first listing reads:

"My Organization—a leading manufacturer of widgets with a record of service to the community."

You smile as you imagine the world seeing this glowing message. Then you scan the rest of the page and you see another entry:

"My Organization sucks—learn how My Organization screwed me royally. Click here to find out why you shouldn't do business with My Organization."

Or you go to a newsgroup and find people criticizing your products.

Or you pick up the business section of your newspaper and find that those newsgroup discussions are being quoted in a story about your company.

Welcome to the new phenomenon of attack sites.

Events like this are taking place all the time. Companies that aren't aware of the potential for attacks in cyberspace may find they have lost their good names.

This chapter and the following two chapters examine the types of communication threats that can befall a company through the Internet. This chapter explores the area of crisis communications and the new kinds of problems the Net can pose through:

➤ Websites.

➤ Attack sites, rogue sites.

➤ Newsgroups and mailing lists.

➤ The rumor mill fed by e-mail.

➤ Spoof sites.

You'll also learn how to handle these attacks with the best thinking from public relations and investor relations experts and attorneys.

Chapter 13 examines stock market manipulation on the Internet, a must-read for investor relations professionals, as well as anyone who invests in stocks and uses the Internet for research. Chapter 14 presents a model for using the Internet to find, monitor, and confront online crises.

■ OVERVIEW

The beauty of the Internet is that it is the world's least expensive printing press. The problem with the Internet is that is the world's least expensive printing press. For $50 or less, a disgruntled customer or a vengeful former employee can post a website that says your company stinks. By the time you find out about it, thousands of people could have been exposed to the message.

"All of this portends that there are communications channels open to employees, consumers, unions, and others by which they can articulate and communicate their messages to a global audience and put the company on the defensive to the point where the company has to respond," says Charles Pizzo, cpizzo@prprnet.com, principal of P.R. PR, Inc., a public relations agency in New Orleans. "It goes back to who owns the printing press. It used to be that you needed to own a printing press to attack a company. Now one, lone activist drinking a lot of caffeine and eating a lot of sugar and put up a hell of a web page in a few hours."*

Some attack sites receive national attention in *The New York Times, The Wall Street Journal, USA Today,* and CNN. Others attack sites attract much smaller audiences.

"It is the not the size of the audience that matters. It is the impact the attack site has on the company's business plan, goals, and operations. If the site were only seen by two politicians and the site influenced them, that would be enough," says Pizzo.

What would the damage be to your organization if a disgruntled person attacked your company and swayed a politician, an employee, a stockholder? The results could be disastrous.

Attack sites are on the rise, according to James Alexander, www.iagency.com, awall@iagency.com, director of eWorks, a service of eWatch! a company that monitors postings in newsgroups and websites for corporate customers. "It is growing."

---

* Interview, July 11, 1997.

He challenged us to search on the word "boycott" in the Alta Vista search engine. We found more than 22,000 websites urging the boycott of everything from tampons to gasoline to the celebration of Jerusalem's founding.

If someone has it out for your organization, they can tell 40 million people about it. "There aren't any editors in cyberspace to police those messages to make sure they are accurate," says Alexander. "There is worldwide distribution. It is not just having a printing press, it is about having a printing press and a distribution center on your desk all at once."

Most damaging, more journalists than ever are going online. The study called "Reporters in Cyberspace," www.mediasource.com, shows 33 percent of all reporters go online at least once a week. "They will stumble on the boycott site. That is a much juicier story than the one they planned on!"

■ WHAT ARE CRISIS COMMUNICATIONS?

Every company can have a calamity. How they deal with it and present their case to the public shows whether they have handled the situation properly. The fine art of managing public opinion during times of stress is the essence of crisis communications.

Companies' images rise and fall when they face a crisis that reaches the front pages of the newspapers. Just hearing key phrases sends shivers up your spine years after the disaster has passed: Exxon Valdez, Bhopal, Tylenol, Three Mile Island. The way a company deals with those disasters can have a lasting impact on the company's sales for many years to come. I know people who still won't buy gas from Exxon because of the way they mishandled the Alaskan tanker spill. Conversely, Johnson & Johnson performed a textbook case on exactly how to manage a crisis so that people today still buy Tylenol with confidence, despite a horrible product tampering scare. A good crisis communications program helps restore a company's image after a crisis has hit. A bad crisis communications program leaves a sour taste in people's mouths for years to come.

What is a crisis?

"For a public company, anything that affects your stock price could be a crisis. For companies that make products, any product defect or threat to human health is a crisis. Overnight you can lose your franchise," says Stuart Z. Goldstein, who is vice president of corporate communications for the National Securities Clearing Corporation in New York, and who formerly worked for Citicorp and American Express.*

"The public no longer distinguishes between product performance and corporate image," he says. "The visual impact of media and the global reach of the internet have created a corporate personality, where every decision or product is seen as a sign of corporate judgment and responsibility."

Traditional crises for companies include product liability, unexpected earnings announcements, employee layoffs, deaths, fraud, and misconduct. You've seen these stories on the front pages of newspapers.

■ THE NEW CRISIS COMMUNICATIONS

Several crisis communications patterns are totally unique to the Internet. These sites come under the heading of "attack" sites but they can also be referred to as "rogue sites" or "advocacy sites":

➤ Crises existing solely on the Internet that are started by disgruntled people (see case studies on Gateway 2000, U.S. Worst, Association of Flaming Ford Owners).

➤ Crises that exist on the Internet and are based on rumors (see case studies on Tommy Hilfiger, Walter Cronkite, LEXIS-NEXIS P-TRAK).

---

* Interview, August 12, 1997.

➤ Crises that start on the Internet and become so inflamed that they reach the mass media (see case studies on Intel and Intuit).

➤ Crises that exist in the real world and the company uses the Internet to spread its message (see case study on Odwalla).

➤ Crises that start in the real world and the company's foes use the Internet to spread its message (see case study on McDonald's/McSpotlight).

➤ Parody sites, also called Spoof sites (not to be confused with the computer security attack, which is called "spoofing"; see Chapter 6).

➤ Fan sites, put up by loyal supporters of products (covered in Chapter 9; see case study on *Star Trek*).

There are ways to combat these crises. This chapter describes these situations and proposes solutions.

■ CRISES THAT EXIST SOLELY ON THE INTERNET

Crises that start and spread on the Internet are becoming the bane of a public relations executive's existence. These crises can be begun by disgruntled employees, upset customers, and even well-meaning citizens who are alerting their friends to what they think are abuses performed by your company. These crises might be solely based in fact, or totally based on rumor. In either case, companies must decide how to deal with the situations. These sites are called "attack sites" because they attack the company.

➤ Disgruntled Employee: The Case of Gateway 2000

Jeff Blackmon, a former employee of Gateway 2000, a computer manufacturer, posted a website called "Gateway2000

Sucks." The site included such information as "Top 10 Reasons Not to Buy a Gateway 2000 Computer." I found out about this site when I used the Yahoo! search engine to find Gateway 2000. In addition to the company's listing appearing, so did the attack site. If you were a purchasing manager for a large company and were doing online research to buy computers for your new building, wouldn't you want to do due diligence and see what the Gateway 2000 Sucks site was all about? Sure you would! Then would you want to do business with a company that has an employee, or former employee, who speaks about the company in this manner? Chances are, Gateway lost sales because of this page, or at least some purchasing agents gave pause before placing the order.

How would you deal with a situation like this?

Technically, people have a First Amendment right to free speech, and can print whatever they like as long as it doesn't violate the laws of libel. Truth is an absolute defense in libel. Unless your organization has a policy forbidding this kind of act, and the employee signs it, you have no way to stop this attack.

In fact, Gateway 2000's lawyers found a clever way to convince Blackmon to take down the site. They filed suit for trademark infringements, not libel. The company gained a temporary restraining order after a judge agreed Blackmon's use of the Gateway logo and cow spots were trademark infringements. Blackmon agreed to remove the site and the company agreed to not seek hundreds of thousands of dollars in damages. In a statement, Gateway says, "Mr. Blackmon is and will always be free to express his honestly held opinions about Gateway and its products." (*San Francisco Chronicle,* October 9, 1996, p. D4).

➤ Protect Yourself

Lawyers say that you should have a company policy that forbids employees from making public statements about the company either during their tenure with the company or after they leave it. Putting up an attack site would violate this policy and expose them to penalties. Make sure employees read the policy and sign it as a condition of employment.

Charles Cresson Wood's Policy: Unofficial websites dealing with Company X products or services are prohibited unless the sponsor of these home pages has a contract signed by the Director of Public Relations. Workers who notice a new Internet reference to Company X products and/or services are requested to promptly notify the Director of Public Relations.

Wood's Commentary: Organizations that don't closely monitor and police these unofficial Web pages could find themselves in legal trouble including misrepresentation, trademark infringement, and copyright violation. This policy is intended to take a strong stand against such infringement and copyright violation.

➤ Disgruntled Customers

Customer service trainers tell an old tale that if people like your product, they'll tell 3 people. If they don't like your product, they'll tell 11 people.

"Hell hath no fury like a customer scorned, or so the saying goes," says Goldstein. "There's a multiplier effect for angry customers that goes something like this: For every customer that writes the CEO, there's 25 who would have written if they knew where to go with their complaint. And unhappy customers will usually tell 10 people about their negative experience. Translated this means, for every 100 letters to the CEO, more than 25,000 people will hear about that complaint."*

With the Internet, disgruntled customers can tell hundreds of thousands of people.

The next set of websites to be discussed involve disgruntled customers. These sites are united by the fact customers had bad experiences with the companies' products and

---

* Interview, August 12, 1997.

services. In each case, the upset consumers posted websites, gathered an audience, and continue to maintain strong presences on the Web. Their stories will not go away.

"If customers have a grievance, the folks on the net are using the net as a level playing field," says James Alexander, director of eWatch, a service of eWorks!* "They are getting very sophisticated. The Blockbuster listing on Yahoo includes the boycott Blockbuster website. Someone realized how Yahoo worked and requested to be listed in the Blockbuster section. The net is the great equalizer."

■ ATTACK SITES

➤ U.S. Worst

U.S. Worst, www.usworst.com, is a well-organized site that attacks U.S. West, a large regional telephone operator. The site's purpose is to help disgruntled customers file complaints against U.S. West.

When consumers first visit the site, they see the supposed company motto "U.S. Worst, bringing you the finest in cup and string communications." They then see a repairman's backside sneaking out from his pants as he squats down. Not a pretty picture.

Despite the opening salvos, the site is all business. Readers can file complaints against U.S. West with regulatory agencies. They can post their gripes online for everyone to read. They can even find out the names and addresses of the chairman, board members, and officers of U.S. West. That includes their office numbers as well as home phone numbers and addresses! Imagine being the chairman of U.S. West when something goes wrong with a consumer's phone at 3 in the morning! Who ya gonna call if the repairman doesn't answer? The chairman!

---

* Interview, July 29, 1997.

RISKY BUSINESS QUICK TIP

Attack sites "suck." That is, many of the sites use the word "sucks" in their titles, as in: AOL Sucks, Nynex Sucks, Kmart Sucks. This list goes on and on. One way to defeat these sites is to register the name of your company and the word "sucks." That way your detractors can't use it.

This site points out several key factors for companies:

➤ It is legal. There is virtually nothing the company can do to take this site down. They are not violating any laws. They are posting public information (the officials' phone numbers and addresses appear in annual reports and other public documents). The ways to file a complaint are also public knowledge. This website simply makes it easy to find the information and act on it.

➤ It can happen to you. Every company has a name that can be bastardized into a parody. "West" for "Worst" is easy. Watch out, Northwest Airlines! To prevent copycats, you need to think of each parody name and register it as a domain name. If you do this, you will take the easy targets out of your opponents' hands.

Attack sites can have a legitimate consumer purpose and there is nothing you can do about it. If the site is libelous or infringes on copyright or trade dress issues, you can sue for damages. Talk to your lawyer for more information.

➤ Association of Flaming Ford Owners

Disgruntled owners of Ford cars have a site they can call their own. The Association of Flaming Ford Owners, www.flamingfords.com, presents news and information about Ford cars and recalls. With a background of red flames, the site jumps off the screen to demand attention. The site also contains a newspaper political cartoon from the *Las Vegas Sun* which shows a television playing the jingle, "Have you driven a Ford lately?" A charred viewer on a couch says "Yes." The political cartoonist is a former Ford owner, according to the website.

As you scroll further down the page you notice the logos of CNN Interactive and *The New York Times*. Both media reported about the site to its millions of viewers. A hit counter at the bottom of the page notes the site has been visited by more than 50,000 people. If you ever wondered if anyone hears about these sites, visits them or takes them seriously, you now have your answer.

Attack sites can claim anyone as their victim. I've seen attack sites against a health club (with information on how to really read a health club contract), computer manufacturers, vacation cruises—the list goes on an on.

Attacks against companies can happen in newsgroups as well as on websites. For example, I conducted an online marketing seminar and needed to demonstrate Deja News, a service that creates a database of every message ever posted to every newsgroup. Since a woman in the seminar worked for a shoe company, a company that has a great website, I decided to search Deja News to find references to the company.

In seconds, we found an entire discussion about their new sneaker. Unfortunately, the messages were posted by "Clydesdales," who apparently are large people. They found the new sneaker came apart after a few days of wear by people who are over 6 feet tall and weigh more than 200 pounds. A store manager who was part of the discussion said he would not carry the sneakers based on these messages.

The woman from the shoe company was mortified.

However, this case is not really a vindictive attack. It is a cry for help. It is an opportunity for the company to find problems and create solutions. If they do the job right, they can create customers for life. Here's how.

"Look at newsgroups as a giant, free focus group," says Katharine Paine, president of The Delahaye Group, of Portsmouth, New Hampshire, a company that measures public opinion online and in newspaper clippings, www.delayahe .com. "It is not a negative thing. You are getting consumer response. That is a valid response. You should be saying 'This is great stuff. This is good consumer feedback. Tell me more!' Welcome and appreciate those comments. We pay good money for that customer response."*

How can you defuse a negative situation?

"If you can determine that what you have is a disgruntled customer, then the best thing you can do is get in touch with the customer and find out what went wrong. You can turn things around," says Shel Holtz, president of Holtz Communications + Technology, www.holtz.com, shel@holtz.com.

Here's what you can say to the person:

"Obviously, something has gone wrong contrary to the way we do business. What can we do to make this right?"

If this goes well, you can turn a complainer into a fan.

"The person goes online and tells people online that the company was paying attention, that they care, and that they want to make things right," he says. "It is an opportunity. If they are disgruntled, they are disgruntled for a reason. People who complain are your best source of information about how to improve what you do.

"It is a no-brainer to figure out that you can turn it into a good experience. The whole notion that someone is listening is very appealing to consumers," Holtz says.

➤ SPSS

Here's how a company changed its policy after reading newsgroups messages. SPSS, a software publisher, monitors discussion groups. They issued an upgrade at a lower price for a limited time. However, people posted messages saying the period was too short for people to get a check cut by

---

* Interview, June 27, 1997.

their organizations. People complained vociferously. The company listened. They went online and said, "We hadn't thought about that. We'd like to take this opportunity to correct it."

"They had a group of people online who are now fans," Holtz says.

Some cases involve people who are convinced the company is 100 percent wrong and won't listen to views that oppose their own. Let's look at a few websites that seem to be here for the long term, much to the despair of their Fortune 1000 victims.

Holtz points to a group of people who fight Nutrasweet on the Internet. "People are absolutely, utterly convinced aspartame will kill you. They are activists, not disgruntled people. They will not respond well to a dialog with the organization. They want the product to be illegal."

Holtz commends the way Nutrasweet, www.nutrasweet.com, is handling the situation. "Nutrasweet uses a good approach by using their home page. It has a link to health issues associated with the product. It is not defensive. It is very upbeat and positive and contains the results of FDA testing," he says. "The people who hate you are going to hate you. The people with an open mind will go to your site to read your side of the story. It is up to you to present the facts to them."

These stories point out an interesting fact. Two types of people post attack sites: people who have open minds and people who have closed minds. People with open minds have had a bad experience with your company, product, or service but can be persuaded to change their minds. People with closed minds can never be convinced there are two sides to a story.

■ PUBLIC RELATIONS SOLUTIONS FOR ATTACKING ATTACK SITES

A client is being attacked on a website that is full of misinformation, lies, and libel. What action would you take?

Kim Bayne, kimmik@wolfBayne.com, www.wolfBayne .com, author of *The Internet Marketing Plan* (New York: John Wiley & Sons, 1997) suggests taking the following steps "If there's no doubt that the site is an attempt to damage the client's reputation":*

1. Make a complete mirror copy of the attacking website, for reference purposes.

2. Find out the Webmaster's point of view. Is this a disgruntled customer, an ex-employee, or a competitor?

3. Create rebuttal pages addressing all accusations and implications. Don't post your rebuttal pages at your own site until you gauge the public's reaction, or you may unwittingly stimulate interest in the attack site.

4. Prepare written statements for your Crisis Communications Team and make sure everyone agrees on how to route inquiries about this particular website, should it become an issue.

5. Telephone the Webmaster and explain your concern about the misinformation. Do not be accusing, angry, or threatening. Ask him to remove the pages. Explain that you would like the opportunity to present your company's view in an unbiased manner at their site. Use your communications skills first to resolve the problem.

6. If you are unable to communicate with the Webmaster, for whatever reason, then it's time to have your company draft a nice letter spelling out the situation and asking for resolution by a certain date.

7. Still not getting results? I'd apply the "three strikes" rule here. If after the third attempt to "play nice," you still don't get results, then it's time to get your company lawyer involved.

---

* Interview, July 1997.

All of this is dependent on a time frame for action, which only the client can judge. Above all, don't drag your heels like some companies do, before they admit this is a problem, says Bayne.

Question: *A client is being maligned in a newsgroup, what action would you take?*

Answer: "The solution is very similar to the attack site case. Make a copy for your records. Try to resolve the issue by identifying motive and a mutually agreeable solution," Bayne says. "Unfortunately, in a newsgroup, the offending post is there for MUCH longer."

It is cataloged at newsgroup indexing sites and it is in a public forum that has much more traffic.

Be ready to reply immediately to any concerns. Don't refute point for point and provide long explanations, which may open you to more criticism. Instead, briefly state your position and offer to answer questions in the newsgroup as they come up. Don't be afraid to answer questions from your market in a public forum. By doing so, you position your company as fair and open-minded, willing to address concerns, rather than ignore them, she urges.

While crises come and go, "Messages and their responses will be logged forever," says Alexander of eWatch.

➤ Sleuthing Closes Down a Rogue Site

Charles Pizzo, cpizzo@prprnet.com, principal of P.R. PR Inc., a public relations agency in New Orleans, used computer searching skills, public relations tactics, and legal maneuvers to pull down a site that attacked a client, a large manufacturing company in the metals manufacturing business.

"We had a policy to scan the newsgroups once a week to check rogue sites. We also search the search engines once a week. However, we got a tip from an employee so we found out about the site a few days early," he says.

Here are the steps Pizzo took to deal with the issue. The first step was to find the site and determine the threat from it.

"We accessed the site and found there was very damaging information on the site. They had snarfed (copied) our logo, data, etc. It looked like the company's official website. It followed the same design elements. But in fact, they created the content, which was very detrimental. It even included a fake interview with the president of the company, included detrimental remarks and made it appear the faked interview had been conducted by a television reporter from a local station," he says.

The next step was to find out who put up the site.

"We looked at the domain name. We wanted to contact the Internet provider and tell them one of their customers had a copyright and trademark infringement and that we wanted them to shut down the site," Pizzo says.

"The site had no visible contact information. No person's name or phone number or address. We opened the documents (with the "view source code" command from the browser's toolbar) to see if clues were embedded on it. They had a feedback mechanism to send e-mail to support them. We were able to get that "mailto" command and see who the mail was going to. Now we had an e-mail address, but no name."

Pizzo then tried to find out as much as he could about this person by using free resources on the Internet.

"We did a search on Deja News on the e-mail address to see if the person participated in newsgroups. She turned out to have posted messages in the weddings newsgroup because her daughter was getting married. She posted notes in the cancer survivor support group and blues music newsgroup. On the rogue website she was careful to not use her name, but on the newsgroup's notes, she used her full name. We could find out where she worked and where she lived. We were able to develop a composite sketch of who this person was based on her newsgroup postings," he says.

"We used www.search.com to find her full address and phone number based on her e-mail address.

"The web page address was long. We kept on backing up a slash to find other sites. We found this rogue website was hidden inside a real estate company's website. We now knew she worked for a Realtor."

Pizzo then copied the site to disk with a software program called Web Whacker.

"If they took down the site, we had it on disk for legal purposes. Cyberspace leaves no trace. We needed to gather the evidence. Before we made the call, we copied the site," Pizzo says.

Pizzo and the company attorney devised a strategy to apply pressure on the woman and force her to remove the offending site.

"The company's lawyer called her up and told her we knew she was a Realtor, that her daughter was getting married, that she listened to the blues, that she was a cancer survivor. Then," Pizzo says, "he unleashed the clincher:

'We're giving you the opportunity to take the website off the net before we do the following,' the lawyer said. 'We are going to tell your boss that you are using their website to promote your personal views against a metals company. We are going to the state real estate board and ask them to revoke your license. We are going to tell the television station and the reporter cited on fake interview on the rogue web page that you are using their names illegally.'

"The site came down in four minutes.

"This all took 4–6 hours to do. I found the information on the Internet. The lawyer told me what the laws were and we built a strategy for applying pressure on the woman. We wanted to make sure the person knew that what they were doing was unethical and that we knew a lot about them," he says. "The industry should know this is a pattern and this is one way it can be undone."

➤ The Case of the Mystery Website

Not all rogue sites can be handled as easily as the previous example. Pizzo and Holtz investigated a rogue site for a Fortune 100 insurance company that claimed the company officials were embezzlers and the company was one of the worst companies.

"The rogue site left no clues. It came from an anonymous ISP who gave free space to people who wanted to complain about companies. There was no feedback mechanism. No way to get back in touch with the person who put up the page. The source code had no clues. There were no links," Pizzo says.

"Based on what kind of things they complained about, we developed a profile of what kind of person put up the page, but we couldn't hone it down to who it was," he adds.

In the interest of fairness, he is not mentioning the company name or the site's address.

➤ Rumors

The most disheartening crises to fight have to be cases based on lies, half-truths, misconstrued information, or just plain misunderstanding.

"A downside of the Internet is the perpetuation of misinformation. If someone gives wrong information that is reported on Bloomberg or is picked up by the general media, that information has the potential to remain accessible on the Internet forever," says Goldstein. "It is critical that we stay on top of and protect our company's institutional memory."

"People view computer-based messages with a sense of authority that it doesn't deserve because it is printed on a screen and looks nice," says Jim Duncan, manager of network and information systems at the applied research laboratory of the Pennsylvania State University.

Companies must make every effort to correct information and dispel rumors as quickly as possible to minimize damage.

➤ Walter Cronkite

At one time Walter Cronkite was considered the most trusted man in America. As the avuncular anchorman of the CBS

Evening News, he was the first reporter to question America's involvement in Vietnam. He is as close to being beyond reproach as any person. Nevertheless, Tim Hughes, a web designer, decided to write what he considered to be a humorous spoof in which he claims that Walter Cronkite spat in his food at a restaurant—a completely fictitious event. While searching the Web, Cronkite came across this essay and was flabbergasted. He contacted his attorneys who convinced the comedy writer wannabe to remove his writing and apologize (*San Francisco Examiner,* April 6, 1997).

This story shows how timely response and pressure from attorneys can resolve a damaging situation.

➤ Tommy Hilfiger

From November 1996 until March 1997, e-mail messages flew around newsgroups claiming that clothing designer Tommy Hilfiger made disparaging remarks about blacks and Asians on CNN and the Oprah Winfrey show. These messages also called for a boycott of the company's products.

Anyone who would have spent two seconds thinking about the sense of these statements would have questioned their veracity. Why would any designer criticize his customers in public? It didn't ring true.

The culture of the Internet seems to dictate that information is believed—even without verification—and is spread rapidly since e-mail costs nothing. People send messages not because they are vindictive, but because they honestly want to help their friends and warn them of computer viruses, online scams, and other information that has a bearing on their lives. In the case of rumors and misinformation, innocent organizations could suffer unless they take quick action.

Tommy Hilfiger, of course, did not make disparaging remarks about blacks and Asians. The rumor mill was in full force, however, and the messages spread from newsgroups to personal mailboxes. The frenzy heated to such a point that reporters at major newspapers heard about the rumor and checked on it. Articles appeared in such national papers as *USA Today,* and the Associated Press repeated the rumor — along with a denial by the company.

Although the situation had been brewing for several months, the company was not aware of it until someone pointed the messages out to the company. Tommy Hilfiger officials attacked the problem quickly. They posted messages in newsgroups denying the rumor and proving that Tommy Hilfiger didn't appear on either TV show! They told newspaper reporters the truth. The message the company posted on newsgroups appears on page 247.

The rumors appeared to stop as quickly as they began. A company official says sales did not seem to be hurt although not everyone got the message: Several boycott sites still attack Hilfiger.

Ron Solberg, president of Easycom, an agency that counsels communicators on how to use Internet and advanced technologies, www.Easycom.com, RonSolberg@compuserve .com points to the Tommy Hilfiger case as an example of a crisis well controlled. "They went to the newsgroup and confronted the people who were spreading misinformation. They headed them off at the pass," he says. "Once you find that people are saying incorrect, damaging or misleading information, you need to take action."

The Tommy Hilfiger case illustrates two important points for all companies:

1. Tommy Hilfiger did nothing wrong — but the company was attacked.

2. Tommy Hilfiger doesn't even have a website — and the company was attacked.

It was a victim of the online audience. This scenario could happen to any company, even if it isn't online. Management must have a plan to deal with rumors, as well as a way of finding rumors early-on. To find rumors in newsgroups, see the discussion on monitoring newsgroups in Chapter 14.

hilfigerco@aol.com (HilfigerCo) wrote:

TO: TOMMY HILFIGER CONSUMERS AND FRIENDS

FROM: TOMMY HILFIGER CORPORATION

SUBJECT: MALICIOUS RUMORS

We are disturbed to learn that an ugly rumor has been circulating about our company.

Since we understand that you have been the recipient of false information we wanted to set the record straight. The facts are simple and incontrovertible. Tommy Hilfiger did not make the alleged inappropriate racial comments. He has never appeared on the Oprah Winfrey show, although the rumor specifically asserts that he made negative remarks in that forum and that Ms. Winfrey asked him to leave. The show's producer has confirmed the fact that Tommy has never been a guest.

Similar rumors have circulated about comments supposedly made on other television shows. All of them are completely false. Tommy Hilfiger has never appeared on Larry King Live or on CNN's "Style with Elsa Klensch" despite persistent misinformation to the contrary.

Whether these rumors are part of a misunderstanding or a deliberate act of malice, they have absolutely no basis in fact. Tommy Hilfiger wants his clothing to be enjoyed by people of all backgrounds and his collections are put together with the broadest cross section of individuals in mind. To reinforce this, he features models of all ethnic backgrounds in his fashion shows and advertisements. Tommy Hilfiger and the entire company are extremely pleased that the brand has been received so enthusiastically by individuals of all ethnic backgrounds around the world. We hope you, too, are a satisfied customer!!

If you have additional questions or concerns, please contact Tommy Hilfiger Corporate Communications at 25 West 39th St., New York, NY 10018.

RISKY BUSINESS ASKS THE EXPERTS

Confronting Rumors

Ron Solberg, president of Easycom, advises a proactive approach to confront rumors.

"Go directly to the people who are leaving the messages. If the message is false, take them to task. You might need to threaten them with libel," he says. "In a moderated newsgroup, talk to the moderator about the material and encourage the moderator to remove these people from the system until they act civil."*

Finally, he advises sending an announcement to the press indicating what is happening.

---

*Interview, July 29, 1997.

Finally, this incident shows what happens when reporters are sloppy and don't check rumors.

■ THE NEED FOR REPORTERS AND EDITORS TO CHECK THEIR FACTS

"The Tommy Hilfiger case could have been thrown away if a reporter had called Oprah Winfrey's producer and asked if Tommy had been on the show," says Alexander. "The material looks polished and professional on the computer screen. Therefore, they think it must be true. This can cause tremendous financial damage."

He points to another rumor in which a cookie company was rumored to have sent cookies to an O.J. Simpson victory party. It took exactly eight minutes for the rumor to spread from a nationally syndicated TV show to the Internet, he said.

➤ The Case of the LEXIS-NEXIS P-TRAK

In 1996, LEXIS-NEXIS, a leading provider of news retrieval services, announced the P-TRAK service. Unfortunately for LEXIS-NEXIS, the online community misunderstood the service due to rumors about its content and thought personal information would be available online for easy access by crooks. The fear was so widespread that the Federal Trade Commission met to discuss measures to protect individuals' privacy. This section describes the crisis and the reaction by the company's public relations department.

LEXIS-NEXIS is a business-to-business online service that has one of the largest databases of news and business information in the world. The company has electronic versions of the full text of hundreds of newspapers from around the United States and the world going back several decades. The company claims its database is many times larger than the World Wide Web. The service is used by many professionals—journalists, lawyers, and public relations professionals are some primary audiences.

In 1996, the company introduced a product that provided the names, addresses, and phone numbers of people in the United States. Initially, the service also included Social Security numbers, but LEXIS-NEXIS discontinued this feature after 12 days. The service was intended to help lawyers find heirs and beneficiaries of estates or help law enforcement agencies find parents who aren't paying child support. It was not available to the general public, and was fairly pricey, at $75 per search.

"P-TRAK actually was a catch-up product for us," says Lesley Sprigg, public relations manager for LEXIS-NEXIS. "All of our major competitors have had similar products, from the same provider, for years. You can surf the web and you'll find much scarier stuff than this, like locators that will provide a map to your house."*

---

* Interview, April 24, 1997.

The product was released in June 1996, and professional librarians began to discuss it in their own newsgroups.

"After being a topic of discussion on a few newsgroups during the summer, e-mails started to be sent to large distribution groups, such as corporate e-mail systems," Sprigg says. "The mostly factual information from the newsgroups was edited. The product name was misspelled. (The product was changed to P-Trax instead of P-TRAK.) Our company's 800 number was changed (printed incorrectly). Erroneous information was added, such as 'they have your medical and credit histories, etc.'"

The original posting read in part:

"Your name SS#, addresses, mother's maiden name, birth date and other personal information are now available to anyone with a credit card through a new Lexis database called P-Trax . . . information could be used to commit fraud . . . allow someone else to use your identity . . . I suggest that we inundate these people with requests to remove our info from the list and forward this e-mail to everyone we know . . ."

"The erroneous e-mail was obviously designed to create anxiety and even revenge. It suggested that the company be inundated, and inundate they did," Sprigg says. All the company's fax machines churned nonstop. They even had to buy additional fax machines to handle the response.

Well-intentioned people sent the erroneous information via e-mail to their colleagues hoping to alert them what they thought was a problem.

"The erroneous e-mail made its way to many venues, posters in barbershops and even in trade publications like Deli News!" Sprigg says.

Then things started to turn ugly.

"Some of our customer service representatives received death threats," Sprigg says.

"Once these e-mails made their way to corporate e-mail systems, we were inundated," she says. At the beginning of the crisis, two of the four people in the PR department were out of town. During the height of the crisis, all four worked from early morning to late evening for nearly a month. "We received calls from every major news outlet in the country.

"After putting a statement on Business Wire, we began posting to the newsgroups that had been discussing P-TRAK. We added another way that people could have their names removed from P-TRAK—through a form on our website," Sprigg says.

The PR department monitored the crisis inside the company's customer service department.

"We were very involved with the customer service department. They really took the brunt. We could tell by the number of calls they were receiving whether the message was getting out. It wasn't our customers who called at first, but our customers did eventually start calling after they'd received the erroneous e-mail 10 times or read about it in the paper," she says.

The company used its website to educate the public about what the product really did and how to remove their names from the list (Figure 12.1).

The company preferred having people fill out the form online since the information could be fed directly into a database and didn't have to be rekeyed, as was the case with the faxed forms.

"Since callers were worried we had everything on them including their shoe size, we included a sample record," she says (Figure 12.2).

LEXIS-NEXIS created links from their home page to news coverage that was balanced. If the article wasn't available on the Web, they cited the publication and author and put in a quote from the article.

"Arc Consulting did some research for us and found that if the concept of online information and the Internet is alien to someone, they are alarmed and uncomfortable with a product like this," Sprigg says.

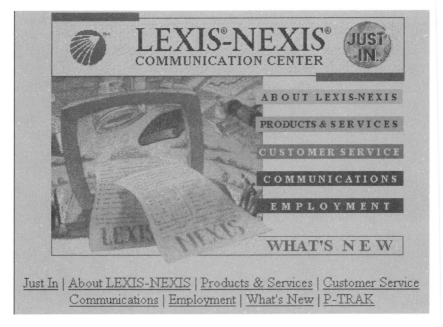

Figure 12.1. LEXIS-NEXIS used its website to clear up misunderstandings about its P-TRAK service. (Copyright © 1997, LEXIS-NEXIS, reprinted with permission.)

For almost a month, P-TRAK took nearly 100 percent of four PR professionals' time. Although the crisis has been settled, fallout remains. As of April 1997, "Just one person handles P-TRAK (part-time), and believe it or not, we still get media calls from people who haven't heard of it before," Sprigg says.

One spinoff problem occurred when the media started reporting on the erroneous e-mail instead of the facts of the story.

"For example, the *L.A. Times* wrote a fairly balanced article and editorial when the story first broke, but in the following months, they've run many stories by uninformed reporters based on the erroneous e-mail which furthered the spread of misinformation," she says. "One of the nicer things

LEXIS·NEXIS®

℞ A member of the Reed Elsevier plc group

Statement on the P-TRAK file from LEXIS-NEXIS
(revised 11/26, 10/25, 10/11 and 9/25, first issued 9/18/96)

Incorrect information is being distributed on Internet newsgroups and e-mail regarding the data displayed in LEXIS-NEXIS' P-TRAK file. P-TRAK is like an electronic "white pages." The only information displayed is the name of the individual, current address and up to two previous addresses and telephone number. In some cases, the *individual's* maiden name may appear as well as the month and year of birth. That is the *only* information displayed in the P-TRAK file. The data included in P-TRAK are records of U.S. residents only.

Contrary to some e-mail messages, the P-TRAK file *DOES NOT* contain any credit histories, bank account information, personal financial data, mother's maiden name or medical histories. This misinformation has also been posted over and over again to various news groups.

An example of a record appears below:

Name: DOE, JOHN E

Current Address: 1066 Anywhere Drive, Dayton, OH 95454

Previous Addresses: 106 Somewhere Drive, Dayton, OH 92454

Birthdate: 9/1965

Telephone number: 555-1212

On file since: 6/1/1994

(continued)

Figure 12.2.   LEXIS-NEXIS Statement on the P-TRAK

The information displayed in the P-TRAK file is the type of information readily available from public information sources such as telephone directories (in print and CD-ROM format) and public records maintained by government agencies. The information contained in P-TRAK is derived from "header" information provided to LEXIS-NEXIS by a national consumer reporting agency. LEXIS-NEXIS markets the P-TRAK file to the legal community for use by general legal practitioners, litigators and public attorneys, as well as law enforcement agencies and police departments. These professionals use the P-TRAK file to assist in locating litigants, witnesses, shareholders, debtors, heirs and beneficiaries.

LEXIS-NEXIS is aware of the sensitivities regarding the potential misuse of information. Business competitors of LEXIS-NEXIS have for some time made Social Security numbers available to users of their services. In addition, Social Security numbers and other information are available on the Internet from a number of sources. Despite this wide availability of Social Security numbers in the market place, LEXIS-NEXIS discontinued the display of Social Security numbers in the P-TRAK file as of June 11, 1996, eleven days after the product was introduced. While Social Security numbers are NOT displayed in P-TRAK, subscribers may locate a record by entering a known Social Security number.

Through its actions, LEXIS-NEXIS is balancing the privacy concerns of the public with the legitimate needs of legal, business and government professionals for access to accurate sources of publicly available information. By discontinuing the display of Social Security numbers in P-TRAK and only providing information that is already available to the public from other sources, the company believes it has responsibly met the expressed concerns of the public. LEXIS-NEXIS is a business to business online service, not generally available to the public.

Figure 12.2. (Continued)

Individuals interested in having their names removed from the P-TRAK file can e-mail their full names, complete addresses and telephone numbers to: P-TRAK@prod.LEXIS-NEXIS.com or mail this information to ATTN: P-TRAK, P. O. Box 933, Dayton, OH 45401. A World Wide Web-based form for deletion is available at *http://www.LEXIS-NEXIS.com/lncc/P-TRAK/index.html.* You may also fax your request to 1-800-732-7672. Name removal occurs on average of 60 days of the request and a letter of confirmation will be sent within two weeks of removal. This information will be used solely to remove names from the P-TRAK database and for no other purpose. Also, for your protection, LEXIS-NEXIS will only accept removal requests from individuals and does not support any third-party removal services.

Figure 12.2. (Continued)

that happened was that *Internet World* magazine chided C|Net for perpetuating rumors and used P-TRAK as an example. C|Net was one of the organizations we kept following up with to try to get them to get the story straight."

■ MORE RUMORS AND CONSPIRACY THEORIES!

The Internet is rife with rumors. Don't believe any of these so-called urban legends.

➤ The $250 Cookie Scam

A woman claims to have ordered a cookie and coffee at a café in a high-end department store. She asks the waitress for the recipe and is informed that the recipe will cost "two-fifty." Thinking that $2.50 is a good price for a recipe for such a delicious cookie, she agrees. A month later, she finds her credit card charged for $250. She vows revenge by sending the recipe

RISKY BUSINESS LESSONS FROM THE FIELD

Here are additional points to consider that could affect your company.

1. LEXIS-NEXIS should have seen this crisis developing long before the product was announced. Marketing research done before, instead of after, the product's launch, would have clued in the marketing department. The online community values its privacy and this product was a threat to that sense. Another company had found itself on the receiving end of a similar spate of bad national publicity several years before for offering a similar service. Lotus had planned to sell a CD-ROM that contained demographics and marketing information on individuals to direct marketers. Privacy groups blasted the company in leading daily newspapers, business press, and trade publications. Lotus originally defended the product but decided to kill it rather than face the continued negative publicity. As a footnote to the story, Lotus sold the product to another company, which quietly released it under a different name and targeted its marketing efforts to its intended audience. Because consumers didn't know about it (until now!), they didn't raise any objections.

   However, LEXIS-NEXIS is not the only organization to forget that history repeats itself. Shortly after the LEXIS-NEXIS situation, the United States Social Security Administration announced they would provide a free service on its website in which consumers could check their Social Security retirement benefits. Senators joined privacy advocates in fearing abuses by crooks. *USA Today* ran a front-page article on this situation. Congress read the article and demanded the agency withdraw this service until security safeguards could be built into the system (*USA Today*, April 7, 9, 1997).

(continued)

LESSONS FROM THE FIELD (Continued)

2. Like the party game "Telephone," in which stories are spread from one person to another and change with each retelling until the final story has no relation to the first, rumors will spread on the Internet even if there is no basis in truth. We have seen so many conspiracy theories spread on the 'Net—Kennedy's assassination, the TWA explosion, and Waco to name a few—that corporate communicators must assume that rumors will spread and messages will be distorted. Communicators must be proactive in finding these rumors and stopping them before real harm is done.

---

via e-mail to everyone she knows and urges them to pass it along.

The truth is that the incident never occurred. The high-end department store originally cited in the story doesn't even have a café.

Why is it that the Internet spawns rumors—and that people believe these writings of people with no last names, and first names like handle123@myisp.com, when they don't believe reporters or government officials?

➤ Dying Boy Wants to Have Largest Card Collection

This rumor started in the real world and spread to the Internet. A dying boy in England wanted to have the world's largest collection of business cards before he passed away. People heard the story and urged their friends to collect cards from their friends and send them to the hospital. That part is true.

However, the boy recovered, left the hospital, and is now 11 years older than when the story began. The hospital continues to receive cards—so many that it must hire a full-time person to sort through the mail. The hospital wishes the story would end, but the Internet seems to have given it a new life.

➤ Procter & Gamble

For nearly 100 years, Procter & Gamble has been fighting rumors that it worships the devil because their logo is the man in the moon. The rumor has spread to the Internet, where the company periodically issues statements defending itself.

➤ Snapple

Snapple beverages show an old-time sailing ship on its label. Someone thought it was the same type of ship used the in slave trade and sent messages to newsgroups claiming that Snapple must be a racist company to use such a symbol. The company denied it was racist or that the ship was used in the slave trade. The incident seems to have disappeared.

➤ TWA Flight 800

When TWA Flight 800 crashed in the waters off New York City, some people didn't wait for the official reports to come out to determine what caused the crash. Instead, these people went on the Internet and spread their own theories based on not a thread of fact. However, these statements were read and repeated. With more repetitions, people actually began to believe these statements were true. It would be one thing to say that teenagers or Internet addicts would believe anything, but no less a respected figure than Pierre Salinger, a member of the Kennedy White House, went on national television proclaiming he had evidence of a government cover-up in the case. His source: messages from newsgroups.

Conspiracy theories have been with us for a long time. Hundreds of books have been written on the assassination of John F. Kennedy. With the advent of the World Wide Web, the world's least expensive printing press, every person can publish his or her own theories—and they have.

Dozens of web pages and hundreds of messages on USENET claim that TWA Flight number 800 was shot down by the U.S. military instead of a "catastrophic mechanical failure" in the words of FBI Director Louis Freeh (*USA Today*, May 5, 1997, page 1).

TWA didn't help matters. Its website didn't even mention the disaster.

"There was no reference to Flight 800. It looks like you are hiding something," says Jolley. "You can't hide on the Internet. The issue is one way to respond is through your website. If you have a high profile incident, you want to respond."

The TWA scenario raises a frightening question: Why do some people believe what they read online even though the source has not proven itself to be credible? Why are these same people so quick to dismiss reports in the news media and comments by elected officials? Is this a failing of the Internet community, or does it mirror a trend in the real world as well? Is this feeling limited to the United States or does it extend to the world?

■ CRISES THAT START ON THE INTERNET AND BECOME SO INFLAMED THAT THEY REACH THE MASS MEDIA

The Internet does not exist in a vacuum. Comments made online can—and do—get repeated in newspapers, magazines, and television news shows. In fact, reporters have been known to search through newsgroups to find leads and sources for stories. If your company has a product flaw, you can bet that people are discussing it in a newsgroup—and that a reporter will find out about it.

"You have to be critically aware that anything that flares up on the Internet is just a day away from appearing in the mainstream media. The Internet is a rich, fertile ground for uncovering juicy stories. You have to keep in mind that if it is online, there are probably journalists who are reading it," says Craig Jolley, principal, Online and Strategic Information Solutions, Dayton, OH, craigj@erinet.com, an information technology management consultant.*

Here are two famous cases in which messages about faulty products started online and spread to the mass media.

➤ Intel

One of America's largest companies fell victim to a crisis on the Internet. For many Americans, one of their first exposures to the Internet came when they read the front page of the *New York Times* or turned on their national TV news show to hear that Intel had produced a faulty computer chip. Intel, which was in the middle of a multimillion-dollar consumer advertising campaign on television, was promoting its theme "Intel Inside" as a sign of quality in a brand-building awareness campaign.

As the crisis evolved through inept handling by Intel, the dozens of jokes floated through newsgroups making fun of this theme. The company was in danger of losing its positive image, and having its massive advertising campaign turn sour as the term "Intel Inside" was becoming a negative. In this example of a classic crisis communication problem, the company didn't understand the potential threat of the Internet to spread crisis from the online community to the mass media of international consumers.

---

* Interview, June 26, 1997.

The problem began innocently enough. Professor Thomas Nicely posted a message in a newsgroup, an online bulletin board, in which he said he had noticed an error in his calculations due to an error in the Intel Pentium chip. In true scientific fashion, he asked if his colleagues could reproduce the error. He wasn't being malicious. He merely wanted to verify his research.

A few days later, two other professors sent messages to the newsgroups verifying the error.

Reporters at trade publications heard about this and reported the story. Being good reporters, they called Intel for a comment. The company said the problem was not serious and affected only a few people.

Reporters called stockbrokers who said the problem definitely was a concern to them. Intel refused to take responsibility for the situation and said it would not refund or replace the defective chip. Over the next several weeks, the problem got worse and worse. Front-page articles appeared in *The New York Times* and the story appeared on national TV newscasts.

At this point, the story seemed to die for a few days. Then IBM announced it would not use Intel chips in its computers. That story was the lead story on the front page of *The New York Times*. Within days, Intel acquiesced and apologized.

Analysis: Intel

"The cause of their mistake was not their refusal to deal with it," says Katharine Paine. "They didn't understand their audience. They thought their audience was the traditional purchasers of components—engineers. What they completely neglected to take into account was that consumers were their customers. Intel completely misunderstood their customers. They spent $250 million on the Intel Inside advertising campaign. That is more than the GNP for 30 countries. The flaw was that they did not understand their audience."

New Rules

A lot of people get into crisis situations because they don't understand the audience. "On the Net, you have to determine what is it going to affect. In other words, if it is going to affect your stock price. Start with Motley Fool (a website devoted to financial information). If you are concerned about the government you need to check out newsgroups for consumer response," she says.

"By checking out the newsgroups, you will have a sense of what is important to that audience. You will understand what the biggest issue is—which might differ from what YOU think the issue is. You might be wondering about the stock price while consumers might be wondering about the environmental impact or the health," says Paine. "Don't make the mistake of listening to the 'loudest person in the room.' Intel listened to the engineers instead of the consumers."

➤ Intuit Gets It Right

If Intel is the classic example of how not to handle a crisis, then the role model for all communicators to follow is that of Intuit, the publisher of the software program Turbo Tax. During the height of the tax season, a consumer posted a message on a newsgroup saying that he found a bug (a major flaw) in the program. Several other people duplicated the bug. The next day, the story made the newspapers and television shows. After all, the story had wide appeal: Many people used the software program and their tax returns could be affected. This wasn't the story of a few computer geeks. It hit mainstream America.

To their credit, Intuit took ownership of the situation. They admitted there was a problem and said they would correct it quickly, send corrected copies to all users at the company's expense, and pay any penalties due to the IRS. The problem went away quickly. In fact, few people even remember this crisis. That's what happens when companies handle crises correctly.

"The true measure of success is the duration of the crisis. Intel with the first Pentium crisis gets an 'F' because it went on for ever and ever and ever," says Paine. "Intuit handled the situation better. "It spiked and went away in three weeks. They did a better job because they made it go away faster."

■ USING THE INTERNET TO SPREAD THE COMPANY'S MESSAGE

Juice maker Odwalla faced a crisis of monumental proportions in 1996 when several children got sick and died after drinking the company's unpasteurized apple juice. The story made headlines around the country for several weeks and was featured prominently on newscasts in several states, including California, where the company is based, and in Colorado, where a child died.

During the early part of the crisis, no one knew for sure why the juice was tainted, or even if the cause of the maladies was the juice.

Odwalla officials used the Internet to get the word out. Not only did they post daily updates and press releases on their website, they also printed heartfelt letters signed by the company president. Anyone who read the messages would be convinced of the company's sincerity to solve the problem and take responsibility for its actions.

When the company created a medical advisory council, they posted the press release online as well as bios of the doctors and scientist on the board.

"Odwalla did a fabulous job. It came from the heart. It was brilliant. They were in touch with their audience," says Paine.

Odwalla survived the crisis, and its products are stacked on many supermarket shelves.

■ YOUR FOES CAN SPREAD THEIR OWN MESSAGES

➤ The McSpotlight Story

One of the most famous crises involving the Internet became known as the *McSpotlight* case. It shows how a small, unknown group of activists in England could attack a large multinational company and spread havoc throughout its worldwide operations. It is also an example of what can go wrong when the lawyers are brought in to resolve a case.

In this case, two people in England who called themselves London Greenpeace (not related to the Greenpeace environmental organization) claimed McDonald's, the fast-food franchise, was guilty of numerous charges. They handed out leaflets with their positions to harried passersby.

McDonald's decided to fight the protesters in court. After three years and a $16 million attorney bill and other fees, McDonald's won the case and was awarded $98,298. However, they lost in the court of public opinion. Millions of people had been exposed to the negative messages, which will not be described here since the High Court Justice declared many of the charges to be untrue. Further, since the pair was not wealthy, the company would never see the court-ordered penalty paid to them.

To make matters worse, the pair continued to hand out leaflets with similar messages after the court case was resolved. They also received considerable attention in the activist community, which could further their own agenda, whatever that might be.

Analysis

Filing a lawsuit was probably one of the worst decisions the company could have made because it gave the protesters a worldwide audience to air their grievances. The pair used the Internet to showcase their claims as well. They created the

McSpotlight website, www.mcspotlight.org, which showed their complaints and "evidence" to viewers around the world. No longer was the audience limited to a few McDonald's in England; the whole world could learn about the purported claims. The McSpotlight site had nearly 41,000 visitors in a 12-week period, including journalists reporting on the case. The site was featured in *USA Today,* NBC TV, *Chicago Tribune, San Jose Mercury News,* BBC2, and many other news services.

McDonald's clearly lost this case, in part because they mismanaged the crisis in the real world as well as the online world. Their website was not used to counter claims, nor did company officials counter claims made in newsgroups. In the absence of company denials, consumers were left to think that the claims must be true.

Postscript

Why would McDonald's—one of the master marketers and molders of public opinion—expose itself to this kind of liability?

Paine considers McDonald's handling of this case to be a failure. "You want the crisis to go away quickly," she says. "Lawsuits prolong the crisis. It also heightens the press." McDonald's also made classic blunders in handling the situation, she says. You need to understand the media you are working with. In Britain, the press is pro little guy, against big business. In Japan, it is the opposite. The exposure did not start with the *Economist,* it started in the tabloids. McDonald's didn't understand the audience."

Another problem with the McDonald's case is that the company had to open its documents to the public. "If you go after a site for slander, libel, copyright infringement, then you are exposing your company by being forced to release internal company documents found in the discovery process," says Alexander. "The foes of McDonald's plastered their site with these documents."

➤ When Do You Bring in the Lawyers?

This case raises several interesting points in handling crises. The first is: When do you bring in the lawyers with heavy clubs or use public relations professionals' kid gloves?

The PR guru Don Middleberg, of Middleberg Associates, who has helped many companies fight online crises, says PR should be the first step in many cases. "If there is a customer service problem, the easiest thing to do is solve the problem," he says.

"This is always a business of humans first. Attorneys always create defensiveness," says Pat Meier, president of Pat Meier Associates Public Relations in San Francisco, www.patmeier.com, patmeier@patmeier.com, who spoke about crisis communications in general, not the McDonald's case specifically. "If you can approach your supposed enemies and deal with them directly, mano a mano [face to face], that's always the best tactic. Our national leaders are understanding that more and more. They don't jump the gun and pull out the big guns immediately. Let's find out what do they really want? Can you provide a solution? Give them an opportunity to vent, but in a way that is not damaging. It might be they have tried to get hold of the company unsuccessfully. The company being attacked needs to look internally and find out why this was not handled and why these customers got so upset they decided to attack the company."

"You bring in the lawyers as a last resort," says Holtz referring to the McSpotlight case. "Now you have everyone and their sister aware of this situation. Bringing in the lawyers is an approach that a lot of companies will be taking because they are familiar with the medium and the consequences of behaving as if they're dealing with traditional media. The online world is unfamiliar; here, many people can talk to each other. As long as they are able to talk to each other, the legal threats can backfire on you real fast. You may succeed in getting the people to take their page down, but 30 more go up. America Online has seen that. It is a court of last resort."

"Lawyers are going to want to say nothing at any point in time. You are going to have to balance that with the need to get the information out," says Jolley. "Probably the biggest value a PR person can provide to their company is when they are developing their crisis communications response, they need to include cyberspace and recognize its potential power for good or bad. Management needs to respond and respond immediately. It can't wait for a couple of days, or even a couple of hours. A person could send these messages to millions of hands."

On the other hand, Pizzo says a lawyer who understands the 'Net can be indispensable. "Communications alone cannot solve every problem. Communicators can facilitate the dialogue between management and legal teams in these matters, educating them about the changing nature of communications in the online era. A lawyer who understands the law regarding libel, slander, defamation, trademark and copyright infringement—and who 'gets' the net—is a powerful resource."

Lawyer Alan Wernick presents a litmus test for deciding when to use self-help or use an attorney. "It is going to depend on the facts. If there is imminent harm to a person or property, then lawyers or law enforcement need to get involved quickly. If there is potential defamation brewing (such as a libel or slander), it might do well to bring in the lawyers to analyze the facts and have them notify the other party of your concerns. If the other party then proceeds, they do so at their own risk and with knowledge that they may be creating legal liability for themselves" (Alan S. Wernick, computer lawyer, copyright, trademark, trade secret and licensing, in private practice at Wernick & Associates, Co., L.P.A. in Columbus, Ohio, 614-463-1400, alan@wernick.com).

"My advice is you need to take a practical commonsense approach to what makes sense for the client. It depends on the facts and the applicable law. Muddying the water for the sake of muddying the water is not necessarily good in the long run. It is usually less expensive to have the lawyer involved in a preventive role rather than a remedial role."

➤ The Case of the Kid Glove versus the Iron Fist

A local utility company found to their horror a website that poked fun at their company. The crisis team met in conference and the lawyers wanted to use their intimidating power to shut down the site. A public relations official wanted to investigate the situation and report back to the committee. She found the site had been put up by the fifth-grade class of a local elementary school that had the assignment to create a Web page. Since everyone seemed to hate the local utility company, it became an easy target.

Imagine the PR fallout if the lawyers had blasted the school with legal threats against a bunch of 11-year-olds! Jay Leno would be telling jokes to this day about the dunderheads from the utility company who went on the warpath against schoolchildren!

Rather than bring in the legal eagles, the PR people contacted the teacher, spoke to the class, took them on a tour of the local facility and donated computer equipment to the school. The kids thought the utility company was great and changed the page to show their new, positive feelings.

The moral of the story is that sometimes the best strategy is to use PR instead of lawyers.

Yet, there will always be times when the silk gloves of PR should be taken off and lawyers need to get involved. "I can't imagine too many cases where companies wouldn't be served by protecting themselves against defamation," says Pizzo.

■ PARODY OR SPOOF SITES

When candidate Bob Dole announced his home page address during a presidential debate, he showed the world that he was a technosavvy kind of guy. What he didn't realize was that a considerable number of web surfers who searched for his home page mistakenly visited a site with a similar name that spoofed Bob Dole and all that he stands for.

While Bob Dole's home page address was www.dole96.org, a spoof site or parody site could be found at www.dole.96.com. Voters used to typing domain names with the "com" extension, probably typed in the spoof site by accident.

These errant typists saw a page that looked professionally designed with a picture of a smiling Bob Dole, the American flag and—what's this??—wallpaper with the Dole pineapple logo. The slogan underneath "Dole-Kemp '96" proclaimed Bob was "the ripe man for the job." In fact, the '96' was printed to read "69." A humorous biography followed. The section on Dole's positions on hot topics of the day yielded equally bizarre results. Click on the button for "Crime" and the Microsoft home page appeared. Click on "Family Values" and you'd see the Marilyn Monroe home page. By this time, even people who hadn't voted since Truman was president would have realized there was something not quite right about this page.

Bob Dole had been spoofed.

A spoof site is a parody created by clever (or not so clever) writers and artists who want to express their views in a humorous manner. Spoof sites lack the venom of an attack site and might not even want to take a company to task. Instead, they want to show their creativity by making fun of the target.

To be fair, the spoofers lampooned every other candidate in the 1996 Presidential election and primary. On Bill Clinton's spoof page, readers were invited to click on a button to see the President's greatest accomplishment. A picture of the President playing golf appeared on the monitor!

The lampooners treated each candidate with humor and without mercy. Tremendous thought went into the words and design of each page. Colin Powell's spoof page used camouflage colors in the logo.

These anonymous authors of these works received publicity in daily newspapers, including *USA Today*. While no one kept count of the actual page hits, one might argue the spoof sites generated more traffic than the candidates' actual home pages. They certainly generated more laughs.

RISKY BUSINESS IN THE FIELD

Stale/Slate

Microsoft started an online magazine called *Slate*. Within days, a parody site called "Stale" hit the web. Major newspapers and trade magazine reported on the new site. Microsoft just rolled with the punches and didn't do anything publicly to close the site. We can only imagine what happened behind closed doors.

Sometimes, parodies exist and there is nothing you can do about them—but laugh.

➤ Spoofs on E-Mail

Spoofs are not limited to websites. One of the most widely read spoofs originated in e-mail and involved Microsoft and the Vatican.

Who would believe that Microsoft would buy the Roman Catholic Church? Lots of people. A clever comedy writer penned a press release announcing that Microsoft planned to make such a purchase. The message spread by e-mail—not a website—to so many people, who then called the company, that Microsoft had to issue a press release denying the rumor! News of the fake press release and Microsoft's response made headlines everywhere. A copy of the original parody appears on page 271. Please note, the Associated Press did not write this story, even though the parody writer included the "AP" symbol.

■ HOW TO RESPOND TO SPOOFERS

While spoof sites like these might be dismissed as trivial pranks perpetuated by harmless college students or David

MICROSOFT BIDS TO ACQUIRE CATHOLIC CHURCH

VATICAN CITY (AP)—In a joint press conference in St. Peter's Square this morning, MICROSOFT Corp. and the Vatican announced that the Redmond software giant will acquire the Roman Catholic Church in exchange for an unspecified number of shares of MICROSOFT common stock. If the deal goes through, it will be the first time a computer software company has acquired a major world religion.

With the acquisition, Pope John Paul II will become the senior vice-president of the combined company's new Religious Software Division, while MICROSOFT senior vice-presidents Michael Maples and Steven Ballmer will be invested in the College of Cardinals, says MICROSOFT Chairman Bill Gates.

"We expect a lot of growth in the religious market in the next five to ten years," says Gates. "The combined resources of MICROSOFT and the Catholic Church will allow us to make religion easier and more fun for a broader range of people."

Through the MICROSOFT Network, the company's new on-line service, "we will make the sacraments available online for the first time" and revive the popular pre-Counter-Reformation practice of selling indulgences, says Gates. "You can get Communion, confess your sins, receive absolution—even reduce your time in Purgatory—all without leaving your home."

A new software application, MICROSOFT Church, will include a macro language which you can program to download heavenly graces automatically while you are away from your computer.

An estimated 17,000 people attended the announcement in St. Peter's Square, watching on a 60-foot screen as comedian Don Novello—in character as Father Guido Sarducci—hosted the event, which was broadcast by satellite to 700 sites worldwide.

(continued)

BIDS TO ACQUIRE CATHOLIC CHURCH (Continued)

Pope John Paul II says little during the announcement. When Novello chided Gates, "Now I guess you get to wear one of these pointy hats," the crowd roared, but the pontiff's smile seemed strained.

The deal grants MICROSOFT exclusive electronic rights to the Bible and the Vatican's prized art collection, which includes works by such masters as Michelangelo and Da Vinci. But critics say MICROSOFT will face stiff challenges if it attempts to limit competitors' access to these key intellectual properties.

"The Jewish people invented the look and feel of the holy scriptures," says Rabbi David Gottschalk of Philadelphia. "You take the parting of the Red Sea—we had that thousands of years before the Catholics came on the scene."

But others argue that the Catholic and Jewish faiths both draw on a common Abrahamic heritage. "The Catholic Church has just been more successful in marketing it to a larger audience," notes Notre Dame theologian Father Kenneth Madigan. Over the last 2,000 years, the Catholic Church's market share has increased dramatically, while Judaism, which was the first to offer many of the concepts now touted by Christianity, lags behind.

Historically, the Church has a reputation as an aggressive competitor, leading crusades to pressure people to upgrade to Catholicism, and entering into exclusive licensing arrangements in various kingdoms whereby all subjects were instilled with Catholicism, whether or not they planned to use it. Today Christianity is available from several denominations, but the Catholic version is still the most widely used. The Church's mission is to reach "the four corners of the earth," echoing MICROSOFT's vision of "a computer on every desktop and in every home."

(continued)

BIDS TO ACQUIRE CATHOLIC CHURCH (Continued)

Gates described MICROSOFT's long-term strategy to develop a scalable religious architecture that will support all religions through emulation. A single core religion will be offered with a choice of interfaces according to the religion desired—"One religion, a couple of different implementations," says Gates.

The MICROSOFT move could spark a wave of mergers and acquisitions, according to Herb Peters, a spokesman for the U.S. Southern Baptist Conference, as other churches scramble to strengthen their position in the increasingly competitive religious market.

Letterman wannabees, such parodies can damage companies because consumers who mistakenly reach the wrong destination may confuse it for the company's real site.

These case studies show the lighthearted nature of parodies. Some companies, however, have been the subject of matters that didn't leave anyone laughing.

Is parody a protected form of expression?

➤ Legal Response

Question: *How far can pranksters go before they cross the line? Your company is being spoofed. What would professional communications recommend?*

Answer: "You have to evaluate each instance individually. There isn't a single answer. Each case is separate," Holtz says. "Who is doing the attacking? Is it serious? Is this something people are going to pay attention to?"

Holtz isn't convinced spoof sites damage companies.

"Some companies have links to their spoof sites to show they aren't concerned, that they're aware of the spoof and that clearly they find it to be inconsequential. Employees will find it no matter what you do. You can use the home page as rebuttal or source of information."

He advises spoofed companies to acknowledge the spoof sites with wording to the effect of: "You might have seen these pages, here is our position on that."

In deciding how to deal with the situation, he would ask these questions:

> Is it worth going to the trouble to force the owner to take it down?
> What is the potential risk?
> Is anybody actually visiting the spoof site?
> If they are visiting the spoof site, are they taking it seriously?

For example, a disgrunted United Airlines passenger who was undergoing a divorce found that his wife had claimed all their frequent flier miles. He complained about the situation on the Internet and urged people to boycott United. No one cared.

If Holtz decided to contact the spoofer, here's what he would try to find out.

"I would start with a discussion about what prompted the individual to post the site. Obviously, something has happened, can we talk about it?" he says. "What you want to do is get it out of the realm of 'You are pissing us off' and into the realm of attempting to resolve the individual's concerns and turning that individual into a customer for life."

"The first step is reach out; the second step is look within," says Meier. "Learn what you can. What is attractive about the site? What makes it compelling? Is there something you can incorporate into your site? A little sense of humor goes a long way."

"Not all spoofs are bad. It depends on the tone of the spoof. If it's in good fun, then I'd say enjoy it. You might even see if you can capitalize on it, in your marketing" says

Bayne. Some companies are not afraid to have fun with their image. It actually creates goodwill in the marketplace. The additional exposure could be helpful. If the spoof is detrimental to a client's image, in that it creates or has the potential to create negative misconceptions that impact sales and stock prices, I would advise differently."

■ SUMMARY

Because the Internet is the world's cheapest printing press, disgruntled customers, employees, and activists can attack your company and tell a worldwide audience. Vigilant public relations and crisis communications officials will deal with these situations and squelch the problems before they get out of hand.

Chapter

13

Market Bull: Online Stock Manipulation

Not many people heard of Zitel, a publicly traded company. Although the stock was traded on the NASDAQ exchange, only a handful of shares traded in an average day.

That all changed when The Motley Fool, an investment forum on America Online (and now the Internet) touted the stock. Record numbers of shares were traded and the stock's price more than tripled over the next few days.

A few months later, the experts at The Motley Fool decided it was time to bail out and told their members. The stock volume swelled again and the price plummeted. To the credit of The Motley Fool, they advise their clients first, before they themselves place trades. That way, they can't be accused of manipulating the market or getting in or out before their clients. Nevertheless, this story shows the power the Internet has over the price of company stock.

This chapter explores the calamities on the Internet that can befall a publicly traded company including:

➤ Current cases.

➤ How reporters use newsgroups.

276

➤ What the Securities and Exchange Commission is doing to fight the problem.

➤ Typical investment scams.

➤ How the SEC is tracking fraud.

➤ SEC guidelines on how to protect yourself.

➤ Investor relations guidelines for the Internet.

➤ Online resources.

◼ CASE IN POINT

The stock prices of publicly traded companies can swing wildly based on information—and misinformation—posted in newsgroups:

➤ Iomega is a hugely popular company that sells the wildly popular Zip drive for computers. The stock soared from 13 to 65 in a little less than three months in early 1996. Online bulletin boards were filled with tips, rumors, and innuendoes from people hoping the stock would go up, as well as from short sellers, who hoped the stock would go down. The company seemed to be at the mercy of these chatters who had their own agenda.

➤ Christopher Reeve, the actor, received funds from Neotherapeutics to run his institute. Based on this information, touts posted messages on bulletin boards claiming that the company was going to make millions. The stock rose from 4.5 to 13 in days.

➤ A person outside the company heard that Iomega was about to launch an advertising program. He jumped to an erroneous conclusion that the company was issuing a new product and told people about the "news" in newsgroups. The stock price moved. According to a company spokesperson, the ad campaign was for an existing product.

> ➤ SyQuest lost 32 percent of stock value in 11 hours after a message on the Motley Fool board announced a rumor that the company would be delisting. The rumor was picked up on Reuters. SyQuest's stock collapsed.

These stories show that publicly traded companies face a series of threats on the Internet. Companies can be victims or beneficiaries of tips in online bulletin boards that have dramatic and drastic consequences on their companies' valuations.

Who were these touts? Stockbrokers? Inside traders? Company officials? Buyers? Sellers? It is hard to say since many messages were signed anonymously or used "handles" (nicknames or e-mail addresses), which are hard to trace, instead of real names. These messengers didn't want to be traced for fear of sanctions by the Securities and Exchange Commission because their missives skirted the laws. They talked about inside information, or rumored inside information, or information they hoped people would think would be inside information. These touts hope greedy investors will latch onto these stories and buy (or sell) the stock in question when they read messages that range in sophistication from product information to out-and-out tout such as:

> ➤ This could be your stock buy of the year!
> ➤ I'm going to ride this train to the gold mine.

Are people taken in by this nonsense? You bet. Look at Iomega, Zitel, and Neotherapeutics and many, many others.

■ REPORTERS AND NEWSGROUPS

While touts target their advice at investors, reporters and editors also scour newsgroups for information and sources.

However, they don't trust anything they read without doing their homework.

Dr. Harry Tracy, publisher of *NeuroInvestment,* a newsletter providing investment research on companies developing neuro/psychopharmaceuticals, monitors the Tech Investor website, which has thousands of bulletin boards in which investors can post information on public companies. Each company has its own bulletin board, which is maintained by Tech Investor. The bulletin boards are not sponsored or edited by the individual companies. People are free to post any information they like. People are identified by their name or handle, which is linked to a page that contains information about the person, which the person supplies. This information is not edited or checked for accuracy by Tech Investor.

RISKY BUSINESS ASKS THE EXPERTS

Here are Dr. Tracy's tips for spotting false or misleading postings:

1. Touts post claims but don't offer information to back them up.

2. Avoid people who talk in extreme terms (e.g., "This stock can't lose. I am sure of it"). Well no one can be sure of anything. You can bet these people are trying to manipulate the stock.

3. If the message isn't signed or has an anonymous return address, disregard the message.

4. Track down the tout, if possible. Tracy said he noticed that one newsgroup writer was attacking a company he follows. One member of the bulletin board traced the source of the message and found the writer worked for a competing company. He was exposed in the group.

Tracy used his newsletter to warn investors about the rumors affecting—and Neotherapeutics, drugs to treat neurological conditions that affect the brain. He's also pointed out that officials at some companies post misinformation about their competitors. Tracy says touts are easily dismissed in the bulletin boards he follows.

"The older members of the group, the people who have been on for a long time, generally know everyone who posts a message. If someone touts a stock, they are quick to attack and ask that person what is the source of his information. They post messages that say, 'Get off our thread. Be serious or be gone.'" In one case, when someone attacked Tracy for his views on a stock, the group members rallied to his defense and told the tout that Tracy was legitimate.

However, not every newsgroup has an unofficial board of editors or advisers to steer new members along the right path. While editors and responsible newsgroup members can alert people to frauds and abuses on the Internet, scam artists are also being pursued by government agencies.

■ INTERVIEW WITH HERB GREENBERG*

Question: *How seriously do you take anything you read about companies in chat rooms?*

Answer: Herb Greenberg, bizinsider@aolcom, KCBS business reporter, columnist for the *San Francisco Chronicle:* Not very because it's all very anonymous and much of it is written by people with a strong vested interest. I think message boards can be dangerous (and this comes from someone who ran them for nearly two years on AOL)! Besides, I don't have time to scroll through chat. I just don't do it. I'd rather do my own research and rely on the sources I know.

_____

* June 1997.

Question: *How do you check out the rumors?*

Greenberg: Online? I don't. Info spread on chat is like getting an anonymous phone call. I've got better things to do.

Question: *What advice would you give to companies that are being attacked or manipulated? Should they respond or deny claims?*

Greenberg: Always respond and speak the truth. Unless you have something to hide. Then I can understand your desire to remain silent.

Question: *Is this problem growing?*

Greenberg: I think the online problems have leveled off from the early Iomega days, because I think people have tired of the boards (unless we're talking about a super-hot stock, but even then, I think many "posters" have tired of the medium).

Question: Any other tidbits, anecdotes, insights would be appreciated.

Greenberg: When I was writing about *c-cube,* I continued to read nasty comments about myself, charges that I was getting paid by the shorts . . . that I should be investigated. etc., etc. . . . eventually the company's biz turned south and all of those folks disappeared.

■ THE SECURITIES AND EXCHANGE COMMISSION TO THE RESCUE

While laws specifically related to online abuses have not yet been written, a representative of the Securities and Exchange Commission told me that if the action is illegal in the real world, you can be sure it is illegal online.

The SEC is aware that scam artists can pose a serious threat on the Internet.

"The Internet has posed a threat now to investors," William McLucas, head of the SEC's division of enforcement, said at a weekly Justice Department briefing. "It's changed the velocity of communications. You can now reach exponentially larger groups of people."

McLucas warned that it is harder for investors to walk away from fraudulent messages posted in newsgroups.

"Sitting at home in the den, looking at the Internet, and observing what purports to be a tremendous investment opportunity that is dressed up with some legalese, people will take out their checkbook, write a check and put it in the mail," McLucas said.

Looking out for bogus investment offers on the Internet is a huge task for the agency, which has 60 professionals who work on Internet-related cases, he said. "Monitoring the Internet would be a daunting task for anybody."

However, the Internet can also help SEC investigators.

"We have an inordinate number of tips and leads from the Internet from people who have seen questionable investment opportunities being pitched," he said (Reuters, May 22, 1997).

■ TYPICAL INVESTMENT SCAMS—WHAT YOU CAN DO ABOUT THEM

One of the most attractive features of online computing is communicating to a large audience without spending a lot of time, effort, or money. By posting a message on a bulletin board, using a chat room, or constructing a site on the Internet, you can broadcast messages to tens of thousands of people. Yet, this powerful tool can cause real problems when used to defraud investors, according to the SEC, which compiled the following information.

While investment con artists have been quick to appropriate online computing as a new way to cheat investors, their online schemes mirror frauds perpetrated over the phone or through the mail. Consider all offers with skepticism.

Investment frauds usually fit one of the following categories:

➤ *The Pyramid* ("How to Make Big Money from Your Home Computer!"). One online promoter claimed recently that you could "turn $5 into $60,000 in just three to six weeks." In reality, this program was just an electronic version of the classic pyramid scheme in which participants attempt to make money solely by recruiting new participants into the program. This type of fraud is well-suited for the world of online computing where a troublemaker can easily send messages to a thousand people with the touch of a button. These "investment opportunities" collapse when no new "investors" can be found.

➤ *The Risk-Free Fraud* ("Exciting, Low-Risk Investment Opportunities"). Invitations have been offered online to participate in exotic-sounding investments, including wireless cable projects, prime bank securities, and eel farms. One promoter attempted to get people to invest in a fictitious coconut plantation in Costa Rica, claiming the investment was "similar to a CD, with a better interest rate." Promoters misrepresent the risk by comparing their offer to something safe, like bank certificates of deposit. Sometimes, an investment product does not even exist—they're scams.

➤ *The "Pump and Dump" Scam.* It is common to see messages posted online urging readers to buy a stock quickly because it is poised for rapid growth, or telling you to sell before it goes down. Often the writer claims to have inside information about an impending development, or will claim to use an "infallible" combination of economic and stock market data to pick stocks. In reality, the promoter may be an insider who stands to gain by selling shares after the stock price is pumped up by gullible investors, or a short seller who stands to gain if the price goes down. This ploy may be used with little-known, thinly traded stocks.

■ THE SECURITIES AND EXCHANGE COMMISSION IS TRACKING FRAUD

In investigating online fraud, the SEC can get a court order to stop scams. The SEC took action in the following cases:

➤ Pleasure Time, Inc. promised astronomical profits in a worldwide telephone lottery. Over two million dollars of unregistered securities were sold to 20,000 investors who were encouraged to recruit other investors on the Internet. The SEC filed a lawsuit and the company's assets were frozen.

➤ IVT Systems solicited investments to finance the construction of an ethanol plant in the Dominican Republic. The Internet solicitations promised a return of 50 percent or more with no reasonable basis for the prediction. Their literature contained lies about contracts with well-known companies and omitted other important information for investors. After the SEC filed a complaint, they agreed to stop breaking the law.

➤ Scott Frye posted a notice that he was looking for investors for two Costa Rican companies that produced coconut chips. He claimed A&P supermarkets had placed an order to buy all the chips he could produce. He was forced to withdraw his notice when his lies were discovered.

➤ Gene Block and Renate Haag were caught offering "prime bank" securities, a type of security that doesn't even exist. They collected over $3.5 million by promising to double investors' money in four months. The SEC has frozen their assets and stopped them from continuing their fraud.

➤ Daniel Odulo was stopped from soliciting investors for a proposed eel farm. Odulo promised investors a "whopping 20 percent return," claiming that the investment was "low risk." When the SEC caught him, he consented to the court order stopping him from breaking the securities laws.

RISKY BUSINESS IN THE NEWS

In November 1996, the SEC filed its first lawsuit to stop securities manipulation over the Internet. The SEC said that a newsletter, *SGA Goldstar,* touted Systems of Excellence (SE), a manufacturer of video teleconferencing equipment. Investors then posted notices on newsgroups. When shares rose above $4 up from 25 cents, the writers and Charles Huttoe, former chairman of SE, sold their stock (*Business Week,* December 9, 1996, p. 114).

Huttoe pleaded guilty to one count of securities fraud and one count of money laundering in November 1996, according to documents filed in federal court in Alexandria, Virginia. He agreed to repay nearly $12 million he had collected in the fraud. He faced a prison term as well, but cooperated with authorities in netting other perpetrators in the ring (*The New York Times,* February 1, 1997). Writers for the newsletter also received stock in the companies they promoted, a fact that was disclosed to readers (*The New York Times,* February 26, 1997, p. C8).

■ SECURITIES AND EXCHANGE COMMISSION GUIDELINES FOR PROTECTING YOURSELF

The following checklist should help you steer clear of online fraud, but first a word about the information these companies are required to file at the SEC and some basic tips.

You should always check with your state securities regulator to see if they have more information about the company and the people behind it, and if your state regulator has cleared the offering for sale in your state.

Because small companies usually present the most risky investments, you should always get as much written information as you can from the company. Check out this information with an unbiased and informed source—your broker, accountant, or lawyer. Your state's securities regulator should be your first stop, but you may also want to visit your local library and talk with the librarian about other sources of information. A number of services provide a constant stream of information about the financial condition of companies.

■ INVESTOR RELATIONS GUIDELINES FOR THE INTERNET

To fight rumors and lies, it is important to use your website to dispense the truth. According to a survey of 2,000 publicly trade companies conducted by Straightline Internet Communications, nearly 80 percent of those companies have websites. A world-class investor relations website contains these items:

> ➤ *Press releases.* They should be posted as soon as you release them to major news organs. Your clients, customers, investors, and employees will want to see original source material in full. By doing this, you begin to control your messages and you dispense

RULES FOR INVESTORS

1. Make sure you know as much as possible about the company, before you invest. Don't ever rely solely on what you read online to make an investment decision.

2. Download and print a hard copy of any online solicitation that you are considering. Make sure you catch the Internet address (URL) and note the date and time that you saw the offer. Save this in case you need it later.

3. Don't believe everything you read online. Take the time to investigate a possible investment opportunity before you hand over your hard-earned money. The following steps will show you how: Check with your state securities regulator or the SEC and ask if they have received any complaints about the company, its managers, or the promoter. See the end of this fact sheet on how to contact these agencies.

4. Don't assume that people online are who they claim they are. The investment that sounds so good may be a figment of their imagination.

5. Check with a trusted financial adviser, your broker, or attorney regarding any investment you learn about online.

6. Ask the online promoter where the firm is incorporated. Call that state's secretary of state and ask if the company is incorporated with them and has a current annual report on file.

7. Ask for other sources of information at your local public library. There are resources that provide information about the company such as a payment analysis, credit report, lawsuits, liens, or judgments.

8. Don't assume that your access provider or online service has approved or even screened the investment. Anyone can set up a website or advertise online, often without any check of its legitimacy or truthfulness.

(continued)

RULES FOR INVESTORS (Continued)

9. Before you invest, always obtain written financial information, such as a prospectus, annual report, offering circular, and financial statements. Compare the written information with what you've read online and watch out if you're told that no information is available.

10. Have you run into a problem? Don't be embarrassed if you think you've been duped—you are not alone. Complain promptly. By complaining early, you will have a better chance of getting your money back, protecting your legal rights, preventing others from losing money, and assisting securities regulators in stopping investment fraud.

11. Be wary of promises of quick profits, offers to share inside information, and pressure to invest before you have an opportunity to investigate.

12. Be careful of promoters who use aliases. Pseudonyms are common online, and some salespeople will try to hide their true identity. Look for other promotions by the same person.

13. Words like "guarantee," "high return," "limited offer," or "as safe as a CD" may be a red flag. No financial investment is risk-free, and a high rate of return means greater risk.

14. Watch out for offshore scams and investment opportunities in other countries. When you send your money abroad and something goes wrong, it's more difficult to find out what happened and to locate your money.

15. If a company is not registered or has not filed a "Form D" with the Securities and Exchange Commission, call the SEC's Office of Investor Education and Assistance at 202-942-7040 or call your state securities regulator. The

(continued)

RULES FOR INVESTORS (Continued)

SEC does not require companies that are raising less than one million dollars to be registered at the SEC, but these companies are required to file a Form D with the Commission. This is a brief notice that includes the names and addresses of owners and promoters, but little other information. Call the SEC at 202-942-8090 to get a copy of the Form D.

16. Remember, if it sounds too good to be true, it probably is.

17. Alert the SEC to possible cases of manipulation.

You can read more about the SEC at their website, www.sec.gov, or call 202-942-7040, or send e-mail to the Office of Investor Education and Assistance at help@sec.gov or the Division of Enforcement at enforcement@sec.gov.

information in a timely manner. If you don't do this, your message will be delayed until the local or trade papers print their versions of your press releases, which could contain errors or perspectives from outside your company that could change people's perceptions of your message. Also, by sending out press releases via PR Newswire or Business Wire, your stakeholders who subscribe to personal news services such as PointCast and My Personal Yahoo will be able to read the releases immediately on distribution.

➤ *Historical press releases.* Old press releases should be kept at your site as additional sources of information. Investors can check the original source material for earnings reports and other matters that could affect the public's perception of your company.

➤ *Annual reports.* Many companies post their annual reports online. The standard formatting technique

RISKY BUSINESS ASKS THE EXPERTS

Investor Relations Advice from Stuart Pearlman*

Because of the specialized nature of investor relations, we spoke with Stuart Pearlman, practice director, Financial Relations of Phase Two Strategies. He had run his own financial and corporate relations firm for 13 years before merging it with Phase Two in June 1997. He had been vice president of corporate communications at Loral Corporation and Chemical Bank. He has also worked for IBM and General Electric Company.

"It's not a new problem. It's just a new technology," he says. "The reality is there are manipulators out there. They will do it on the Internet, as well as with every gossip sheet in your industry."

To fight online crises, he advocates taking proactive steps to open lines of communication with key audiences.

"You need to communicate regularly with shareholders, analysts, portfolio managers, vendors, suppliers, customers and employees on the nature of key issues of business. It is important to highlight what matters, admit what is not working (that's good communications). Ignoring problems or glossing over them leads to bad communication," he says. "The goal is to get and keep everyone on the same page. If you do that well, the rumor mill won't hurt you over the long term. The company has proven to be worthy of belief. It sounds like apple pie," says Pearlman, "but companies that don't do this don't win."

When rumors or unannounced information find their way to online forums, he suggests following the game plan created with the company's long-term interests in mind.

---

* Interview, July 1997.

(continued)

RISKY BUSINESS (Continued)

"You have to have policies on what you will or won't do, regardless of where the rumors start. It should not be the policy of the company to comment on rumors. There will always be rumors. You'll spend all your time commenting on rumors. You'll be in a reactive mode. You have to have a sense of what your messages are," he says. "There are no requirements to disclose things until they near reality. Traders love rumors. How much time are you going to spend responding to rumors instead of working on the critical issues about the company that really matter for investors?"

What should you do in a crisis? Follow your game plan, he advises.

"Suppose the stock is erratic. People will call you and ask what is going on: the *Wall Street Journal,* traders, investors and money managers. First of all, you need a system to handle calls."

Here's what Pearlman advises:

1. The switchboard needs to know to whom they should direct calls.
2. PR people must know what is going on.
3. Don't respond to rumors. You don't tell them anything that isn't public.
4. If it is public, tell everyone at the same time. Use blast fax, Business Wire or PR Newswire, and follow-up calls.
5. If any material things happen, you *must* disclose them promptly and completely.
6. You cannot comment to one reporter beforehand. *Period.*
7. There are clear directions on how to do things in investor relations and corporate communications business.

(continued)

RISKY BUSINESS (Continued)

There are not shortcuts and no exceptions can be made. Once you do that, it is a very slippery slope.

What would you do if a competitor prints misstatements about your company?

"If they publish something that is not true, you are not going to comment on it. Why dignify a ridiculous comment by commenting on it?"

Is silence seen as assent?

"No. IBM has been the subject of lots of rumors over the years. Look where they are today," he said. "The stock is near an all-time high, despite being near record lows as recently as a couple of years ago."

If your company makes a mistake, he advises to confess quickly.

"My rule of thumb is 'When mistakes are made, admit them and correct them.' There's a saying: 'Wall Street will forgive you for disappointments but punish you for surprises.' That isn't really true. Wall Street will punish you both for surprises and for disappointments. However, it is easier to regain credibility from a disappointment, especially if you admit and correct your mistakes."

To help fight negative images about a company, Pearlman advises companies to create internal support for their plans.

"The most compelling people to speak about the company is its own employees. They should be told what is going on at the company," he says. "Employees should know what is considered confidential and what can be discussed outside. They should know where the company is going as a business and where to get help when they get a question (i.e., Investor

(continued)

RISKY BUSINESS (Continued)

Relations, Public Relations or External Relations) so the appropriate, trained people can respond to questions."

A common concern in newsgroup postings is projections on company's earnings. What should management do about announcing projected earnings?

"You don't want to predict earnings, but analysts get paid for this activity," he says. "Businesses are protected somewhat by 'Safe Harbor' laws which enable management to discuss where they believe the business is going, but things could change for a number of reasons. It allows managers to say, 'This is our best guess or our most reasonable expectation.' 'Safe Harbor' protects management so that they can comment with analysts and journalists without undue consequences if their predictions don't come true."

In devising an investor relations strategy, Pearlman asks companies to consider these questions:

"What kind of business are you in? What kind of reputation do you want to build? You are really in the business of managing the reputation of the comany. Base it on facts and reality. That can be tough to do, but you have to. The goal of investing is to build shareholder value over time and return on equity over time."

---

seems to be Adobe Acrobat. This free software program must be downloaded from the Adobe site and installed, a one-time process that takes about 15 minutes. Straightline reports that only 54 percent of publicly traded companies post their annual reports online.

➤ Case histories.
➤ Testimonials.

➤ Reprints or links to newspaper articles, television and radio transcripts.

➤ Audio interviews with company officials.

➤ Product literature.

➤ Company background and executive bios.

➤ Any other material that tells the truth about the company.

➤ Stock ticker. Public companies frequently list the stock price on their home page.

➤ Contact information for investor relations, public relations, media contacts, and product managers. Many websites don't make this information easily available, which is an oversight that inconveniences reporters and stakeholders who want to contact company officials to check claims they read in newsgroups.

■ SUMMARY

Newsgroups and web pages are being used to tout stocks. You must protect your company by:

➤ Monitoring newsgroups.

➤ Correcting errors and misstatements.

➤ Decide to respond or ignore messages.

➤ Alert the SEC to possible frauds.

➤ Use your website and e-mail newsletters to spread news about your company.

Remember that a good offense is the best defense. Additional strategies for responding to crises are contained in the next chapter.

ONLINE RESOURCES

Securities and Exchange Commission, www.sec.gov, contains news about new scams, how to fight fraud, and online resources. The SEC's Edgar database, www.sec.gov/cgi-bin /srch-edgar, contains annual reports, prospectuses, and other reports required of public companies.

NASDAQ, www.nasdaq.com, maintains a free service to see if someone is a legitimate stock broker, 800-289-9999.

Daily Stocks, www.dailystocks.com, is a great starting page for information about companies. It includes links to investment services and news services.

The law firms of Fensterman & Fensterman and Ziegler, Sagal, & Winters publish the Stock Investor's Fraud Resource website, www.stockbrokerfraud.com/, which describes in detail the three common types of stockbroker fraud. The Stock Investor's Fraud Resource also provides facts about recovering losses from brokerage firms that mishandle your money.

Bloomberg News, www.bloomberg.com, displays business news so you can check claims.

S&P Equity Investor Service, www.stockinfo.standardpoor .com, prints news and stock picks.

USA Today Money, www.usatoday.com/money/mfront.htm, shows news and data.

Yahoo! Finance, www.quote.yahoo.com, contains news, stock quotes, and data.

Crisis Communications: The New Online Crisis Communications Plan

Crisis communications plans need to be adapted to include the online media. Whether the crisis starts online or in the real world, online resources can be used to find the crisis and deal with it. This chapter will show you how to use online tools to fight crises and how to integrate the plan into the overall crisis communications plan, which should include all media including the Internet. This chapter presents a step-by-step plan for fighting online crises with advice from the experts in these areas:

➤ Precrisis planning.

➤ Anticipating the crisis.

➤ Using the Internet to find potential crises.

➤ Determining the severity of the situation; is it a crisis?

➤ Responding to the crisis.

➤ Measuring success in handling a crisis.

➤ Finding Online resources.

■ PRECRISIS PLANNING

Companies must have policies for dealing with crises. From a set policy, all strategies can flow smoothly. Consider having a policy based on openness and honesty. This sounds simplistic, but it wasn't always the case, nor have all companies adopted this simple guideline.

"Crisis communication is about distributing information, not withholding it," says Katharine Paine, www.delahaye .com, president of The Delahaye Group, a learning communications measurement and analysis company. "That wasn't the case 10 years ago when the rallying cries were: 'Put the press off.' 'Storm the barricades.' 'Don't respond.' 'Withhold information.' The corporate culture that is open and forthcoming will defuse the situation."*

Stuart Goldstein, sgoldstein@nscc.com, vice president of corporate communications for National Securities Clearing Corporation, in New York, which is the responsible for all posttrade processing for stocks, bonds, mutual funds, and other financial transactions, agrees. "In a crisis, the question is, are we reacting to today's realities or are we in a position to influence them? Today, many PR departments still approach a crisis with a 'let's circle the wagons' attitude.

"We need to recognize that the Internet is dramatically transforming our world and the way we communicate. It's expanded the quantity, quality and speed of information that's distributed worldwide," he says. "To be effective, companies must be in a state of information preparedness. This strategic approach requires anticipating and planning for 'if p then q' scenarios long in advance. I think the key here is to preempt

---

* Interview, June 27, 1997.

or try to influence the impact of a crisis as it's occurring. This is a very different way of doing PR."*

Good crisis communication planning at this stage includes these steps:

1. All message management is worked out in advance.

2. A spokesperson is identified and company employees know whom to contact in case of a crisis.

3. Messages are created to address the individual concerns of key communities: analysts and shareholders each have different concerns.

4. Delivery methods are in place (e-mail, fax, phone).

5. Databases of audiences have been created.

The team to put this activity together would include senior management and database managers who compile the lists and distribute the information to those targeted groups. Legal counsel is also recommended.

■ ANTICIPATING THE CRISIS

Nearly every company can anticipate a crisis situation. Company layoffs, disappointing earning results, executives indicted, discrimination suits, product delays, tainted products, you name it, it can happen to you. The best plan for dealing with a crisis is to plan for it in advance.

Pat Meier of Pat Meier Public Relations, patmeier@ patmeier.com, www.patmeier.com, anticipated a problem with a company's product launch and took steps to defuse a potentially dangerous issue.

"Kansmen's Little Brother allows a boss to see how employees are using the Internet and how much time they are

---

* Interview, August 12, 1997.

spending at each site. It also makes it possible to block unproductive Internet activities during business hours. "This could upset some people and it certainly could fly in the face of what some journalists believe as well," says Meier. "We anticipated possible reaction to a client's product by having audio on the website. We posted an interview with the sales manager with his vision for the product and all the situations where there is a great need for this product."*

Audio has an added dimension lacking in print. "An audio interview allows for the passion to come through in a way that doesn't come through in a press release. Anyone can check it out," she says. "This is something that is controversial that allows us to give a lot more depth and explanation to the product." The interview lasts 20 minutes and is divided into five-minute segments: how a manager can establish a policy, the technology, how the program works, and places where it has been implemented. Meier, an experienced television talk show host, interviewed her client. The PR agency publicized the site to the media by sending postcards and e-mails.

James Alexander, director eWatch, jalex@eworks.com, www.ewatch.com, 914-288-0000, a company that provides Web monitoring services, advises his clients to ask these questions when they move into crisis mode:

Step 1. Diagnosis—The Information Gathering Stage

➤ Where is it being discussed (a newsgroup a website, e-mail)?

➤ How many messages?

➤ Is it in a high-profile group, or an isolated group?

➤ What is the issue?

➤ Can you focus it to a single problem?

---

* Interview, July 1997.

> ➤ How will it impact the company?
> ➤ How will it impact the sales?
> ➤ How will it impact the employees (death threats, bomb scares)?
> ➤ How will it impact the vendors?
> ➤ How will it impact the clients?
> ➤ How will it impact the stock price?

"You need to go through this exercise to determine response. Put everything on the table. A decision has to be made. What will the company do about this?"

Step 2. Prescription

> ➤ Are we going to respond or not?
> ➤ If we don't respond, what can we do on the periphery?
> ➤ Can we have the ISP shut the person (group) down?
> ➤ How can we solve the problem?
> ➤ Is a legal settlement appropriate?

"When a company responds, the newsgroup stands at attention. That has serious implications. The first few days of the crisis are the most stressful because you don't know how big it will grow," says Alexander. "Every crisis starts with one person."

■ USING THE INTERNET TO FIND POTENTIAL CRISES

The Internet has many tools to help you find crises including:

> ➤ Newsgroups, online bulletin boards.
> ➤ Search tools for newsgroups.

➤ Websites.

➤ Search engines that scour the websites for references to your company.

➤ News services that automatically alert you to stories about your company, competitors, and industry.

This section explains how to find crises on the Internet, World Wide Web, and Usenet Newsgroups. The next section describes how to respond to these messages.

➤ Monitoring Newsgroups

Newsgroups are online bulletin boards on the Internet. More than 25,000 newsgroups discuss topics ranging from computer programming to teaching dyslexic children, to self-help groups for survivors of breast cancer. Members of these groups post messages on these electronic bulletin boards with help, advice, news, and opinions. As seen in Chapter 12, several major crises for Intel, Intuit, Tommy Hilfiger and LEXIS-NEXIS actually started in newsgroups. If the company had been aware of these messages in their incubation stages, they might have averted crises that landed these stories on Page 1 of major newspapers.

"Newsgroups and mailing lists are early warning systems of crisis," says Paine. "To effectively plan for crises, you need to know what is out there. You don't have time to do research in the middle of a crisis. It is too late. You need too determine which news groups are talking about you. The best defense is a good offense.

"Five years ago, no one was thinking about monitoring newsgroups. Today, if you manage a brand, opposition groups and special interest groups are on the Internet each morning trying to create a crisis every day, everywhere in the world. Each exposure gives them an opportunity to question your right to exist, your right to pollute, or whatever. The reason a crisis becomes a crisis, is because the companies mishandle it," Paine says.

➤ The Internet Changes Everything

"You have to realize the Internet is a media where people are engaging one another. Whether you have an active presence is irrelevant. People are sharing information and various topics, which include your organization. You need to be part of that community. If you have potential customers, suppliers, friends, foes, you need to be there and monitor what is going on," says Craig Jolley, principal, Online and Strategic Information Solutions, Dayton, Ohio, craigj@erinet.com, information technology management consultant.

There are several ways to monitor messages in newsgroups quickly and effectively.

➤ Newsgroup Monitoring Tools

With more than 20,000 newsgroups, it is impossible for any organization to individually monitor each message on every newsgroup. Fortunately, tools and services can help find messages that relate to your company.

DejaNews

This is a database of every message posted to a newsgroup since March 1995. DejaNews, www.dejanews.com has 100 million articles, accounting for more than 175 gigabytes of disk space. This is equivalent to approximately 120,000 400-page novels. The database is updated several times a day.

This service can be searched by topics (e.g., oil, renewable energy, irrigation), company name (e.g., Reebok and Time-Warner) or e-mail address (dan@janal.com). Typing in a search term yields an index containing the date, title, and e-mail address of the author, as well as the newsgroup in which the message was posted.

You can scan the newsgroups and titles to see if the match looks like a good hit or a false hit. A good hit mentions the company being searched. For example, a mention of Time-Warner in the television or stock newsgroups makes sense and the searcher should review the message. A false hit sounds like the company but isn't. A search of renewable energy for a utility company might provide links to articles about vitamins and health-related products, which would be a false hit.

By clicking on the headline of the article, you can see the entire message. If other people responded to that message, you'll be able to read those as well. The message and responses are called a "thread." By reading the thread, you can see exactly what the gist of the message is and whether you need to respond. If you decide to respond, you have the option of sending a message to the entire group and join the thread. You could determine that it is best to send a private note to the original writer of the article. In fact, you can even see all the messages that writer ever posted to any newsgroup. Simply click on the hyperlink with his e-mail address. By reading those messages, you might be able to begin creating a profile of that person and decide how to build rapport. For example, if the writer has posted to newsgroups dealing with science and computer newsgroups, you would probably use a different approach than if he posted to newsgroups dealing with racism, hate speech, and satanic cults.

Searches can be based on time periods so you find the latest information.

In my seminars, participants have found many interesting articles. One person found that his publicly traded company was the subject of interest in a stock market newsgroup. The article asked for information about the company and he could readily provide it.

A second person, who deprogrammed cult members, found many relevant articles on his topic and searched the additional postings of those writers. One person had submitted dozens of articles to newsgroups dealing with satanic cults. That information helped him determine whether and how to deal with that person and his comments.

A third person working for a utility trade group searched for "renewable energy," which happened to be the topic of this year's national high school debate. She found dozens of students searching for information on that topic. She was able to supply it easily.

You can use the DejaNews database without cost. The site is supported by advertisers who sell banner ads.

eWatch

This service will spot references to your company on news-groups and websites and send you daily reports. The eWatch service fee starts at $295 a month.

"eWatch Classic tells you what consumers and professionals are saying and reading about your services, products, industry and competitors. You'll hear rumors before they start to spread. You'll be among the first to find out about negative or inaccurate information—instead of the last," says James Alexander, director eWatch, jalex@eworks.com, www.ewatch .com, 914-288-0000. The parent company is called eWorks! Inc.

By using eWatch, company clients have found numerous situations that demanded monitoring or responses. The company's roster of clients reads like a Who's who of the Fortune 1000, with many publicly traded companies that need to be sensitive to what people are saying about their company.

"Companies want to connect to their consumers. They want to be aware of this. Monitoring is just one way to find out how to reach these people," says Alexander. "It is important to know what is going on."

➤ Monitoring Websites

Reading, reviewing, and responding to websites is an essential part of a crisis communication program. You need to watch your competitor's sites for misinformation, news sites for reports of new problems and personal pages of consumers who might post inaccurate information. All of these sites could lead to misleading data as well.

Monitoring sites can be done with software programs that copy pages or entire sites and store them on your hard disk. You can determine how often to check the sites and how you would like to be notified. Programs in this category include Web Whacker, www.ffg.com, and Netbuddy, www.netbuddy .com, Web Ex, www.travellingsoftware.com.

If incorrect information is printed, you should contact them and set the record straight. For personal pages, you might ask them to link to your site or to other Web resources that show your company's point of view (e.g., newspaper articles, white pages, analysts' websites). As mentioned, eWatch also monitors websites for a fee.

➤ Monitoring Online News Services

Hundreds of newspapers and trade publications appear on the Internet. In fact, publications that once appeared on a weekly schedule might now have daily updates on their websites. Never has there been such a demand for new information—or such an easy way to distribute that information on a timely and cost-effective basis than by the Internet. In the past, stories wouldn't appear in the newspaper until the following day; now these articles can be written and printed within minutes the news event. In a matter of minutes, your employees, stockholders, and dealers can know about an event that could have major implications for your company. Shouldn't you know about it too so you can respond effectively?

Online clipping services can notify you for free of newspapers that report on your company or industry. The news can be downloaded to your e-mail box or hard disk; or you can manually go to the service and see the news on a personal screen. Try using these free programs: Pointcast, www.pointcast.com; Hotbot, www.hotwired.com; Excite, www.excite.com; and Infoseek, www.infoseek.com, these programs let you search dozens of online versions of newspapers from their sites. LEXIS-NEXIS sells two services, Requester and InfoTailor, www.lexis-nexis.com, which are more comprehensive than the other services. LEXIS-NEXIS's services track hundreds of news sources, compared with a handful for the free services.

If you use these services, you'll know about news as it happens.

➤ Reporters Need to Be Monitored

You also need to track what reporters are saying about your company and the crisis. Journalists participate in several newsgroups, mailing lists such as car-l, and forums on CompuServe such as jforum. Additionally, they post queries for sources for stories they are writing on Profnet, a service of PR Newswire, www.profnet.com.

When a USAir plane crashed in Pittsburgh several years ago, a reporter from Detroit went into the CAR-L mailing list and asked if the tail fin number could be used to find the maintenance records through the National Transportation Safety Board website.

"We don't know what he was looking for, but chances are the PR people at Boeing and USAir didn't have an idea that he was nosing around," Jolley says. "A Detroit-based broadcast reporter wouldn't be on the normal list of reporters for USAir. Nevertheless, he could have found the information, filed his report and uploaded a copy to NBC national."

ProfNet

The service of PR Newswire that is invaluable to PR people, especially in times of crises. Profnet takes queries from reporters who need sources to help comment on the news. These queries are sent via e-mail several times a day to PR people who subscribe to the service. PR people can then see what stories reporters are working on, what slant they are taking, and what kinds of sources they need. Reporters also post their deadlines and how they prefer to be contacted: phone, fax, or e-mail. PR people then know how to contact these reporters and give them the information they need via the preferred media.

■ DETERMINE THE SEVERITY OF THE SITUATION: IS IT A CRISIS?

Finding out what is being said is the first step in working with newsgroups.

The next step is to determine the credibility of the people making the loudest noise. On electronic discussion groups, everyone's comments seem to have the same weight because everyone can type a message and respond. In reality, long-time members of the group know who is credible and who is not.

The moral here is to not jump to the conclusion that a crisis is brewing when in reality only a few irresponsible writers are seeking an audience that has already dismissed them. On the other hand, newcomers to a group who have no track record, could be there solely because they had a problem with your product and are looking for help. They are not cranks, but customers who are alerting you to a problem. Fix the problem and the situation will go away.

"The next criterion is 'What is the impact on your target audience?'" Paine asks. During the 1996 Olympics, the media blasted IBM because of a computer network snafu.

"IBM's customers said no one could bring up a network in five days. The general response from IT [International Telecommunication] managers was 'They got 95 percent of that thing working in five days, I'm impressed.' IBM realized there was no crisis," she says.

These cases show that even though there might be negative messages, you might be able to let the situation pass.

■ RESPONDING TO CRISES

Once the decision to act has been made, it is important to act quickly to squelch minor problems before they cross over to the mainstream media and become big problems. Different strategies are needed for newsgroups, websites, reporters, and stakeholders.

"You must be proactive, aggressive," says Meier. "You cannot shrink from these things. If you are a public company you have to take a stance. That is our philosophy whether it is online or in print. These things have to be addressed officially. Silence is assent."

"The biggest benefit a PR person can have is to set up a plan and recognize that it requires an immediate response that is decisive and lives up to legal and securities concerns, but needs to be responded to immediately," says Jolley. "If your surveillance activity uncovers any hint of trouble you must react quickly. You must present credible, factual information as quickly as possible. Do it publicly if you can."

Late in the game, LEXIS-NEXIS identified the original sender of misinformation in its P-TRAK controversy.

"By the time they did that, the cancer was starting to grow and fester. While they corrected the source and figured they had done their job, it was the burning ember under the sofa that was just smoldering that they didn't see," he says. "You need to nip it in the bud as soon as possible. When it hits the fan, you are a step behind."

➤ Newsgroups

To maximize your company's response, you must establish credibility with a newsgroup's members by becoming a trusted member of their community—before the crisis hits.

"Here is where people get into trouble. Instead of just monitoring this conversation in cyberspace, in targeted areas you need to take proactive steps and become credible member of that community prior to anything good, bad, indifferent happening. Because when it hits the fan, it is difficult for a company to come in and establish credibility," says Jolley. "There should be a member of the organization who is charged with becoming a member of that organization and provide helpful information and become credible. This is not unlike the physical community, be it a neighborhood or community organization, there are people you get to know and trust because they have been part of the conversation and are plugged in. You will filter the information they provide through the lens of past interaction with that individual."

For example, in the Public Relations forum on CompuServe, a Business Wire representative answers questions about the company. She states up front that she works for Business Wire. She doesn't downplay competitors. If a crisis should befall Business Wire, she would be the person who comes on and says, "This is the real story." She would be believed because of her participation in the community.

"If she hadn't been active, she'd be seen as a shill. People would say 'Of course she is going to say that.' If you have a relationship with her, you understand she is giving the company line, but I trust her," Jolley says. "Participating can pay off benefits in the long run."

For some companies, this is a luxury that they cannot afford. When crises hit, they must enter the newsgroup discussions and demonstrate their credibility and willingness to provide information by posting messages, linking to websites and news reports about the case, and making key officials available for comment.

To build this trust, the organization should appoint a person to speak for the company—and the other employees should be placed on notice that they don't have the authority to answer questions online. This will ensure that the organization speaks with one voice and that a central authority has control of the communication message (see Chapter 2 for company policies on authorizing a spokesperson and controlling employee use of newsgroups).

To establish credibility with the groups, the spokesperson needs to take these steps:

1. Spend time in the newsgroup learning about the culture of the group.

2. Always establish identity as the representative of the company.

3. Create a signature block, or online business card, that contains your name, title, company, phone, and e-mail contacts.

4. Once the crisis hits, "Jump in and use your credibility with facts and figures," says Jolley.

"In the LEXIS-NEXIS situation, the trade publications looked at the issue, analyzed the situation and agreed with LEXIS-NEXIS. One of the things I would have done was negotiate rights to the articles and distribute them on the Internet. Then when I went out to deny the misperception, I would have offered those individuals (the people who questioned the service) to send them the document and publish it in the forums. I would also have them come to the website (which LEXIS-NEXIS did), but that requires the marketplace take action to find the information. I would be proactive. Now it isn't the company just saying it, but experts who have no axe to grind and no conflict of interest are backing up the message."

➤ Building a World-Class Website for Handling Crises

A world-class website fights crises by having these content areas:

➤ Press releases.

➤ Letter from chairman.

➤ Links to newspaper articles, online columns, news broadcasts online.

➤ Links to unbiased sources (e.g., trade associations, medical groups, scientific organizations).

➤ Letters from customers.

➤ Testimonials.

➤ Contact information.

"If you make a broad range of information available on your website, reporters can easily verify facts and check on rumors or innuendo," says Goldstein. "You also have to think about using push technology—faxing and e-mail databases, that will allow you to distribute text, audio or video to key constituencies or members of the media."

➤ Access Issues

You need to monitor who is coming to your media website by placing a password to protect the area on the site. People who don't have the password can't get into the site. Chrysler and Fuji are two companies that password protect their media site, along with a number of oil companies.

"If you ask people to register, then you can have reports on which reporters are coming to the site and what they are looking at. You can put two and two together. They might be on to a story," says Jolley. "Within last 24 hours, we've fulfilled bios on the CEO five times the normal rate. Why is this happening? Could it be there is a rumor in cyberspace? Maybe it is a coincidence. Now you can build scenarios."

"If you have a potential crisis looming, you can't leave any stone unturned," he says. "The key is to try to go into a surveillance mode to identify emerging patterns that are abnormal."

Before deciding on this approach, consider the downside. If you limit access to the site, your other communities—employees, stockholders, dealers, and the community—won't

RISKY BUSINESS ASKS THE EXPERTS

Pat Meier's Six Tips for Fighting Crises

Websites can and must be used to get the word out. Here are Pat Meier's recommendations for turning your website into a powerful tool to fight crises.

1. If you are a public company, ask your public affairs division to put up a chat area on your website so that any sort of crises can be addressed by senior management in real time. Active Presenter by Software Publishing Company allows companies to host press conferences on their websites.

2. Link to complementary sites and ask them to link to your site. They can host a news blurb and a link back to your site.

3. Send a copy to your attorney for approval before responding to anything. There is no going back once you put your words in writing. You can't say, "What I meant to say was."

4. Use meta tags (HTML commands that include descriptions and keywords of your company's web pages) on your website to lead people to this issue. Anyone who is searching under the topic of controversy should go directly to your site.

5. Consider using audio. "Words make the music. It really is inflection. That's why I believe in audio on the Internet. Things can be interpreted in a number of ways," Meier says. "It is much easier to create rapport when you heard the words. It is much harder to do in print. You can't underline or italicize with e-mail. As e-mail becomes more creative and formatted, this will occur. By itself, it can be misinterpreted."

6. Read and reread the message.

be able to read your material. Consider the benefits and risks to each audience before adding a password. If you do add a password, you will need to distribute the code to each reporter, a time-consuming task. What happens if they misplace the password? I see a lot of problems with this approach, but for some companies that are victims of activist groups and gadflies, it might be necessary.

➤ Create Your Own Newsroom and Messages

Companies also must become creators of news to help correct misinformation. "The truth is that cost pressures and consolidation in the media has reduced the number of independent news sources. You may have one news story that is syndicated and printed in 10 newspapers," says Goldstein.

"The opportunity side of the Internet is that you can begin to operate as your own news organization, generating credible, factually accurate information. By creating direct channels of communication, you leverage coverage with mainstream media and provide an avenue where shareholders or average citizens can get accurate information.

"The Internet lets you do this in a way that no other media can. In fact, with other media there is no guarantee you can get your message printed or reported on the air. With the Internet, you can use your website to present audio and video of your CEO," he says.

Another advantage the Internet brings to communicators is that they can present their side of the story as the news is happening. "You can get ahead of the story. In the worst-case scenario, you are coming out at the same time," Goldstein says. "If you don't do this, your story is printed the following day on page three instead of on page one. You don't get the same attention."

Now you have a medium that can help you maintain instant communication. "The Internet is a means to distribute the information," he says. "When a crisis develops, companies will merely have to push the button and deliver the information to their doorstep as the info is going out over the news channel."

➤ Create Unique Messages for Each Audience

Because you can track messages from each target group, you need to create individualized messages that answer each group's questions. "We shouldn't overlook that competition for influencing public opinion will reach new heights with the Internet," Goldstein said. "Outside interest groups will be better organized and have the same sophisticated arsenal of technology tools—leveling the playing field.

"To effectively communicate, companies will need to research and target their messages. You will be able to track newsgroups, newswires . . . and even press calls. You'll be able to see what's influencing your share price or how stakeholders are reacting to news stories. You'll track for trends. Survey research will help you better understand perceptions about issues. And you'll be able to use this information to target and deliver messages on different issues to various stakeholders and opinion leaders," says Goldstein.

➤ Distributing Information

It is important to have lists containing the names, addresses, phone numbers, and e-mail addresses of your key audiences so that you can distribute information to them fast. These audiences include:

➤ Reporters and the issues they cover.

➤ Online gurus: forum hosts, mailing list owners, on-line evangelists (people who post many messages in newsgroups), and ISP operators. "You need to start engaging these folks who are the gateways. You need to prove to them that the information is wrong and ask them to be diligent on their behalf," says Jolley.

➤ Stakeholders—stockholders, employees, analysts, decision makers and others who have an interest in the company.

Pat Meier urges clients to use their websites to present information. Here are her suggestions:

➤ Launch an e-mail campaign to the most critical press and analysts. Meier advises the length to be never more than a page. "Give enough of the message in the e-mail and a full URL to read more about it and link back to the site," she says. Never add an attachment to an e-mail which she calls "the kiss of death." Don't make the media work for it.

➤ Include your own e-mail address and answer your mail. Not answering e-mail is like calling a press conference and not showing up. "Be available," she says.

■ MEASURING SUCCESS IN HANDLING A CRISIS

How do you measure the success of your crisis communications efforts? In addition to keeping your job, there are four other measures:

1. How long does the crisis last?
2. What kind of comments are being posted to newsgroups?
3. What effect has the crisis had on stock price and product sales?
4. How long does the crisis last?

"A crisis on the Internet may spread more rapidly, but measuring it is not different from other crises," says Paine. Here is a simple formula.

1. Monitor the messages over time.
2. Look at the percentage of positive messages and negative messages.
3. If there are more negative messages than positive, then you have a problem.

"If the messages are even, then you are lucky. You will never have 100 percent favorable. . . . One vital part of understanding how to respond and measure a crisis is to understand the audience and what they consider to be the problem. It might be different than what you consider to be the problem," says Payne. "You might think the problem is your stock price. Your customers might think the problem is customer service."

"The true way to measure your success in handling a crisis is to measure public opinion among several constituencies before, during and after the crisis," says Goldstein. "Research and overnight polling will be as natural in gauging and guiding your success, as turning the lights on in the morning."

■ SUMMARY

The Internet can be used to monitor and fight crises. Many free or low-cost tools and services are available to help companies monitor developments. Unlike other media, the Internet allows companies to create individualized messages for targeted audiences at a low price.

ONLINE RESOURCES

Public Relations Society of America, www.prsa.org, contains useful links to publicity reference materials.

Afterword

The Internet is a useful, valuable, fun, and interesting place, and, with this book, no longer a scary place.

Hopefully you have now learned, to the extent possible in this world of changing Internet technology, how to use the Internet and avoid its risks or at least to spot the legal landmines before you land on them and find your company or yourself blown up. The Internet is a challenging, interesting, and valuable personal and business tool, which can be used to enhance the value and facilities of your business to create wealth and value.

To be sure, there are unknowns, and, as technology changes and people and companies try to use the technology to their own benefit, or to the detriment of their competitors, legal and technological issues will appear. However, through the examples, questions, and, hopefully, answers, provided here, you and your business will be in a better position to know what you can do, what you can't do, and areas where there is uncertainty, in order to better run your business and personally use the Internet.

WHAT WILL THE FUTURE BRING?

High-speed chips have begat high-speed computers, enabling immediate, no waiting communications, and instantaneous transfer of information in digital form. All forms of information, music, video, and sound can now be shot around the world without a trace on the Internet. The only thing scientists haven't yet figured out how to digitize and E-mail across the world is the "smell of the flowers," which we are all too busy to smell.

As chips get faster and new computer programs and hardware enable a faster, better, and more efficient transfer of information, how will we cope?

First, there will undoubtedly be some who won't, some who will be stalked, spammed, spoofed, and stopped. Hopefully through information such as you have gathered here, you will learn by their mistakes or lack of caution. By spreading the word about the dangers and steps that can be taken to protect ourselves, future generations of Internet computer users will be less vulnerable to the system.

Second, technology, which unintentionally created many of the problems, may come up with some solutions. The technology which allowed some with less than honorable intentions to take advantage of others, may also have solutions to discourage or stop some of the risks. Scientists continue to develop hardware and software for tracking and identification, and blocking devices, to trace, discourage, or capture the offenders or their activities. As children and adults become active on the Internet and take advantage of its facilities—browsing the Internet, sending and receiving E-mail, advertising, and communications—we will need more information about blocking, sorting, tracing, screening, and anti-spamming devices, to protect ourselves or identify the offenders or offending materials.

DIGITAL DATA IS PILING UP AROUND US

Also, the incremental, but exponential, addition of huge amounts of digital information and material available on the Internet, stored in our read and unread E-mail, and deeper and bigger web sites, Internets, intranets, and extranets will create an immense need for storage media. However, instead of moving in the direction of erasing and reusing the media for more current and valuable digital information, storage media has becomes cheaper, and more readily available, so that the cost of sorting through and "separating the chaff from the wheat" we want to save, may be more expensive, particularly when the value of the time necessary for human beings to think about it is factored in against the cost of more memory. As a result, more and more is stored and saved, yet remains digitally available.

Unfortunately, the Internet and its progeny, while wonderful at storing and making available gazillions of gigabytes of information and material with a click of a link, or the spider of a search engine, is not at all good at discarding, or even dating, the information that is there. We have enough trouble with knowing whether information available on the Internet is reliable, for example, that its author is who it claims to be, that its author is competent, or that its translator or poster did so accurately and without bias. But the biggest problem is that as all of this available information continues to build up, and much of what may have been accurate and reliable at one time will be simply old and outdated. But how will we know? How will we be able to discard or discount, or avoid having to wade through, read, and receive, the huge amounts of digitally stored information which our browsers and search engines can bring to our screens in an instant.

Therefore, as more information is available on the Internet, and more users want individual home pages, business pages, and organizational pages, we will need better search engines and spiders to find what we are looking for, and some way of dating, classifying, and sorting information by its "age on the net" and, hopefully, its reliability, to remove the risks and uncertainty present there.

CAN OUR LAWS COPE?

As technology has changed with the advent and widespread use of the Internet, many new legal issues arise. Is the use of an Internet domain name a violation of law? If it is, then is it under U.S. trademark laws or the law of all the countries accessing the Internet? Is making available music, pictures, or books, for viewing or downloading, infringement of the copyright in the book, music, or video? Is the use of hidden codewords, called *metatags,* or the use of repeated words printed out on a black background in black letters virtually, so that the user of the Internet cannot see them on a web site, yet attracting the attention of Internet search engines, unfair competition? Is it acceptable under the law to design your web site so as to "frame" another web site on your site, by having it appear through a window or frame on your site. These are all new and original legal issues never before decided and not supported by either existing laws or previously decided law cases.

Never before have the laws and courts been faced with so many new challenges and questions as to whether opportunities for exploitation and/or creativity are legal or illegal under U.S. law.

Some have suggested that the laws of the world need to leap ahead and be changed to make corrections for abuses of the Internet, and to avoid opportunities for harm or injury through the Internet. Others argue that our old and existing laws will develop and be construed by courts to apply to new technology. Undoubtedly both will take place. The courts will be called upon to weigh new fact situations created as a result of new technologies, and state, national and international legislators will call for new laws to prevent abuses and control the growth of crime and unfair competition that might otherwise take place on the Internet.

For society it means an ever-increasing need to know the laws, and know your rights and obligations under the laws, to protect yourself and your business from being stalked, conned, libeled, or blackmailed on the World Wide Web.

The web provides challenges and opportunities. As its capabilities and opportunities become more and more widespread, we will have to continue to learn and educate ourselves about our rights and the limitations of technology and law in order to guide our lives in the future. It will be an interesting challenge.

What used to be called the White House Science Policy Committee, high-level government officials dealing with the science policy, was reconstituted a few years ago and given a modern name, the Information Infrastructure Task Force (IITF), to articulate and implement the Administration's vision for the National Information Infrastructure, to look at the transfer of information as new technologies are used for communication, particularly digital transmission made over Internet. The Working Group on Intellectual Property Rights subcommittee of the IITF put out a paper analyzing the intellectual property laws, suggesting various amendments to take care of its perceived inability of the laws to cope with new technologies. As yet, none of their recommendations have been implemented. The wheels of politics, and the education of congressman and congresswomen do not move at Internet speed.

The original report of the Working Group had a wonderful quote from Thomas Jefferson (the first head of the U.S. Patent Office), from the Jefferson memorial in our Nation's Capitol. I commend it to all who are concerned that the laws won't keep up with the changes in society, as a mantra:

I am not an advocate for frequent changes in laws and constitutions. But laws and institutions must go hand and hand with the progress of the human mind. As that becomes more developed, more enlightened, as new discoveries are made, new truths discovered and manners and opinions change, with the change of circumstances, institutions must advance also to keep pace with the times. We might as well require a man to wear still the coat which fitted him when a boy . . .

I am a strong believer in the ability of old laws, inherited from our framers and the Common Law of England, and modified from time to time with technological change, to cope with changes in the technology of the future. For example, courts have used the copyright laws over the years, and applied them as new technologies came to be: video tape recorders, video games, on-line services, and Internet framing issues, and even 80-year-old low-tech judges understand the facts sufficiently to interpret and apply the laws. For example, historical concepts of trespass law, which evolved for keeping your neighbor off your property, have been applied in Cyberspace to spamming issues.

I am a strong believer in the future. The laws of the past will control the acts of people using the technology of the future.

San Francisco
NEIL A. SMITH
Limbach & Limbach L.L.P.

Index